T0398838

Advance Praise for *National Identity and Partisan Polarization*

"*National Identity and Partisan Polarization* is a critical work that brings scholarly rigor and insight to the most troubling force threatening democracies today: nationalist movements that seek to divide a nation's citizens into 'us' and 'them.' Eric Uslaner uses data like a scalpel, laying bare the ethno-religious roots that are nourishing contemporary forms of asymmetric polarization, where parties on the right are increasingly pushing conceptions of the state based not on democratic principles but on exclusivist assertions of white Christian identity. Getting clear about the source and nature of this threat is vital for the health of democracies not just in the US, where these problems are particularly acute, but throughout the world. Uslaner provides a clear diagnosis of the dangers, and this book is vital reading for anyone concerned about the health of democracy today." —**Robert P. Jones**, CEO and Founder, PRRI

"If you want to understand why politics has become increasingly and dangerously polarized, Ric Uslaner's new book provides important insights. As Uslaner explains, people with an 'exclusive' national identity often perceive grave threats from 'outsiders,' which has unleashed challenging political forces. Donald Trump is one manifestation of national identity politics, but there are many others around the world. Uslaner makes clear that national identity and perceived threats to it play a critical role in our current predicament. That not every country's politics has been as consumed by tribalism provides some hope for better management of these forces." —**David Madland**, Center for American Progress, and author of *Re-Union*

"Eric Uslaner did it again. One of the most prolific political scientists of our generation, has deciphered the link between national identity and political polarization in a wide-ranging study that includes ten different countries. Beyond being a gifted scholar, Uslaner has earned a reputation for his phenomenal writing ability, which he demonstrates in the book. Like its predecessors, this book will soon become one of the pillars of contemporary comparative political research." —**Ami Pedahzur**, The University of Texas at Austin

"This book creatively explores the sources of political polarization across ten countries and over various time periods. It is a fine example of scholarship that zeroes in on the effects of diversifying societies on political outcomes. Based on a wealth of data sources and via sophisticated data analysis this book reveals that the determinants of polarization are found in the type of national identity electorates possess, rather than in the countries' institutional variation as oftentimes claimed. Guided by the idea as to who counts as a 'true member of society,' the book powerfully demonstrates the importance of being moored to a sense of belonging, community, and identity in shaping people's political choices." —**Markus M. L. Crepaz**, University of Georgia

"There is no doubt this is a hugely important book. In the current era, there is an urgent need to understand better why a feeling of national identity seems such a powerful attitude. This volume bring everything together to arrive at this understanding. It offers the accumulation of a lifetime of profound scholarly work. The combination of historical evidence and a profound knowledge of data and statistical analysis is more than impressive. This book brings also a powerful moral message: it demonstrates how important education, and the universal access to education are. The evidence, assembled in this volume is just overwhelming and conclusive; and it sheds new light on current debates. The bright side of the story is that education indeed has the power to have an effect on people's minds, and on the way our future society will look like. Uslaner shows in this volume what political science can do, based on rigorous methods, and how this work can lead to a more just society. Maybe that is the most important contribution political science has to offer." —**Marc Hooghe**, University of Leuven (Belgium)

"At a time when researchers talk about a dispersed identity when borders are disappearing, and citizens try to belong to many, often difficult to define, places, Eric M. Uslaner's book *National Identity and Partisan Polarization* is indispensable reading. It shows the processes of redefining national identities and using political identities in political communication. Comparing the indicated approaches in different countries increases the book's value, showing the role of specific factors." —**Agnieszka Turska-Kawa**, University of Silesia in Katowice

National Identity and Partisan Polarization

ERIC M. USLANER

OXFORD
UNIVERSITY PRESS

OXFORD
UNIVERSITY PRESS

Oxford University Press is a department of the University of Oxford. It furthers
the University's objective of excellence in research, scholarship, and education
by publishing worldwide. Oxford is a registered trade mark of Oxford University
Press in the UK and certain other countries.

Published in the United States of America by Oxford University Press
198 Madison Avenue, New York, NY 10016, United States of America.

© Oxford University Press 2022

All rights reserved. No part of this publication may be reproduced, stored in
a retrieval system, or transmitted, in any form or by any means, without the
prior permission in writing of Oxford University Press, or as expressly permitted
by law, by license, or under terms agreed with the appropriate reproduction
rights organization. Inquiries concerning reproduction outside the scope of the
above should be sent to the Rights Department, Oxford University Press, at the
address above.

You must not circulate this work in any other form
and you must impose this same condition on any acquirer.

Library of Congress Cataloging-in-Publication Data
Names: Uslaner, Eric M., author.
Title: National identity and partisan polarization / Eric M. Uslaner.
Identifiers: LCCN 2021057276 | ISBN 9780197633946 (hardcover) |
ISBN9780197633960 (epub) | ISBN 9780197633977
Subjects: LCSH: National characteristics—Political aspects. |
Political culture. | Citizenship. | Identity politics. | Welfare state |
National characteristics—Political aspects—Case studies. |
Political culture—Case studies. | Citizenship—Case studies. |
Identity politics—Case studies. | Welfare state—Case studies.
Classification: LCC JC311 .U75 2022 |
DDC 320.54—dc23/eng/20220204
LC record available at https://lccn.loc.gov/2021057276

DOI: 10.1093/oso/9780197633946.001.0001

1 3 5 7 9 8 6 4 2

Printed by Integrated Books International, United States of America

To Debbie and Avery, who make it all worthwhile

Contents

Preface

This book started by accident. After I finished my previous book, *The Historical Roots of Corruption*, I became fascinated by forces that were emerging around the world as people and their leaders were becoming increasingly focused on identity. Nationalism was rising and people were becoming less tolerant of minority groups and refugees. The most immediate example in my own mind was how Donald Trump and his Republican followers denigrated people of color, of different religion or sexual orientations, and immigrants in general. I set out to examine how these biases shaped Trump's support. That led me to consider what Trump and his supporters considered the bases of national identity. The American National Election Study in 2020 included questions on what people thought was necessary to be "real Americans." I thus estimated a statistical model of support for the two major candidates and found that a measure of identity was strongly related to vote choice. What surprised me is how powerful the relationship turned out to be, greater than party identification, ideology, positions on specific issues, or attitudes toward individual minority groups.

That led me to wonder if the same dynamic was working elsewhere. And shortly after I developed this model, the Pew Research Foundation conducted a study of national identity in 14 other countries. Bruce Stokes of Pew kindly gave me his data set in advance of public distribution, and I found that a sense of identity was important in many other countries. From there two major issues remained. First, I had to select the countries I would examine for a larger project, this book. I made my choice on the basis of the following criteria: (1) the importance of national identity to political choice in the country; (2) whether a party with measurable support focused on nationalism; (3) whether the political or social culture in a country favored a more "inclusive" or "exclusive" sense of identity; (4) the overall level of polarization in the country; (5) how politics in the country has developed over time to stress this issue; and (6) whether I could obtain survey data for the country. An "inclusive" identity means that people of all origins and backgrounds are accepted as members of the society, while an "exclusive" identity gives priority to members of the country's majority population.

To make the project manageable, I had to restrict the number of countries. I chose 10 nations, starting with the United States. I have spent most of my career working on my home country, know it the best, and there are multiple data sets that I could use. Second was Great Britain. I have both academic and personal contacts there, having worked with and lectured at the University of Manchester for many years. I have many friends there and most notably my wife was born and raised in London, so I know the country well. Britain in 2016 had a referendum leading to withdrawal from the European Union, and vote choice on that ballot reflected strong nationalist sentiments. In both the United States and Great Britain, one major party's leaders and supporters favored a more "exclusive" identity and the other an "inclusive" identity. The parties on the right on issues of identity also took conservative positions on economic and social issues.

Most of the other countries are in Europe. Sweden is the least divided country among the 10 I consider. Equality has been central to Swedish society for centuries and the country was one of the first to admit immigrants and to provide for widespread social security. France is a central case because both major parties have given way to new ones—a centrist party replacing the left bloc and a right-wing nationalist party (the Front National). Unlike the United States and Great Britain, nationalist ideology was not strongly correlated with other issues. This is also the case in Germany, although there the nationalist party (the Alternatif für Deutschland) is a small minority. Yet this tiny party has pushed both major parties, on the center-left and the center-right, to more nationalistic positions on identity. Austria is the only Western European country I examine where a right-wing nationalist party (the Freedom Party) has entered the government and its ties to Germany's former Nazi regime make it a case worthy of examination.

The other countries in Europe are the former Communist nations of Hungary and Poland, chosen because they are among the most prosperous former satellites of the Soviet Union and because they have long histories of strongly inclusive nationalism. In both countries, right-wing nationalist parties have threatened both ethnic and sexual minorities and have been threatened with expulsion from the European Union. The main sources of political conflict are ethno-nationalist in both countries.

I also include two non-European countries for two key reasons. First, I know them well and second, because ethno-nationalism has become the dominant force in their political and social realms. The first is Israel, where I lived as a Fulbright scholar in 1981–82 and where I have visited, lectured, and have many friends. The traditional left-right divide on economic and security issues has given way to a debate as to whether Israeli non-Jews should have full citizenship rights. The second is Taiwan, where I have lectured and also have friends. There the main issue has always been one of identification—either as Chinese or Taiwanese.

I have been fortunate enough to obtain data, much of it not publicly available, on each of these countries. These data sets together with narratives about history, politics, and social cleavages in each society, form the basis of what follows.

I owe special debts of gratitude to people and organizations that have shared data with me. I am grateful to Bruce Stokes, Margaret Vice, Neha Segal, and Kelsey Starr of the Pew Research Center for their data; to John Sides of Vanderbilt University for access to the Democracy Fund surveys; to Elizabeth Theiss-Morse for her data on Perceptions of the American People; to Jennifer Benz and Marjorie Connelly of The Associated Press-NORC Center for Public Affairs Research; to Jerry Hansen and Kris Hodgins (of the Gallup Organization, to which I serve as an unpaid adviser);, to Ashley Jardina and Robert P. Jones of the Public Religion Research Institute; and Nicolas Sauger, Doug Rivers, Chris Curtis, Henrik Ekengren Oscarsson, Richard Karlsson, Agatha Kraz, Manuela Blumenberg, and Markus Wagner for their data. I am also grateful to the American National Election Studies and the Cooperative Congressional Election Studies for access to their data; to the United Kingdom Data Services for their data; and to GESIS-Berlin for data and translation. I have a special debt to William Zinnser, author of *On Writing Well*, who taught me much of what I know about composition: Use short sentences and paragraphs, contractions, the first person, few adjectives and almost no adverbs, avoid the passive tense, and tell stories as well as presenting history and quantitative analyses.

I am also grateful to Nils Holtug, Bo Rothstein, Morris Levy, Bryan Gervais, Roberto Foa, John Sides, Wen-Chin Wu, Marc Hooghe, Kerem Ozan Kalkan, Kathy Cramer, Debbie Schildkraut, and Chris Welzel for their comments and to Bezalel Newman and Sara Shemali for their research assistance. I also appreciate the opportunities to present webinars through Agnieszka Turska-Kawa of the University of Silesia in Katowice, Poland; and to Tristan Claridge of the Social Science Research Group, New Zealand.

Let me also add some friends, colleagues, and former students who have helped shape my thinking and my world over my many years as an academic: Mitchell Brown, Kerem Ozan Kalkan, Richard Conley, John Gates.

Bob Maranto, Martha Bailey, Robert DiClerico, Ali Carkoglu, Gabriel Badescu, Paul Sum, Kim Sonderskov, Eduard Ponarin, Peter Chang, Tristan Hightower, Charles Green, Oguzhan Dincer, Yoji Inaba, Kimmo Grönlund, Kathy Kretman, Chong-Min Park, Michael Mumper, Peter Kinberg, Barbara Segnatelli, and my colleagues and staff in the Department of Government and Politics at the University of Maryland—College Park, where I began teaching in 1978. I owe particular debts to Dave Bobrow, Mark Lichbach, and Irwin Morris, my former department chairs, and to staff including Cissy Roberts, Stefanie Drame, Mike Mansfield, Mary Keener, Kathleen Klein, and Judy Ludvigsen, as well as to librarian Judith Markowitz. It has also been a pleasure to work with David McBride, Amy Whitmer, and Emily Benitez of Oxford University Press. I am also grateful to Olympic Air, which announced a two-hour delay on September 8, 1981. That led me to something totally out of character for me—to start talking to the person ahead of me on the check-in line, who (as I say in the next paragraph) has been the most important person of my life, the woman I married about 18 months later.

Most important is my family to whom I dedicate this book: my fantastic wife of almost 40 years, Debbie, and my wonderful son Avery—and to the non-human members, the late canines Bo and Amber and to our new cat, the amazing Banjo.

1

Foundations: The Question of Identity

When I was in elementary school, we still started each day with a prayer—specifically the Lord's Prayer. Like most young Jewish kids, I also went to Hebrew school, after school two days a week and on Sunday mornings to prepare for my bar mitzvah. But we never said the Lord's Prayer. One day I asked my Hebrew school teacher, a distinguished older gentleman named Mr. Stein, why we never said the Lord's Prayer. He answered: "It's a Christian prayer." I was puzzled. Our elementary school population was at least 80 percent Jewish. We sang Christian melodies at Easter and Christmas, but never any songs for Passover or Chanukah. And now I realized that we even said Christian prayers. I did not feel part of the community. I was not one of "us," but one of "them." My identity was not the same as the one I was expected to belong to.

I felt a bit out of place but the problem was not so severe in the United States of the 1950s and 1960s. I still identified as an American and, as Huntington (2004) argues, people of different backgrounds could be considered as part of a country as long as they adopted norms and social values of the country. This is an inclusive view of belonging to a society. Higham (1956, 20) wrote: "Over the centuries, America had developed a fluid, variegated culture but incorporating alien peoples into its midst, and the experience had fixed in American thought a faith in the nation's capacity for assimilation . . . The ancient Christian doctrine of the brotherhood of man proclaimed the ultimate similarities between all peoples and their capacity for dwelling together in unity."

An alternative view of "belongingness" is that people have "exclusive identities." They need to share common characteristics such as religion and national origin; simply accepting norms is not sufficient. Majorities feel threatened by minorities that have different backgrounds from themselves. This perspective is based upon the idea that every society has its own "national identity" based upon objective criteria. People of different backgrounds cannot readily assimilate and the majority population fears that this identity is threatened by people of different backgrounds.

National Identity and Partisan Polarization. Eric M. Uslaner, Oxford University Press. © Oxford University Press 2022. DOI: 10.1093/oso/9780197633946.003.0001

This view has become salient throughout the world, from Donald Trump's campaign in the United States to Brexit in the United Kingdom to Marine Le Pen in France and to Alternatif für Deutschland (AfD) in Germany, political movements in Western countries have made inroads in electoral politics in Western societies—and outside the West. These movements have all stressed the primacy of national identities—what makes someone an American, a Brit, a Frenchman/Frenchwoman, a German, even an Israeli or a Taiwanese. This politics of national identity has reshaped issues of what political parties stand for with whom they stand. Who is an American, a Brit, a French person? Who belongs to a society, who is entitled to the benefits of "belongingness," and how can societies protect themselves against "threats" from people who don't fit into the majority's definition of a "true" member of society?

What, then, constitutes a "true" member of a society? There is no single criterion for belonging to the majority. The answer will vary from one country to another and even over time in the same nation. There is a question that has been asked in a large number of surveys: What is a "true X?" The alternatives vary across surveys. The most consistent alternatives—and the theoretically most important—are being born in the country, having ancestors born in the country, being white, and being of the dominant religion. But these are not the same across time or countries. The conflict between "us" and "them"—who is a true member or not—varies across time and space. In the United States and most of Europe, you should be white and Christian, and also have ancestry in the country over time.

Yet this is hardly the case in Israel (where it is important to be Jewish, not Christian) or Taiwan (where there are few Christians and even fewer whites and where many people identify as Taiwanese even if their families came from mainland China). And objective criteria are far less salient in Sweden—where observing social norms is more important than are objective criteria.

I shall consider the nature of "belongingness" and "deservingness," as well as which criteria are most important for national identity in different societies, how identity is measured across surveys (what criteria are important and which ones are not), the consequences of different criteria for identity for electoral choice, and how measures of identity are linked with other values. Specifically, I argue that identity has become more closely linked with other issues in the United States, only modestly linked in most of Europe, and uncorrelated with other values in Central and Eastern Europe.

While it may be appropriate to consider positions on identity as part of a right-wing ideology in the United States (and to a lesser extent in Western Europe), such an argument would not hold at all in Central and Eastern Europe. The more strongly issues of identity are linked with other issues, the more likely the policies adopted by a governing party emphasizing identity (the Republicans in the United States) will be overturned if they lose power. But when identity is less strongly connected to other issues, the less likely restrictionist policies will be changed if one mainstream party is replaced by another (as in Western Europe). When there is little correlation between issues of identity and economic issues, restrictionism policies will become very difficult to change.

Polarization is the division of the electorate and a country's political parties across a range of issues. My major concern is how the sense of national identity shapes political choice (voting behavior wherever available or partisan identification when not) and later how identity is related to policy position on immigration and the provision of benefits to people (that is, who is seen as "one of us"). Is the sense of identity "inclusive" (anyone who lives in a country is considered "one of us") or "exclusive" (must you or your ancestors be born in the country and/or belong to the majority race/religion/ethnic group)? Across the world, people have become divided on issues of nationalism, belongingness, and deservingness. This is reflected in their partisan choices (which reflect, not determine, support in elections). In some countries, nationalism is associated with other issues, elsewhere it is not.

The rise in nationalism across the world has led some observers to believe that democracy itself is in trouble. If both the public and its leaders cannot agree on who is a "true" member of society and who is deserving of government benefits, people may lose faith in the capacity of their institutions to make effective public policy. When the leader of a party that pursues an explicitly "exclusive" perspective on identity gains power, that leader may even try to restrict who can enter the country, who can claim its benefits, and even who might participate in its politics.

Examining over 3500 surveys across 77 democracies throughout the world, Foa (2020, 12–13) reports that dissatisfaction with democracy has risen almost 10 percent from the 1990s to 2020 and traces the decline both to economic crises and increased immigration levels. Satisfaction with democratic performance has fallen to about half of the population in the long-established governments of Western Europe and the Anglo-American countries (Foa, 2020, 16–19). The drop in satisfaction is stronger in the former Communist countries of Central and Eastern Europe, including Hungary and Poland, which I explore below. Foa (2020, 25) attributes this to the ruling parties' focus on "platform[s] of nationalism, social welfare, and anti-immigration." As I argue in the next section, the leaders of these parties emphasize not just exclusivist identities but are also authoritarian, seeing their adversaries as enemies of the population and the state.

Levitsky and Ziblatt (2018, 3) argue: "Democracies may die at the hands not of generals but of elected leaders—presidents or prime ministers who subvert the very process that brought them to power." Erhardt, Wamsler, and Freitag (2020, 62) show that Europeans whose sense of national identity is more exclusive tend to be more authoritarian and less supportive of democratic governance. I am not as pessimistic as these analysts, at least with respect to the survival of democratic institutions. I share the worries about the prominence of issues of who is considered a true member of society and who is deserving of the country's benefits. The idea of identity is the major problem facing governments and citizens today, regardless of the institutional frameworks in which they operate. These are the questions that prompted me to write this book.

The Question of Identity

I will first consider a wide range of countries for which the identity question has been asked and then focus on a series of countries for more detailed analysis. This latter group was chosen on the basis of two criteria: the salience of the issue of identity to the country's politics and the availability of good data on identity and political choice.

The only way to measure national identity is to ask people in each country what they consider to be critical for being a "true X." This means that the measure of national identity will not be the same across countries. There is no single criterion for "belongingness"—either over time or across countries. These countries are

1. The United States, where identity has been measured the most often, where the basis of identity has changed over time, and where it is has become a central issue under the Presidency of Donald Trump. Identity has also become strongly related to other issues as the American public has become polarized.

2. Great Britain, where issues of identity loomed large in the debate over the debate over the withdrawal from the European Union and where I have two data sets to examine this issue.

3. France, where a party stressing exclusivist nationalism (the National Front) has surged to become one of the two major parties.

4. Germany and Austria, which had histories of extreme nationalism (Naziism), but now the party in Germany stressing an exclusivist nationalism is on the fringes while the mainstream parties are more moderate—but pushed to limit immigration by the fringe. In Austria, the nationalist party has entered the government.

5. Sweden, which has the most liberal and inclusivist "belongingness" ideology, but has developed a minority party, the Swedish Democrats, who resemble the strong nationalist parties of other European parties and whose leader mimics Trump in promising to "make Sweden great again." They have pushed the major parties to the right on issues of immigration and benefits.

6. Hungary and Poland, former Communist countries, have lurched to the right on issues of immigration and an exclusivist vision of "belongingness," as leaders and followers fear Muslim immigration and Jewish influence and also take rightist positions on moral issues—but favor generous social welfare benefits for the majority populations.

Others have reported data on whether societies are inclusive or exclusive and before I turn to my own analysis, I summarize what we know. Perhaps the most important recent survey is that conducted by Pew in 2016 and its director, Bruce Stokes (2017, 33), which finds that for 14 nations, people generally place a low priority on the exclusive categories of where one was born (32 percent of Americans and 33 percent of Europeans agree), with Hungary (52 percent) and Poland (42 percent) as notable exceptions and Germany (13 percent) and Sweden (8 percent) showing the lowest share agreeing. For sharing the dominant religion, 32 percent of Americans, 34 percent of Poles, and 29 percent of Hungarians agreed while just 13 percent of British people, 11 percent of Germans, and 8 percent of Swedes concurred. For the more inclusive criteria, following traditions is important everywhere, especially in Hungary (68 percent) and Poland (56 percent) but least important in Germany and Sweden (29 percent and 26 percent).

I have obtained surveys from contacts in these countries. I also include Israel and Taiwan in my analysis because the issue of national identity has become central to Israeli politics and has always been essential in Taiwan. In Israel, the right-wing Likud party has promoted legislation that would prioritize citizenship for Jews above Arabs and Druze members of society. In Taiwan, many people who have Chinese ancestry now identify as Taiwanese rather than Chinese. In each of these cases, the majority ethnic group felt threatened by the minority. Threat is the major concern for all parties adapting exclusivist nationalist ideologies, and I will expand on this below.

I have one survey from Israel (the 2016 Pew survey; Stokes 2017). I have all of the data available in English for Taiwan: they only allow me to estimate thin models, but they do include the key issue of identification as either Taiwanese or Chinese. Finally, I will update the American results with 2020 data from the Voter Study Group and the American National Election Study when they become available (although I do report the pre-election survey here). As a consultant to the Gallup organization, I also have time series data on the importance of immigration to both Democratic and Republican party identifier over time and show that the salience of this issue has increased over time—even before Donald J. Trump became the Republican nominee.

The traits shaping identity do vary over time. In the United States, the shares of respondents saying that it is important to be a Christian or to be born in the country have declined substantially over time (I will consider this in detail below). And the nature of who belongs to out-groups also varies over time In the United States, some people in the past were not seen as "true Americans." Italian-Americans "were an uncivilized" and "racially inferior people, too obviously African to be part of Europe" (Staples, 2019). Irish-Americans were perceived as "drunken, belligerent, and foolish" and in cities "thrown together with free Negroes" (Ignatiev, 2008 [1995], 2).

Jewish Americans were "a marginalized group, and wound up neither black nor white" (Slayton, 2017). In the 1930s my mother had to wear a cross to work to hide her identity. Eventually each of these ethic groups "became white" (Ignatiev, 1995; Slayton, 2017; Staples, 2019). Over time these groups were accepted as "true Americans," but others replaced them as out-groups: Muslims, Latinos, immigrants more generally, gays and lesbians, and even intellectuals in cities. The assimilationist ideal that was widely accepted after World War II has been challenged by arguments that some people are "true Americans" and others are not—as reflected in the rise of Donald Trump. In 2019 Trump argued that some American Jews were more loyal to Israel than to the United States (Nahmias and Jaffe-Hoffman, 2019).

Who is a true X is important because it shapes both electoral politics and debates over who should benefit from government programs. Attitudes toward specific out-groups do not matter as much as overall measures of national identity. Yes, views of Muslims, Latinos, immigrants, gays and lesbians, and urban intellectuals—who work with their heads rather than their hands (Cramer, 2016)—or even African Americans (Abramowitz, 2018; Jardina; 2019; Tesler, 2016b) matter, but as shapers of national identity. Overall identity is a far more powerful determinant of politics in a country than attitudes toward specific groups.

The notion of national identity incorporates views of minorities—people don't associate "them" with "us." So for 2016 in the United States the out-groups include Muslims, immigrants (most of whom are Latinos), people who are not Christian fundamentalists, and those who benefit from policies designed to reduce inequality (mostly minorities more generally), as well as attitudes toward racial minorities and even authoritarian attitudes (see Tables 1.1 and 1.2).

Wherever national identity has become a central factor in political discourse, it reflects a reaction against out-groups and a sense of threat that the status of in-groups is in danger from minorities. In the United States, many people see "true Americans" as native-born white Christians (Theiss-Morse, 2009, 87). White Christians, long a major player in social and political life, are no longer a majority and are a declining force in electoral politics (Jones, 2017). The threat to the power of fundamentalist Christians in American politics is more multi-faceted in the United States than in Western Europe, where religion is less a part of one's identity.

People feel threatened when they believe that their identity group may become outnumbered by people of different backgrounds. When this occurs, they will seek to exclude people who are different from themselves from the country or, once they live in the country, will not want to live near them or spend their own resources to help support them. The more people base identity upon these "formal" characteristics of other people (race, religion, country of national origin), the less they will want to live near them or spend resources on them (Larsen, 2011; Massey and Denton, 1993; Uslaner, 2012).

The major forms of identity are "inclusive" and "exclusive." The latter are based primarily upon ethnicity, where one was born, and religion, while the former is formed by observing the customs of a country and feeling a member of society (Bonikowski, 2017). Hacker (1955) saw the United States as a liberal society where anyone could succeed regardless of where they were born, what their race was, and of any religion. This ability to succeed was made possible by the fact that America was never a feudal society (cf. Sombart, 1976). Citrin and Sears (2014, 2) add that Americans have accepted "economic inequality, and the boundaries of government action that limited the development of a welfare state. But the definition of American identity implicitly was inclusive; anyone could belong to America if he or she embraced the civil religion, spoken in English."

Huntington (2004, 47) argued: "Identifying America with the ideology of [the American] Creed [was] a 'civic' national identity as contrasted with the ethnic and ethno-cultural national identities of other countries." Yet both race and religion did matter in the early American Republic, so that both "inclusive" and "exclusive" identities marked the country for most of its history. This conflict made America different from Europe, since its countries had mostly exclusive identities. The battle between inclusive and exclusive identities has been present throughout American history and was particularly strong during periods of the greatest immigration (such as the late 19th and early 20th centuries). It continues to this day and now divides the parties in America and we now see similar patterns in Europe and elsewhere.

Societies with more exclusive identities are usually marked by strong ethnic or religious divisions. Minorities may live in a nation but are not considered "true" members of the society (Miller, 1995). Citrin and Sears (2014, 80) argue that an ethnic nation (notably Germany) "defines membership on the basis of descent . . . the nation is a marriage of blood and soil; primordial criteria determines whether one is born a national, not simply being born in the country." Bilefsky (2018) described a small town in Quebec that introduced a code of conduct aimed at Muslim immigrants requiring them to adapt to local culture: "We listen to music, we drink alcoholic beverages in public or private places, we dance and at the end of every year, we decorate a tree with balls and tinsel and some lights," the code explained. "The only time you may mask or cover your face is during Halloween." Yet the village had no immigrants at all. It was a response to a feeling of threat that didn't exist.

Jones and Smith (2001, 48–49) present a good statement of the division between inclusive and exclusive identities:

The civic model, which first arose in the West, assumes a sense of political community for all its members, including common institutions and a single code of rights and duties. It also assumes a demarcated territory in which all its members live. 'Historic territory, legal-political community, legal-political equality of members, and common civic culture and ideology; these are the components of the standard Western model of the nation.' Alongside this dominant Western ideal there also arose, a non-Western ethnic model that was first and foremost a community of common descent. 'Whether you stayed in your community or emigrated to another, you remained ineluctably, organically, a member of the community of your birth and were forever stamped by it.' In this model, national identity was more a matter of ascription than civic choice, with the Western emphasis on laws and institutions replaced by linguistic and cultural elements. 'Genealogy and presumed descent ties, popular mobilization, vernacular languages, customs and traditions: these are the elements of an alternative, ethnic conception of the nation.'

People living in the more homogenous countries such as France, Germany, Poland, and Hungary tend to stress ancestry and bloodlines (with Sweden being a notable exception; Jones and Smith, 2001, 49). If you grew up in a family outside your country of origin, you may have noticed that older people will be less likely to see themselves as members of where they currently live, while their children will see themselves as connected to where they live. When I gave a talk at Goteborg University in Sweden a few years ago, I asked two older taxi drivers who had lived in the country for several decades whether they considered themselves Swede. One from Mali and the other from Afghanistan gave the same response: "No, but my children see themselves as Swedish. They go to university without paying tuition, they are accepted by native born friends and are happy to be here" (cf. Jones and Smith, 2001, 57).

An inclusive identity is important because it promotes social cohesion, the ability of people of different backgrounds to consider others as members of the society and to provide them with the benefits of the social programs its government provides. An exclusive identity will exclude a large share of the benefits to some members of the society and this will cause division and reduce social cohesion (Holtug, 2021, 136). When a society is divided because more people emphasize an exclusive identity, the society will also reduce the influx of immigrants (see below). I will also show that societies with inclusive identities will be more likely to have universalistic welfare policies while countries where most people favor inclusive identities will restrict such benefits to people who look like the majority (Holtug, 2021, 140; Rothstein and Uslaner, 2005 and the sources below on deservingness).

The idea of exclusivity is based upon a fear that the dominant culture is under threat. If culture is based upon ancestry, where one was born, or the religion one follows, minorities may be considered to be a threat to the dominant culture. This is the heart of ethnocentrism and the opposition to immigrants from areas where people do not share the same background as the majority. Sumner (1906, 13) explained such a view: "Ethnocentrism is . . . this view of things in which one's own group is the center of everything, and all others are scaled and rated with reference to it . . . Each group nourishes its own pride and vanity, boasts itself superior, exalts its own divinities, and looks with contempt on outsiders. Each group thinks its own folkways the only right ones, and if it observes other groups have other folkways, these excite its scorn."

Bartels (2018) examines feelings of threat among 10 European nations in 2014–2015 and finds that cultural factors, rather than worries about the economic impact of immigrants, are important. Rathbun and Powers (2017) report similar findings for Europe and the United States—people are more worried that their culture will be reshaped than that their own economic situation will be worsened by people of different backgrounds. Dislike of Muslims and Jews are important determinants of feelings of cultural threat. Sniderman and Hagendoorn (2007, 44) argue that in the Netherlands they "are viewed as dark, foreign, intrusive, working class, and deviant. Difference and deviance are the constituent elements of the other . . . 'They' will take what is 'ours,' without making reciprocal contributions . . . or exercising restraint and self-control."

Throughout Europe, but especially in Austria and France, a visceral hostility to Jews was supported by layers of racial, cultural, religious, and socioeconomic prejudices, sedimented over centuries but also aggravated or reframed by new anxieties and insecurities. This type of anti-Semitism bound together the majority of the transnational forces of the "new" radical right (fascism predominant among them) in the interwar years, turning them into willing accomplices in the brutal campaign of genocide against the continent's Jewish communities in the 1940s. Islamophobia was reinvented and revitalized as a potent exclusionary ideology upon which the radical right has radically redefined and narrowed the notion of "us" in opposition to "them," mixing race with culture, prejudice with rational arguments about integration, compatibility, and absorption capacity.

In France, Marine Le Pen, who in 2011 succeeded her father in the leadership of the Front National (FN), capitalized on moral panic about Muslim street prayers and the availability of halal meat (a moral panic that her party had helped create in the first place) and began speaking about an "invasion" of France, deliberately invoking the parallels of the German attack on the country in 1940 (Kallis, 2018).

Anti-Semitic attitudes also define much of political life in Hungary. Hungarians saw their identity as incompatible with Jewish and as a battle between the two ethnic communities. The Communist party saw "the Jewish question" as antithetical to Hungarian traditions. The successors were even more hostile to the Jews, seeing the leaders of its community as too much aligned to the Communist party, who stressed the memory of the Holocaust to make Hungarians feel guilty (see my analysis and Kovacs, n.d., in chapter 8).

Zick, Kupper, and Hovermann (2011) report very high levels of both anti-Jewish and anti-Muslim sentiments throughout Europe—in Poland, Hungary, Germany, France, and Great Britain. Less than 20 percent of the population of Poland and France believe that Islam is compatible with their own culture, while over two thirds of Europeans find that Muslims treat women as inferiors and feel that many Muslims treat terrorists as heroes. Their most important findings are that (1) anti-Semitism and anti-Islamist feelings are highly correlated and (2) both types of prejudice are strongly related to homophobic, anti-same sex marriage, and anti-immigrant attitudes. They report that ethnocentric attitudes are highest among authoritarians who might be willing to compromise democracy and who believe that that "it is a good thing that certain groups are at the top, while others are at the bottom," as one might expect from a social dominance orientation.

These results are strongest in countries that have more of an exclusive than inclusive identity. In countries with a legacy of Communism, dictatorial rule has been replaced by right-wing authoritarians who prey upon the nationalist attitudes of their populations (see especially the discussions of Hungary and Poland below). The leaders prey on constituencies that are biased against Jews: Almost a quarter of Hungarians hold negative opinions of Jews.

Even as many Europeans are biased against both Muslims and Jews, the wrath is mostly aimed at people of the Islamic faith (see the discussions of individual countries below, especially Austria, Germany, Hungary, and Poland). Sniderman, Hasgendoorn, and Prior (2004, 47) argue:

 . . . increasingly, the strains over immigration in Western Europe are being cast in terms of a division between European majorities and Muslim minorities . . . A perception that [national] culture is threatened is the dominant factor in generating a negative reaction to immigrant minorities . . . Culture is a condensation of shared convictions as to what is right and should be valued and what is wrong and should be prohibited. Oversimplified and erroneous images of the "other" play a part in conflict between national majorities and Muslim minorities groups.

Anti-Muslim sentiments are especially strong among people who believe that theirs is the only true religion and who are also biased against other immigrants (Kupper and Zick, 2010, 85). They argue that "religious teachings themselves contain some problematic aspects that sometimes present justifications for inequality and the devaluation of specific groups."

In some countries—notably France and Germany now—people distinguish between Jews and Muslims by seeing Jews as European and thus able to integrate into their societies. States may support Jewish religious institutions as they give funds to Christian churches and organizations—although this is not the case in Hungary and Poland. On the other hand, Islam is regarded as a "totalitarian ideology," Muslims are seen as a threat to Christian culture and immigrants are expected to return to their countries of origin (Bar-On, 2018, 9). Betz (2018, 98–99) writes about fears of Islam among Europeans: "The radical right's nativist discourse on Islam has all the ingredients of a moral panic, designed to evoke anxieties and fears and thus reinforce already existing sentiments of cultural and symbolic insecurity and disorientation among the general public, reflected in the notion that one no longer feels at home in one's own community and country."

Greven (2016, 5) argues that nationalists see all sorts of minorities as "them":

In Hungary, one target is therefore the Roma minority, while the Tea Party and Trump highlight Mexicans and other immigrants from Latin America. Islamophobia (much more prominently than antisemitism) characterizes rightwing populists' positions regarding the immigration (and integration) of Muslims everywhere, but in the United States it is informed less by the current influx of refugees than by the threat of terrorism. In the United States, Betz (2018, 7) states: "Nativism originated as a social movement inspired by Protestant revivalism, which advanced a far-reaching reform agenda including temperance and the abolition of slavery."

Hungary's identity is reified by emphasizing the exclusivist nature of the Christian religion. Judaism and Islam are heathen religions. Hungarians' right-wing leader, Viktor Orban, sees the two in alliance to undermine the nation's religious heritage. The most prominent Jew born in Hungary (now living in the United States) is the billionaire George Soros. Soros has set up foundations to support democracy in the former Communist countries of Central and Eastern Europe. He also founded the Central European University in Budapest, which had a center for the study of Judaic history. Orban saw Soros as a threat to him both domestically and internationally. He forced the university to close and move to Vienna. He also accused Soros of sponsoring the immigration of Muslims to Hungary as part of a conspiracy between Islam and Judaism to undermine Christianity and to his autocratic rule (Witte, 2019) and of being the "chief instigator of a deliberate plot to replace white, Christian Europeans—and Hungarians in particular—with brown-skin Muslims" (quoting Applebaum, 2019, 39).

Explanations for Identities

What shapes people's senses of identity? There are three major accounts of the roots of "tribalism" and polarization.

The first is institutional. From Duverger (1954), we have the argument that countries with parliamentary systems and primarily national elections, especially when elected on a single ticket, should have more polarized political systems. Nations with the following characteristics should be more moderate: a federal government and single-member districts where voters choose legislators by majority rule and must respond to the demands of constituents from their districts rather than from the party (see also Hall and Lamont, 2013); with presidential leadership, and first-past the post elections should be more moderate (Duverger, 1954). The latter will have more moderate parties that will have to work together to enact public policies, especially if the legislative and executive branches are controlled by different political parties (Lee, 2019).

The two other explanations discussed next are not institutional. The countries I examine have different sets of institutions and patterns of polarization. Institutions don't shape the level of polarization in a country. Duverger's argument does not hold today. Without institutional change, parties have become more polarized in the United States and the United Kingdom. Polarization happened as the bases of the major parties diverged, even as the institutions didn't change. If division were the source of conflictual parties, Sweden (with a parliamentary system without individual constituencies) should have the strongest level of polarization.

Institutions don't shape polarization. Presidential systems with single-member districts and first-past-the-post elections used to have moderate parties. Since the 1980s the American parties have become more polarized (Abramowitz, 2018; Bartels, 2018), even before Trump emerged on the political scene. Seib (2016) finds a continuity of support in the electorate for right-wing nationalism from Patrick Buchanan to H. Ross Perot to Sarah Palin to Donald Trump.

The parties are polarized on a wide range of issues, from who should count as a "true American" to who is deserving of government support and also includes economic, social, security, and immigration policy. Citrin and Wright (2009) find that the importance of white Christian identity for being a "true American" shaped support for Republican candidates and opposition to legal immigration even in the 1990s. We see a similar pattern in the United Kingdom.

Institutions don't predict levels of polarization very well: Austria has parties polarized over a wide range of issues with a nationalist party in government. France has a complex electoral system with parties polarized on nationalism and on some domestic and foreign policy issues. Hungary and Poland are governed by parties with exclusivist positions on nationalism but converging on most other issues. Israel and Taiwan have competing parties with one party emphasizing an exclusivist position on identity and the other a more inclusive position in parliamentary systems. So there is no direct pathway from institutional design to partisan conflict.

A second explanation is that American politics is essentially tribal and not ideological (Fiorina, Abrams, and Pope, 2011). Mason argues (2018, 15, 55) that identities shape partisan affiliations independent of positions on issues. She argues that issue positions may increase support for one's own political party but are not responsible for the roots of negativity toward the opposing party. Mason (2018, 118–121) claims that the only policy issue that shaped voters' decisions was abortion, but there is no evidence that views on right to life were as critical as other issues in 2020.

A third explanation is tribalism, and issue positions are strongly related. People dislike the other side because its supporters are "them," not "us" in terms of religion, race, and ethnicity—and because these demographic traits are strongly linked to the values that both the leaders and supporters of the opposition hold. This is the position that I shall present throughout the book. Tribalism, Mason (2018, 58) argues, is rooted in demographic and religious differences but is not strongly connected to issue positions and values. Immigration and prejudice are only mentioned as part of an overall measure of issue constraint with no independent effects. These issues are not as powerful as identities or social ties. In 1972 the simple correlation between ideology and party identification was .31 and remained below .43 until 1996. It increased above .6 (when it was almost .7) in 2019. In 1972 about half of strong Republicans considered themselves conservative and 30 percent of strong Democrats said that they were liberal. By 2016, 77 percent of strong Republicans were conservative and 52 percent of strong Democrats were liberals.

In the United States, where I live, people in my home county of Montgomery County, Maryland look and think and vote very differently from folks in Nebraska. It is a very diverse county, with many Jews, Hindus, other Asians, Catholics, African Americans, and Muslims. It is highly educated, among the wealthiest in the country, and Republicans have a hard time finding candidates to run for office in a place where all elected officials are liberal Democrats. There are very few evangelicals or Republicans. People are more likely to go to an ethnic restaurant or a theater than to a wrestling match or a family restaurant. They select candidates who want to restrict gun ownership, favor women's rights and gay rights, and even vote to increase taxes on themselves (see also Hetherington and Weiler, 2018).

The link between demographic traits and issue positions is strong. I show in Table 2.1 in the next chapter that a sense of identity was the strongest predictor of Americans' vote choice in 2016—and I have also found that our tribalism is well predicted by (in order of statistical significance) political ideology, positive or negative feelings toward minorities (African Americans, Asians, Muslims, Hispanics, and Christian evangelicals), support for government spending on social programs, age, favoring government programs to increase income equality, support for gun control legislation, and beliefs that minorities face discrimination. Simply, tribalism and issue positions are strongly related, not independent of each other as part of a broader syndrome of "negative partisanship," in the terminology of Abramowitz and Webster (2018). The direction of causality may be in question, but the overriding issue is that tribalism and issue positions are highly correlated.

This increase in tribalism and ideology cannot be attributed to institutions, since the structure of most political systems has not changed much over time even as attitudes have (as I discuss throughout the book). If structures ruled, one might expect that tribalism would be greatest in a country such as Sweden and least in the United States and the United Kingdom, according to the logic of Duverger. However, just the opposite is true. Sweden is the least polarized country I discuss and the United States (followed by the United Kingdom) has the greatest polarization. As Hopkins (2018) has argued, political life in the American federal system has become increasingly nationalized in the past several decades.

See Figures 1.1 and 1.2 for portraits of these linkages. In Figure 1.1 I outline how an inclusive and an exclusive sense of identity is related to issue positions on nationalist and other issues. The story is simple: Both inclusive and exclusive identities may be related to a variety of issue positions, but strong polarization across issues is most likely to be found when one political party is inclusive and the other favors an exclusive identity. We have no single measure of polarization: Instead it is measured when a wide range of issues are highly correlated with each other and especially with national identity. There is no simple relationship between inclusive and exclusive identity and institutional structures. The measure of identity is Bonikowski's (2017), based upon the 2013 International Social Survey Program's indicators of whether being a true member of society reflects religion, country of origin, or national ancestry.

Identity in the United States does have historical roots. There is a weak correlation between the share of the statewide vote for Trump in 2016 with the votes for the anti-immigration Know Nothing Party in 1856, but a slightly stronger link between the Trump vote and the estimated Klan membership

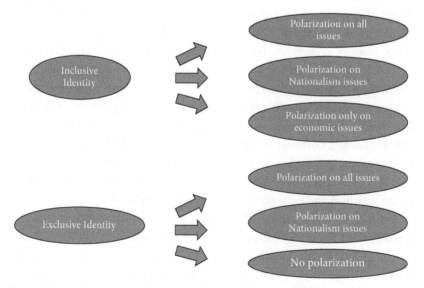

Figure 1.1 Inclusive versus Exclusive National Identity and Polarization

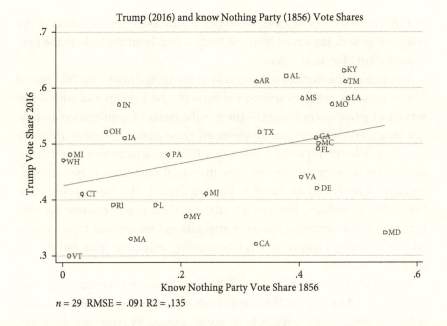

Trump (2016) and know Nothing Party (1856) Vote Shares

n = 29 RMSE = .091 R2 = ,135

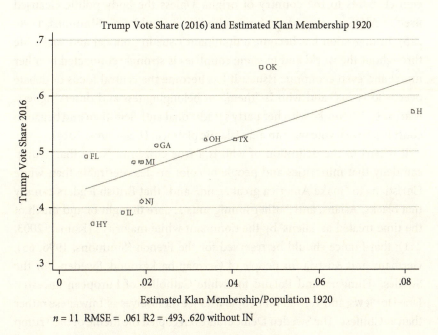

Trump Vote Share (2016) and Estimated Klan Membership 1920

n = 11 RMSE = .061 R2 = .493, .620 without IN

Figure 1.2 Trump and Know Nothing Party Vote Shares

in 1920 (from data in Jackson, 1967) (see Figure 1–2). The weakness of the relationship with the Know Nothing Party is largely attributable to the dramatic shift of Maryland voters.

Throughout the world, and especially in the United States, the "us" versus "them" dynamic revolves around the issue of who belongs and who is deserving of government support—the specific issues of immigration and racial antagonism. Mason barely mentions these issues. Abortion (Mason's issue) has fallen in importance since the 1970s, replaced by immigration and race as core issues in politics. We argue that racial attitudes have become preeminent in American discourse in the past decade. This has happened not just in the United States but throughout the world as people became less concerned with the economic effects of migrants and more about their cultural adaptation. What matters most is where immigrants come from rather than their sheer number.

Jean-Marie Le Pen, the founder of the Front National in France, said: "Just as AIDS posed a danger to the human body, so too immigrants posed a metaphorical threat to the French body politic purged by returning these foreign elements to the country of origin. Unless the body politic cleansed itself of AIDS, foreign ideas, foreign bodies, it would die" (Simmons, 1996, 225). Immigration has become a dominant issue in political and social life throughout the world and in some countries is strongly connected to other moral and even economic issues. It has become the central focus of debate over who is "us" and who is "them," of belongingness and deservingness. Marine Le Pen broke with her party's traditional anti-Semitism and began to court the Jewish vote with an anti-Islamic platform (Beuazamy, 2014).

It is part of the definition of who is a true citizen of X, so that Trump can deny that minorities and people of color are less desirable than white Christians to "make America great again," and "that British leaders can say that blacks, Asians, and " other immigrants . . . are thought of and much of the time treated as 'aliens' by the dominant white majority" (Kumar, 2003, 241); that France should be reserved for the French (Simmons, 1996, 65), Germany and Austria for people of German background, Sweden "for the Swedes," Hungary and Poland for white Catholics of European ancestry, Israel for Jews, and Taiwan for people who see themselves as Taiwanese rather than as Chinese. The Sweden Democrats even copied the theme of the Trump campaign in the United States and promised to "make Sweden great again," selling T-shirts with this motto to its supporters (AFP and Snell, 2018).

For Germany, an exclusivist orientation refers to "the notion of a 'cultural nation'" as Germany defined itself during the nineteenth century (Hjerm and Schnabel, 2012). The country, write Schierrup, Hansen, and Castles (2006, 147), was torn between moderate leftists who advocated recognizing "the permanence of immigration through measures designed to offer equal rights and ultimately citizenship to immigrants" and moderate conservatives who worried that this policy "would undermine the principles of national identity based on German descent and not being a country of immigration." More than 70 percent of Germans believe that it is critical for minorities to adapt to the nation's culture (Eatwell and Goodwin, 2018, 138).

The same rhetoric is being used around the world. For each of the countries I examine, the distinction revolves around race, ethnicity, and religion. So immigration and racial policies (especially deservingness) center around the distinction about who is a true member of a society. It is not surprising that these movements are linked, because Trump campaign manager Steven Bannon has worked with nationalist parties throughout the world with the same overall message.

In the United States: When Bannon took over Trump's campaign, he ran "a nationalist, divisive campaign in which issues of race, immigration, culture, and identity were put front and center" (Green, 2017, 208). And "Trump's . . . victory is better understood as the death rattle of White Christian America—the cultural and political edifice built primarily by white Protestant Christians—rather than as its resuscitation" (Jones, 2017, 3). Additionally, "Christian nationalism operates as a set of beliefs and ideals that seek the national preservation of a Christian identity" (Whitehead et al., 2018). Trump also accused Jews who voted for Democrats of dual loyalty to Israel and the United States (Sullivan, 2019). By recreating a Christian America, Trump presumed he was "making America great again" (Serwer, 2019). Trump's support derives from the views of his voters, who see the American flag as an essential symbol of the country. Sixty percent of Trump supporters in 2016 associate the flag with Republicans while only 30 percent of Clinton voters link the flag to their party (Ballard 2021). Eighty percent of Americans share the view that migrants must adapt to American traditions (Eatwell and Goodwin, 2018, 138).

In the United Kingdom: "Some people do not abide by British values and traditions such as "the Union Flag, football, and fish and chips," said the British Prime Minister (Cameron, 2014). Immigrants must conform to British culture—and this view was endorsed by over 80 percent of people who were most insistent on leaving the European Union (Eatwell and Goodwell, 2018, 157).

In Austria: A Freedom Party document in 1997 stated: "The language, history, and culture of Austria are German" and called for "Austria for Austrians,"

"Austria first," and "Stop immigration" (Backes, 2018, 11). Morrow (2000, 34) writes: "The FPO presents itself to some audiences as a movement of the 1990s, a decisive break with anti-democratic authoritarianism . . . yet also to signal a desire to keep faith with a cultural and historical tradition which sees little to be ashamed of an Austrian National Socialist past."

In France: "Being on the right meant an attachment to traditional values . . . and to our national culture, . . . a feeling of sacrifice, love of family, esteem, for work well done, a taste for order, authority, hierarchy, attachment to individual liberty, admiration for glory, tenderness for the weak, and the oppressed" (Simmons, 1996, 64). The National Front's slogans became "Defend the French" and "only the Europeans who belong to the historic groups . . . can possibly join the nation today" (Simmons, 1996, 63, 163). The party became the focal point of debates on French identity, emphasizing exclusionary conceptions of communities and denouncing the anti-colonial and integrationist values of the left (Stockmayer, 2017, 14).

The FN became preoccupied with "the defense of national identity against its enemies, both interior and exterior, mainly immigrants and especially Muslims and immigrants, and the forces of 'cosmopolitanism' and 'globalization'" (Mayer, 2018, 436). With the decline of Communism, Islam became the far right's preoccupation (Mayer, n.d., 52).

"In the southern city of Beaucaire, the mayor has refused to allow alternatives to pork in school lunches for Muslim and Jewish students because [b]eing French means eating pork" (McAuley, 2018b). Eatwell and Goodwin (2018, 138, 157) wrote: "A key problem Muslim migrants faced in France was assimilationist approach which required them to adopt French culture and identity . . . The historic separation of church and state caused further problems over girls wearing hijabs to schools, which [Front National leader] Jean-Marie Le Pen was happy to exploit" and that more than 80 percent of voters insisted that sharing their nation's culture with immigrants is important. Le Pen proposed "a rearmament of the country . . . in the face of unbridled globalization." This program depended upon the state acting a as a "community of values, a foundation of the social welfare state" for the benefit of people of French origin, not immigrants (Betz, 2015, 84).

In Germany: the AfD invokes "Christian occidental values" (Backes, 2018, 6) and warns against "the decay of bourgeois culture and values" (Minkenberg, 1992, 60). Backer (2000, 95) has written: "The German extreme right has responded to this challenge with a conservative counter-attack, expressed via a renewed interest in German national identity. Based on the reassertion of values and virtues traditionally associated with the Germans (such as hard work and sense of duty), it rejects all that is seen as 'un-German,' ranging from new technologies to foreign immigration."

In Hungary: Prime Minister Orban has declared himself "as a defender of traditional Christian and national values" (Erlanger, 2021) and a supporter of "white, Christian culture against the nonwhite, non-Christian migrants and their 'cosmopolitan' liberal protectors in Brussels, Berlin, and other Western European capitals" (Kagan, 2019).

In Poland: The Polish Prime Minister demanded in a 2017 television interview: "Poland First," and in both Hungary and Poland the foreign-born population is miniscule (less than 5 percent). People still expected migrants to conform to local customs and religion (by more than 90 percent (Eatwell and Goodwin, 2018, 141, 157).

In Sweden: "We want to reshape Euro Bevara Sverige Svenskt [BSS], Keep Sweden Swedish and re-Christianize it" (Santora, 2019). The right-wing Bevara Sverige Svenskt (BBS) party's name translates to "Keep Sweden Swedish" (Wildfeldt, 2018, 6). Swedes were the least likely people in Europe to insist that immigrants adapt to Swedish society. Yet more than 60 percent still were willing to do so (Eatwell and Goodwin, 2018, 157).

In Israel: Some of the more religious Israelis have called for "the exclusive right of the Jewish people over Greater Israel" (Perliger and Pedazhur, 2018, 6), and the right-wing coalition of Likud and the religious parties in 2018 enacted a law making only Jews full citizens of the country, denying that status to the Druze, an Arab community that has been loyal to the country and served in the armed forces (Rasgon, 2018).

In Taiwan: The old party of Kuomintang, which favors ultimate reunification with China, is seen by a large share of people as "out of touch with modern Taiwanese life" (Chien, 2021).

In addition to inclusivity and exclusivity, there are other forms of identity that have different foundations. Schildkraut (2011) considers alternatives such as respecting political institutions, pursuing economic success through hard work, letting other people say what they want even if they disagree with you, doing volunteer work, feeling American, being informed about local and national politics, being involved in local and national politics, being able to speak English, and having American citizenship. Some of these traits are shared by almost everyone living in the country (economic success, giving others their own positions, speaking the language, and citizenship). Others are observed by only a few (such as volunteer work and being informed or involved in politics). But they don't distinguish between "us" and "them" the way the inclusive/exclusive divide does.

I next discuss each country in detail and then move to statistical analyses of each country. I first link arguments of national identity and issues of policy to vote choice, party affiliation, and (in Britain the vote on the Brexit referendum) and then to a consideration of how national identity leads to perceptions of which people deserve benefits from government.

My argument is simple: Identity is critical but it is *not* independent of policy positions, especially on issues such as immigration and race. The variations are not shaped by electoral systems. The United States and the United Kingdom, the only countries in the sample with first-past-the-post electoral systems, are the most polarized. The two policies that stem from the issue of identity are deservingness and immigration.

There are mixed results on the effects of ethnic diversity on government spending for welfare. Fenwick (2019) finds that countries with high levels of immigration also spend more on welfare benefits—and this result may reflect the more tolerant and left-leaning governments such as Sweden, where immigration and universalistic social welfare policies go together. Yet who the immigrants are may also matter. Hopkins (2010) finds that welfare programs aimed at poor people will be lower when there is a rapid rise in the rate of immigration by people who look different from the majority (notably Hispanics) in American communities. (See also my findings for support of right-wing parties in Chapter 10).

The most deserving people are the ones most willing to work. Yet many people combine their ideas of willingness to work with ethnocentrism. Magni (2018, 4) argues that many immigrants are not as hard working as citizens of the host country and are thus not as deserving as natives. In most European countries, natives see immigrants as unwilling to improve their own situations and therefore are not worthy of government support. Western publics see "old people, the sick and disabled, needy families with children, and underemployed" as deserving of government support but immigrants who do not seek work as less deserving of assistance (van Oorschot, 2010, 35).

Petersen, Slothuus, Stubager, and Togeby (2010) write: "If a recipient is in control of his own situation but still requests help, it suggests that he or she is intentionally trying to evade making an effort. If a recipient . . . has demonstrated a willingness to contribute, it suggests that he or she is in general willing to make an effort and, hence, is not trying to evade doing so in the particular situation." Van Ooorschot (2006, 25–26) argues that the government should not support people who are "are assumed to be lazy, unreliable, and/ or addicted to drugs and alcohol . . . Programmes targeted at groups with no negative images—such as widows, elderly people, and physically disabled people—[should be] supported by the American public" and these people are generally presumed to be of the majority.

Gilens (1999, 169) finds that the primary determinant of white Americans' opposition to welfare is their perception of blacks as lazy. Cramer (2016) makes a similar argument for the United States when she claims that many people, especially intellectuals and bureaucrats, are not hardworking. Not deserving government support thus includes people who put out little effort and people who simply don't work with their hands.

Many people see minorities as the people who put out little effort (also look at Sweden). Throughout Europe, working class people have become more alienated from the mainstream parties supporting immigration because they see migrants and their supporters as usurping their contributions to the nations' economies: "people who see themselves as economically-underprivileged also tend to feel culturally-distant from the dominant groups in society and to envision that distance in oppositional terms, which lend themselves to quintessential populist appeals to a relatively 'pure' people pitted against a corrupt or incompetent political elite" (Gidron and Hall, 2017, S59).

If the recipient is from the same ethnic/racial/religious group as the majority population, natives will be more likely to support providing assistance to the group (Krimel and Rader, 2020; Reeskens and van Oorschott, 2012; Senik, Stichmoth, and Van der Strateten, 2009, 347). This is especially the case for Europeans when the immigrants are from the Middle East or otherwise look different from the majority population. People are also more willing to block assistance to minorities if they are not Christian (Lahav, 2004, 118, 178) and when the share of immigrants has spiked in recent years (Alesina, Murard, and Rapoport, 2019, 29, 40, 41).

When the majority strongly identifies with its own background, it will be more likely to limit its benefits to the majority population and to block assistance to immigrants of different backgrounds (Alesina and Tabellini, 2021, 25). Levy (in print) argues that while there is no overall correlation between levels of immigration and support for welfare spending, there is a relationship between support for migration and the share of immigrants who are Hispanic.

Immigration concerns who may enter the country, and deservingness tells us who benefits from government programs. Societies with an inclusive sense of identity will be willing to accept immigrants from a wide variety of backgrounds if these new residents accept the values and customs of the majority. Countries where most people have an exclusive sense of identity will try to restrict immigration to migrants of their own background (cf. Wright, 2011). They will see immigrants of different backgrounds as less educated and as attempting to change the values of their new homes (see Alesina and Tabellini, 2021, 24; and the discussion of individual countries in the chapters to follow).

Both deservingness and the decision to allow people of diverse backgrounds to migrate to a country are more likely to be based on the ethnocultural characteristics of people than on the effects of new entrants on the economy (Rathbun, Iaknis, and Powers, 2012). Yet there is an economic dimension to immigration policy. The wealthier and more equal countries are more likely to admit new immigrants from diverse backgrounds. And the voting base for nationalist parties in all of the countries covered here is largely composed of blue collar voters (see the discussion of individual countries: see Schaefer, 2017; and Rathbun, Iaknis, and Powers (2012, 23).

Even in much more tolerant Sweden, the rising Sweden Democrats focused on "how unassimilated migrants were eviscerating not just the nation's cultural identity but also the social-welfare heart of the Swedish state" (Becker, 2019).

The architect of Trump's campaign, Steve Bannon, based his campaign on "themes and phrases from European populists to rally the make-America-great-again faithful" (Witte, Morello, Mahtani, and Faiola, 2019). And he went on to advise European parties on national identity (Horwitz, 2018). Trump allied himself with the two Italian parties and their opposition to both the European Union and immigration (Kingsley, 2018).

These movements all focused on how there is a sense of threat feared by the majority population. Most Germans do not consider Muslims to be a part of their country. Only 20 percent of German Muslims are citizens and more than half of the native population see themselves threatened by the culture of an alien religion (Dlezal, Helbling, and Hutter, 2010).

More generally in Europe, Fetzer (2012, 7) found in surveys that people "who believe that the foreign born threaten them economically are much less likely to support immigration or immigrants. Individuals who feel deprived relative to another immigrant or native-born group exhibit hostility to migrants."

Trump did not, but did question whether American Jews voting for Democrats demonstrated a lack of loyalty to the Jewish people (Sonmez, 2019). He had a long history of attacking Muslims, Mexicans, and African Americans (Lopez, 2019)—anyone who is different from his most devoted supporters, who are evangelical Christians in rural areas.

What are the bases of these fears? The answer is three-fold, although the reasons are interrelated. First, the out-groups are culturally distinct from the majority population. They look different, may speak different languages, follow different religions, and even if they are not objectively different may have alternative world views shaped by where they live and how they make their living. Second, they are seen as less deserving of government benefits than are the majority population—often they are seen as lazy and not worthy of the support for government programs. Third, they are seen as an *increasing threat*.

It is not simply that minorities are numerous. The share of Muslim immigrants is very small in the United States but is growing in Europe, where they are increasingly not welcome. But their share is growing. People fear change, as they do in the United States. The key trend in the United States is the decline of the share of the population that identifies as born-again Christians (Jones, 2016). When people feel that their values are under attack by people who do not share their beliefs, they mobilize in an attempt to counteract these trends (Bean, 2017; Hansen, 1984). This is why nationalist parties have been faring so well in Europe and why evangelical turnout increased strongly in 2016 in favor of Trump.

In Belgium, voters of N-VA (the New Flemish Alliance) and Vlaams Belang are substantially more likely to adhere to a dominant Flemish identity. When it comes to explicit nationalist motives, we observe that the effect for holding a dominantly regional identity is very strong, and anti-immigrant sentiments are also important determinants of the vote for these parties (Hooghe and Siters, 2020). Religious voters should support the nationalist Likud in Israel in 2019, and people who identify as Taiwanese rallied behind the Democratic Progressive Party in Taiwan when they feared efforts by China to force unification.

The impact of fear is strongest in countries with homogenous populations. In more homogenous countries there has not been pressure to develop policies that emphasize assimilation. But attitudes toward assimilation can change over time, as they did in the United States. When jobs were plentiful, people welcomed immigrants and immigration did not play a large role in

American politics. This view was prominent in the United States for many years (as a multiethnic society) and is still dominant in Sweden. There is no strong dividing line between "us" and "them," and minority members of society can readily assimilate into the larger culture.

Higher levels of immigration throughout the United States and Europe led to a situation "in which the ideals of liberal democracy feel like foolhardy surrender. Liberal democracy is designed to flatten out social hierarchies, making this kind of majoritarian backlash all but inevitable. This helped lead Poland's Catholics, a once-dominant group, to support a political party that had promised to subvert the courts. It may have also led European and American whites who feared losing what they viewed as their special place in society to support leaders who promised to control immigrants and minorities (Fischer, 2018). See also Betz (2018) and Kallis (2018) for survey evidence on anti-Muslim sentiment in Europe and the worry that Muslims might become so numerous as to threaten Christian culture.

This politics of national identity has reshaped issues of what political parties stand for with whom they stand. Who is an American, a Brit, a French person? In the analyses to follow, I consider these issues by examining what shapes national identity in the United States, Western Europe, Central and Eastern Europe, Israel, and Taiwan. I present models of vote choice for the major parties, some fringe parties, and for the United Kingdom's vote on withdrawal from the European Union. I seek to understand how identity shapes vote choice (or where such data are not available, then party identification).

I use instrumental variable probit when possible so that I can consider what shapes national identity, as well as vote choice. Finally, I examine factors shaping attitudes on identity at the aggregate level. I also examine how identities stressing a common heritage of religion and ancestry may lead to greater support for authoritarian and nationalist parties and for more restrictive immigration policies.

The sample sizes are small, so these analyses are more suggestive than definitive, but they do point to a syndrome of how nationalist attitudes shape both preferences and voting. I emphasize that the measures of identity will vary from one country to another, since people in different places have alternative priorities for what constitutes a "real X"–and because not every alternative is examined in every survey.

The key arguments I make are as follows. Prior to 2016, immigration did not shape vote choice in contemporary American politics (although it was salient in earlier periods). American politics had become increasingly polarized on a wide range of issues since the 1980s, and since the election of Barack Obama in 2008 American politics had become divided by race and the racialization of other issues such as health care. But immigration or national identity had not emerged as a central issue in American campaigns until recently. In 2016 it became the most important determinant of vote choice in the Presidential election.

Immigration and national identity were more important dividing lines in European politics. However, the issues were critical to smaller parties, which were labeled as "extreme right-wing" and which mostly received a small share of the vote (under 20 percent). In the Nordic countries, there has long been agreement among the major parties supporting universalism in social welfare policies (rather than focusing on who is deserving).

The same "depolarization" occurs in Britain (Adams, Green, and Milazzo, 2012), where there are only minimal divisions on immigration policy among the Labor, Conservative, or Liberal Democrat parties–or their supporters. Throughout Europe, opposition to immigration and to the European Union was restricted to fringe parties such as the French Front National, the German AfD, the Norwegian Progress Party, the Dutch Freedom Party, the True Finns, and the Sweden Democrats (Schäfer, 2017) and the United Kingdom Independence Party (UKIP).

More recently, right-wing parties have won larger shares of the vote, gaining power in Austria, Italy, Hungary, and Poland, displacing the right wing Republicans in France with the National Front, and the AfD emerging as a threat to the more centrist parties in Germany. The Freedom Party in Austria entered the government in 2017. In the 1991 regional election in Vienna the party received 22.6 percent of the vote and became the second largest party in Vienna (Betz, 1993).

There are divisions on immigration policy between the left and the right in most European countries. These divisions are not as wide as those between the mainstream parties and fringe populist parties. They are stronger than the conflicts between Republicans and Democrats in the United States under Presidents George H. W. and George W. Bush and Ronald Reagan and their Democratic opponents, but are much weaker than the splits between Trump and Hillary Rodham Clinton in 2016.

Fringe parties in Europe have pushed the mainstream parties (both conservative and socialist) to the right on immigration. In most of Europe nationalist parties have averaged less than 15 percent of the vote, while pushing center-left and center-right parties to nationalist positions on immigration. In Western Europe—with the exception of Austria and France— these nationalist parties have remained distinct minorities, while in the former Communist countries of Central and Eastern Europe, they have emerged as governing parties (Eiermann, Mounck, and Giutchen, 2017, 5, 7).

Troianovski (2016) argues (emphasis added)

> ...the firmness of the mainstream parties' commitment to European integration has helped drive the dissent to fringe parties. It has allowed nationalists and populists to win over people disenchanted with the mainstream, pro-EU consensus, to such an extent that *euroskeptic language is creeping into major parties, too, in some places as they seek to stop voters from moving away.*

This dynamic reduces the impact of national identity in the models of the two party vote (or party identification) that I estimate. The connections between issues of national identity and other issues have important consequences for immigration policy. National identity and other issues are strongly linked in the United States today and there are strong divisions between the parties on both. The narrow victory of Trump (and the Republicans more generally) might give way to a Democratic majority (with a Democratic President) in 2016 and then 2020. The strong polarization between the parties–specifically the different interpretations of what makes a "true American" between Republicans and Democrats—may lead to a substantial shift in policy on issues related to identity—especially immigration.

This rise in an exclusivist ideology constitutes a reaction against the movement in the post-World War 2 West to atone for the Holocaust and to welcome immigrants from all over the world.

The issue of "deservingness" has also been important in many European countries, even those with reputations as more tolerant of refugees and minorities more generally. In Norway, Denmark, Sweden, and the United Kingdom, majority whites do not see immigrant as "deserving" social welfare benefits, even in states with universal programs (Larsen, 2011; Kumlin, 2017; Mudde and Kaltwasser, 2013). Immigrants do not share the same culture or the work ethic of natives, as Larsen (2011, 347) finds. Johnston et al. (2010) agree that cultural values are more important for deservingness than are economic conditions (in their analysis). So do Brooks and Manza (2007) in their study of Sweden and the United States. Brooks and Manza (2007) and Levy and Wright (2021) also find that values of national identity and toward immigrants of different backgrounds than the majority are more critical to feelings of deservingness than are economic conditions.

In Western Europe, immigration and issues of identity have been salient in some countries (France, Hungary, Austria, Spain, Greece, Italy, the Netherlands, Norway, Denmark, and Sweden, Switzerland, the United Kingdom), but not in others (Ireland, Portugal). There are two key factors that shape whether issues of identity are polarized. First, how salient politically are issues of immigration and identity? Second, are these issues part of the agendas of the major parties or are they confined to fringe parties, as in France? Bornschneier (2012) argues that these issues are confined to the fringe National Front in France but divide supporters of the major parties in Germany. In 2017, however, the National Front moved from the fringe to the mainstream as the rightist alternative. By 2017 the party of French national identity was also the party of the right. Its candidate was Marine Le Pen, whose positions on immigration were similar to those of Donald Trump.

Where there is a strong effect for nationalism on the left-right vote—or on left-right party identification—this issue has become central to party polarization on identity (though not necessarily on other issues). When there is not a strong relationship between nationalism and left-right voting (or partisan identification), either (1) nationalism is not a salient issue in a country's politics (the United States before 2016, Central and Eastern Europe and Asia today) or (2) nationalism may be salient to some voters, but only to voters of fringe extremist parties (as in France before 2017, most northern European countries before 2017). The strong effects for nationalism in the United States in 2016 indicate that these cultural concerns have become more salient and divide the voters of the major parties. The rise of nationalism in countries such as France and the Netherlands indicates that these cultural concerns have displaced other social and economic issues (and the traditional parties) as the main source of political conflict. Parties that had previously been minor (and extremist) have now become mainstream.

From the surveys I have estimated the share of respondents who give different characteristics as requirements for being a true member of society. In almost all of the countries sampled, a significant share of the population answered "being born here." They were France (46 percent), Greece (77 percent), Hungary (82 percent), Italy (79 percent), Poland (80 percent), Spain

(52 percent), Sweden (80 percent), the United Kingdom (57 percent), and the United States (53 percent).

Only Australia, Canada, the Netherlands, and France (29, 40, 42, and 46 percent) had minorities saying that it was not important to be born in the country. A much smaller share of respondents said it was important to share the country's dominant religion: 79 percent (Greece, 69 percent) Hungary (71 percent), the Netherlands (71 percent), the United Kingdom (40 percent), and the United States (51 percent). All of the other countries had less than 31 percent making this argument, with the lowest being Sweden and Spain (about 18 percent). See Table 1.1.

The entries for other countries in Table 1.-2 are minus signs for significant coefficients that are negative (national identity leads to greater support for right-wing parties) or plus signs positive (for left-wing parties). A zero indicates an insignificant effect. No entry means that there was not a survey for that country in the data set. An asterisk indicates that the coefficient is significant, but barely. A strong sense of national identity should be associated with support for rightist parties. The measure of national identity is a country-by-country set of factor scores for the importance of being born in the country and sharing a country's true religion (as well as observing the nation's customs).

The strongest impacts are for Western European countries. In the European Values Survey (2008/2009), strong national identity leads to support for conservative parties in most Western European and Anglo-American countries. There is a similar pattern for party support in the ISSP modules for 1995, 2003, and 2013 as well as the Pew survey in 2016. National identity leads to voting for or political identification with conservative parties in most Western European countries. There are sporadic insignificant coefficients (notably for Portugal, but also for Austria, Ireland, Spain, and the United Kingdom in the 1995 ISSP) but most Western European and Anglo-American countries (other than the United States) have significant negative coefficients. And there is evidence of ideological polarization from national identity in Western Europe well before we observe it in the United States.

The measures of national identity used in the analyses for Table 1.2 are factor scores of measures of national identity in the surveys. For the Pew surveys, the measures are being born in the country, sharing the dominant religion, and following customs.

For the ISSP surveys, the measures of identity that load highly are cultural and ethnic questions such as being born in the country, having lived

Table 1.1 Country Averages for Characteristics for Being a True Member
of Society for Countries Included in Analysis

Variable	Identity Born Here	Identity Dominant Religion	Identity Observe Customs
Country			
France	.464	.212	.840
Germany	.306	.306	.700
Hungary	.819	.685	.945
Poland	.801	.706	.976
Sweden	.202	.179	.643
United Kingdom	.567	.379	.880
United States	.537	.513	.853

Table 1.2 Overall Importance of Citizenship Factors for Countries Examined
in Depth from ISSP 2003

Variable	Important					
	Born Here	Ancestry	Live Here	Religion	Feel Member	Factor
Country						
Austria	.753	.578	.774	.531	.885	−.360
France	.611	.492	.707	.176	.920	−.425
Germany	.574	.481	.662	.371	.744	.690
Hungary	.712	.792	.766	.837	.971	−.885
Israel	.517	.524	.820	.841	.906	.534
Poland	.888	.817	.844	.718	.970	1.456
Sweden	.482	.300	.558	.172	.822	−2.030
Taiwan	.661	.514	.735	.261	.923	−.130
United Kingdom	.734	.515	.726	.659	.740	−.189
United States	.774	.552	.811	.172	.922	.620

most of one's life in the country, being a member of the country's dominant
religion, and having ancestry from the country. Measures that do not have
high loading are more issues of civic-mindedness: simply being a citizen, respecting institutions, speaking the nation's language, and feeling oneself as a
member of the country (see Table 1.3).

Table 1.3 Overall Importance of Citizenship Factors for Countries Examined in Depth from Pew Christian Survey 2017

Variable	Identification Criteria				
	Born in Country	Identify with Customs	Share Dominant Religion	Important Keep Culture	Identity Factor
Country					
France	.212	.840	.212	.840	−.038
Germany	.306	.697	.306	.697	−.253
Hungary	.684	.945	.685	.945	.253
Poland	.706	.956	.706	.956	.250
Sweden	.171	.643	.171	.643	−.397
United Kingdom	.379	.878	.486	.880	.056
United States	.511	.853	.700	.852	−.045

Country	EVS 2008/2009	ISSP 1995	ISSP 2003	ISSP 2013	Pew Global 2016
Europe / Anglo-American Countries					
Australia		−	−	−	
Austria		0	−	−	
Belgium	−				
Canada			−	−	−
Cyprus	0				
Denmark	−		−	−	
Finland	−		*	−*	
France	−		−	−	−
Greece					−
Ireland		0	−	−	
Italy	−				−*
Luxembourg	−				
Malta	0				
Netherlands			−	−	
New Zealand		0			
Northern Ireland	−*				
Norway	−	−*	−	−	
Portugal	0			0	
Spain		0	−	−	−
Sweden	−	−*	−	−	−
Switzerland	−		−	−	

Table 1.3 Continued

Country	EVS 2008/2009	ISSP 1995	ISSP 2003	ISSP 2013	Pew Global 2016
United Kingdom	–	0	–	–	–
(West) Germany	–		–	–	
Former Communist Countries					
Albania	0				
Armenia	0				
Belarus	+				
Bosnia	0				
Bulgaria	0	0		–	
Croatia	–			–	
Czech Republic	0	0		0	
(East) Germany		+		0	
Estonia	–			0	
Georgia	0				
Hungary			–*	–*	–*
Kosovo	–				
Latvia	–			–	
Lithuania	–*			–*	
Macedonia	0				
Moldova	–				
Montenegro	–				
Poland	–*	0		0	0
Romania	0				
Russia				0	
Slovenia	–*	0	–*	–*	
Slovakia	+	0			
Ukraine	–*				

Country	EVS 2008/2009	ISSP 1995	ISSP 2003	ISSP 2013	Pew Global 2016
Europe / Anglo-American Countries					
Australia		–	–	–	
Austria		0	–	–	
Belgium	–				
Canada			–	–	–
Cyprus	0				
Denmark	–		–	–	
Finland	–		–*	–*	

(continued)

Table 1.3 Continued

Country	EVS 2008/2009	ISSP 1995	ISSP 2003	ISSP 2013	Pew Global 2016
France	–		–		–
Greece					–
Ireland		0	–	–	
Italy	–				–*
Luxembourg	-				
Malta	0				
Netherlands			–	–	
New Zealand		0			
Northern Ireland	–*				
Norway	–	–*	–	–	
Portugal	0			0	
Spain		0	–	–	–
Sweden	–	–*	–	–	–
Switzerland	–		–	–	
United Kingdom	–	0	–	–	–
(West) Germany	–		–	–	
Former Communist Countries					
Albania	0				
Armenia	0				
Belarus	+				
Bosnia	0				
Bulgaria	0	0		–	
Croatia	–			–	
Czech Republic	0	0		0	
(East) Germany		+		0	
Estonia	–			0	
Georgia	0				
Hungary			–*	–*	–*
Kosovo	–				
Latvia	–			–	
Lithuania	–*			–*	
Macedonia	0				
Moldova	–				
Montenegro	–				
Poland	–*	0		0	0

Table 1.3 Continued

Country	EVS 2008/2009	ISSP 1995	ISSP 2003	ISSP2013	Pew Global 2016
Europe / Anglo-American countries					
Australia		–	–	–	
Austria		0	–	–	
Belgium	–				
Canada			–	–	–
Cyprus	0				
Denmark	–		–	–	
Finland	–		*–	*–	
France	–		–	–	–
Greece					–
Ireland		0	–	–	
Italy	–				–*
Luxembourg	–				
Malta	0				
Netherlands			–	–	
New Zealand		0			
Northern Ireland	–*				
Norway	–	–*	–	–	
Portugal	0			0	
Spain		0	–	–	–
Sweden	–	–*	–	–	–
Switzerland	–		–	–	
United Kingdom	–	0	–	–	–
(West) Germany	–		–	–	
Former Communist Countries					
Albania	0				
Armenia	0				
Belarus	+				
Bosnia	0				
Bulgaria	0	0		–	
Croatia	–			–	
Czech Republic	0	0		0	
(East) Germany		+		0	
Estonia	–			0	
Georgia	0				

(continued)

Table 1.3 Continued

Country	EVS 2008/2009	ISSP 1995	ISSP 2003	ISSP 2013	Pew Global 2016
Hungary			−*	−*	−*
Kosovo	−				
Latvia	−			−	
Lithuania	−*			−*	
Macedonia	0				
Moldova	−				
Montenegro	−				
Poland	−*	0		0	0
Romania	0				
Russia				0	
Slovenia	−*	0	−*	−*	
Slovakia	+	0			
Ukraine	−*				

Country	EVS 2008/2009	ISSP 1995	ISSP 2003	ISSP 2013	Pew Global 2016
Europe/Anglo-American Countries					
Australia		−	−	−	
Austria	0		−	−	
Belgium	−				
Canada			−	−	−
Cyprus	0				
Denmark	−		−	−	
Finland	−		−*	−*	
France	−		−	−	−
Greece					−
Ireland		0	−	−	
Italy	−				−*
Luxembourg	−				
Malta	0				
Netherlands			−	−	
New Zealand		0			
Northern Ireland	−*				
Norway	−	−*	−	−	
Portugal	0			0	
Spain		0	−	−	−

Table 1.3 Continued

Country	EVS 2008/2009	ISSP 1995	ISSP 2003	ISSP 2013	Pew Global 2016
Sweden	–	–*	–	–	–
Switzerland	–		–	–	
United Kingdom	–	0	–	–	–
(West) Germany	–		–	–	

Former Communist Countries

Albania	0				
Armenia	0				
Belarus	+				
Bosnia	0				
Bulgaria	0	0		–	
Croatia	–			–	
Czech Republic	0	0		0	
(East) Germany		+		0	
Estonia	–			0	
Georgia	0				
Hungary			–*	–*	–*
Kosovo	–				
Latvia	–			–	
Lithuania	–*			–*	
Macedonia	0				
Moldova	–				
Montenegro	–				
Poland	–*	0		0	0

Country	EVS 2008/2009	ISSP 1995	ISSP 2003	ISSP2013	Pew Global 2016

Europe/Anglo-American Countries

Australia		–	–	–	
Austria		0	–	–	
Belgium	–				
Canada			–	–	–
Cyprus	0				
Denmark	–		–	–	
Finland	–		*	–*	
France	–		–	–	–
Greece					–

(continued)

Table 1.3 Continued

Country	EVS 2008/2009	ISSP 1995	ISSP 2003	ISSP2013	Pew Global 2016
Ireland		0	–	–	
Italy	–				–*
Luxembourg	–				
Malta	0				
Netherlands			–	–	
New Zealand		0			
Northern Ireland	–*				
Norway	–	–*	–	–	
Portugal	0			0	
Spain		0	–	–	–
Sweden	–	–*	–	–	–
Switzerland	–		–	–	
United Kingdom	–	0	–	–	–
(West) Germany	–		–	–	
Former Communist Countries					
Albania	0				
Armenia	0				
Belarus	+				
Bosnia	0				
Bulgaria	0	0		–	
Croatia	–			–	
Czech Republic	0	0		0	
(East) Germany		+		0	
Estonia	–			0	
Georgia	0				
Hungary			–*	–*	–*
Kosovo	–				
Latvia	–			–	
Lithuania	–*			–*	
Macedonia	0				
Moldova	–				
Montenegro	–				
Poland	–*	0		0	0
Romania	0				
Russia				0	
Slovenia	–*	0	–*	–*	
Slovakia	+	0			
Ukraine	–*				

Table 1.3 Continued

Country	EVS 2008/2009	ISSP 1995	ISSP 2003	ISSP 2013	Pew Global 2016
Europe / Anglo-American Countries					
Australia		–	–	–	
Austria		0	–	–	
Belgium	–				
Canada			–	–	–
Cyprus	0				
Denmark	–		–	–	
Finland	–		–*	–*	
France	–	–	–	–	–
Greece					–
Ireland		0	–	–	
Italy	–				–*
Luxembourg	–				
Malta	0				
Netherlands			–	–	
New Zealand		0			
Northern Ireland	–*				
Norway	–	–*	–	–	
Portugal	0			0	
Spain		0	–	–	–
Sweden	–	–*	–	–	–
Switzerland	–		–	–	
United Kingdom	–	0	–	–	–
(West) Germany	–		–	–	
Former Communist Countries					
Albania	0				
Armenia	0				
Belarus	+				
Bosnia	0				
Bulgaria	0	0		–	
Croatia	–			–	
Czech Republic	0	0		0	
(East) Germany		+		0	
Estonia	–			0	
Georgia	0				

(continued)

Table 1.3 Continued

Country	EVS 2008/2009	ISSP 1995	ISSP 2003	ISSP 2013	Pew Global 2016
Hungary			_*	_*	_*
Kosovo	–				
Latvia	–			–	
Lithuania	_*			_*	
Macedonia	0				
Moldova	–				
Montenegro	–				
Poland	_*	0		0	0
Romania	0				
Russia				0	
Slovenia	_*	0	*_	_*	
Slovakia	+	0			
Ukraine	_*				

Data taken from International Social Survey Program 2013 and other surveys as noted.

Symbols: – indicates that significant coefficients are negative (national identity leads to greater support for right-wing parties); + indicates positive (for left-wing parties); 0 indicates an insignificant effect; no entry means that there was not a survey for that country in the data set; * indicates that the coefficient is significant, but barely.

The overwhelming share of respondents answer positively to the civicness ideals, but there are far fewer positive responses for the cultural-ethnic measure. And the results vary by country. In Western Europe, especially Sweden, the cultural-ethnic questions are far more important for the factor analyses but the share of natives who insist upon them is smaller than in other countries, especially in Eastern Europe. Western Europeans are more concerned with immigrants identifying with the host country, but are more willing to believe that immigrants can adapt. They are less likely to feel threatened by people from different cultures.

2

The United States

Issues of race and immigration became more salient as the two major parties became more polarized at both the mass and elite levels in the 1980s and 1990s (see especially Abramowitz, 2018). The parties had previously been divided internally on issues of immigration and race, with Southern Democrats and Eastern Republicans being more moderate on both issues. In the 1980s there were fewer Southern Democrats and almost no Eastern Republicans. Yet even many conservative Republican leaders such as Ronald Reagan and both Bushes were supporters of immigration reform.

A key shift in the tilt of the Republican party's position came in 1994 when Governor Pete Wilson of California sponsored propositions leading to legislation that established "a ban on affirmative action, a prohibition on bilingual education, and an effort to exclude undocumented immigrants from public services" (*The Guardian*, 2020).

The lieutenant governor of Texas, Dan Patrick, was quoted in *The Texas Observer* in 2006, when he was running for a State Senate seat, describing undocumented immigrants as invaders and saying that the main "problem we are facing is the silent invasion of the border. We are being overrun. It is imperiling our safety" (Fernandez, and Montgomery. 2019). He has blamed the spread of the coronavirus in Texas on African Americans who have not been vaccinated and added: "Last time I checked, over 90 percent of them vote for Democrats in their major cities and major counties, so it's up to the Democrats to get . . . as many people vaccinated" (Gregorian, 2021).

Together with Trump's attacks on both illegal and legal immigration, his travel bans on Muslims, and the Republicans' attacks on immigration more generally, this issue rose to the forefront of partisan conflict in the United States. In 1995 approximately 30 percent of the identifiers for each party believed that immigrants work hard and help the country. By 2010 this view was held by 60 percent of Democrats in the public but just 35 percent of Republicans, and in 2020 over 90 percent of Democratic identifiers supported this position but just 40 percent of Republicans did (Samuels, 2021).

National Identity and Partisan Polarization. Eric M. Uslaner, Oxford University Press. © Oxford University Press 2022.
DOI: 10.1093/oso/9780197633946.003.0002

Trump's rhetoric "can . . . be seen as representing both a longing for previous status quo of a more White America and a defense of traditional arrangements. During the course of his anti- immigrant rhetoric, Trump also frequently argues that immigrants ignore and flaunt traditional American societal norms . . ." (Brewer, 2016, 258). He "appealed to people who were absolutely convinced that white Americans are losing out relative to others" (Eatwell and Goodwin. 2018, 31). And his rhetoric was aimed at keeping out of the country "anybody who's not white, not Protestant, not what they saw as a native-born American, an old-style American" (Iling, 2018). So people felt that "Trump's appeal to 'make America great again" was a call to exclude some groups of people from belonging or feeling like Americans (Vavrek, 2017).

In leaner times people looked at immigrants as threats to the culture (Higham, 1996, 217, 233), so assimilation became more contentious. Now each party is searching for an issue that would give it an electoral advantage. In the more homogenous countries, immigrants are rarely welcome and there are sharper divisions between the major parties. Serwer (2019) capsulized the two conceptions as follows: "[First] . . . the U.S. is the champion of the poor and the dispossessed, a nation that draws its strength from its pluralism . . . [Second] America's greatness is the result of its white and Christian origins, the erosion of which spells doom for the national experiment."

In the United States, partisan polarization was well under way by the turn of the 20th century (Abramowitz, 2019). The Democratic party's supporters included the very people the Republicans saw as out-groups: minorities, immigrants, gays and lesbians, and urban intellectuals. Attitudes on issues affecting these groups became intertwined with policy positions that already divided supporters of each party.

Donald Trump won a narrow victory in 2016, and the Republicans supported his policies on issues of national identity. Republican voters had already moved toward the positions he advocated, so the parties became polarized on these concerns as well. Positions across issues, including those of identity, were strongly determined by one's partisanship. In 2018 evangelicals felt less threatened, since they were already in power, and their turnout declined. Voting levels for the supporters of the Democratic coalition—largely women, young people, and minorities—increased, and the party recaptured the House.

Elsewhere the "threat" may come from immigrants who are ethnically and religiously different and who compete for scarce resources, as in France and Germany. France and the United Kingdom each had elections in 2017. In France, both of the major parties failed to win enough votes in the first round of the presidential election to contest the second round. Former Socialist Emmanuel Macron ran a centrist campaign (and ultimately became the president of France). Marine Le Pen of the National Front, a party that emphasized French identity and opposition to immigration and to the public display of religious symbols (notably by Muslims) won the other place in the run-off.

The 2017 election was (as the 2016 election in the United States) largely shaped by national identity (factor score of the importance of birth in France and family origins). No other variable came close to predicting the final vote in 2017 (using data from the Centre des Etudes Europeanes provided by Nicholas Sauger of Sciences Po, Paris). National identity in turn was shaped by opposition to free trade in the European Union and calls to reduce immigration.

The overall level of polarization was lower in France than in the United States (not surprising since Macron ran as a centrist on economic issues). Attitudes on social issues (gay marriage, gay adoption, abortion) and an overall measure of ideology were moderately associated with vote choice and less strident positions on national identity.

I constructed the national identity measure by constructing an index of factors people believe to be central to American identity: other countries should be "more like us"; how one feels when one sees the American flag; whether identity is based upon ancestry, speaking English, adhering to American customs, and identifying as an American. A sense of national identity overwhelms other factors believed to be central to Trump's victory, perceptions of the economy, authoritarianism, racial attitudes, and positions on trade and immigration. Negative attitudes toward immigrants and Muslims and the belief that there is too much emphasis on inequality did shape the vote—but mostly through nationalistic sentiments. The sharp split on nationalism between Republican and Democratic voters indicates that political polarization extends well beyond economic concerns.

The model I estimated by instrumental variable probit is in Table 2.1. Other variables such as party identification, Christian fundamentalist identification, and opposition to free trade also shaped vote choice, but none were anywhere close to national identity in shaping vote choice.

I constructed a two-equation model of voting behavior in 2016 from the American National Election Study with the first dependent variable being vote choice in the presidential election and the second reflecting the major predictor, feelings about American heritage (see Table 2.1). The "American factor mode" is a composite measure of whether other countries should be more like the United States and if one wants to fly a flag, must have been born in United States, have American ancestry, speak English, follow American customs, and identify with the United States. It reflects an exclusivistic framework for belonging to America and divides the country into "us" and "them." For Trump, the "us" is restricted to white Christians of European heritage who see themselves as Americans first and foremost. The Democratic coalition is much more diverse.

The American factor was the single most important factor shaping the 2016 vote, even more so than party or religious identification. But these

Table 2.1 Instrumental Variable Probit 2016 American Election Democracy Fund Survey

Variable	Coefficient	Std. Error	z
Vote 2016			
American factor	1.424****	.038	37.02
Party ID 3 point	−.056****	.014	−.418
Fundamentalism	−.628****	.185	−3.39
Favor free trade	−.036**	.017	−2.09
Immigrants harm culture	−.200****	.041	4.82
Feeling thermometer Muslims	−.002	.002	−1.21
Constant	1.114****	.201	5.70
American factor			
Party ID 3 point	−.004	.007	−0.60
Favor free trade	.096	.086	.11
Immigrants harm culture	.276****	.016	16.85
Feeling thermometer Muslims	.008****	.001	10.35
Favor more equality	−.005	.012	.040
Worry too much inequality	1.48****	.014	10.34
Generalized trust	.028	.022	1.26
Constant	−1.83****	.091	−20.08

American factor: Other countries should be more like the United States, want to fly US flag, must be US-born, have American ancestry, speak English, follow American customs, and identify with the United States.

$N = 2007$ −2*; Log likelihood factor = 5309.36; Wald Chi Square: 2123.40.

* $p < .10$; ** $p < .05$; *** $p < .01$; **** $p < .0001$.

factors were significant, as were favoring free trade and attitudes toward immigrants in general and toward Muslims in particular. The American factor itself reflects attitudes toward immigrants, especially Muslims, and the belief that minorities and urban dwellers worry too much about inequality and are willing to spend your money to help themselves.

In Table 2.2 I present a model with similar findings from the Democracy Fund survey. The national identity factor is again by far the most powerful determinant of vote choice, but here the effect of party identification is strong. Born-again Christians were also more likely to vote for Trump—and also to have high loadings on the national identity factor. National identity is shaped

Table 2.2 Instrumental Variable Probit 2016 American Election Democracy Fund Survey

Variable	Coefficient	S.E.	z
Presidential Vote Dummy			
National Identity factor	−1.150****	.036	−31.54
Party identification	−.325****	.021	−15.26
Ideology	−.172****	.049	−3.53
Born again Christian	.369****	.076	4.86
Gay marriage	−.168**	.079	−4..13
Abortion	−.097**	.054	−1.78
Constant	1.973	.210	9.38
Party identification	−.059****	.009	−6.88
Variable			
Ideology	.063****	.018	3.50
Born again Christian	.246****	.033	7.39
Abortion	.010	.023	.44
Immigration factor	.329****	.021	15.47
Race majority factor	.091****	.017	5.43
Feeling thermometer minorities	−.061****	.015	−4.00
Proud factor	−.120****	.015	−7.85
Authoritarianism	−.224****	.016	−13.68
Constant	−.011	.070	−.16

* $p < .10$ ** $p < .05$ *** $p < .001$ **** $p < .0001$ −2*LLR = 7665.10 N = 3252

by attitudes on immigration, authoritarianism, pride in America, and being a born-again Christian. The national identity factor is shaped by variables that fit the Trump campaign of "America First"—including authoritarianism. Authoritarianism matters because Trump supporters saw the supporters of Hillary Clinton and the Democratic party as not sufficiently committed to strong moral standards.

In Table 2.3 I summarize the results for the other models I estimated for the United States. There are moderate effects for national identity on vote

Table 2.3 Effects of National Identity on Vote Choice and Party ID in American Surveys

Survey	Survey Year	Dependent Variable	t / z Ratio
American National Election Study Pilot	1991	1988 Vote	−5.39**
International Social Survey Program	1995	Party identification	−1.06
	2003	Party identification	−6.70**
	2013	Party identification	−2.44*
General Social Survey	1996	1992 Vote	−.55
	2014	2012 Vote	−3.84**
Theiss-Morse	2006	2000 Vote	−1.44 cultural factor
			.76 institutions / values factor
Americanism (Schildkraut)	2006	2004 Vote	−1.28 race factor
			2.11* activity factor
			−3.68** feeling factor
American National Election Study	2016	2016 Vote	−37.12***
Pew Global	2016	Party identification	−8.22***
Associated Press / NORC	2017	Party Identification	−16.46***
Democracy Fund	2017	2016 Vote	−31.54****

$* p < .05; ** p < .01; *** p < .0001.$

choice in 1988 and 2012 (ANES 1991 Pilot, General Social Survey 2014). However, identity was not a significant predictor of vote choice in 1992 (General Social Survey) or 2004 (Schildkraut Americanism survey), although there are modest effects for whether "feeling American" constitutes being a "true American."

In 2016 (Pew Global) and 2017 (AP/NORC), national identity has a strong effect on party identification, and in the Democracy Fund survey (2017) there is a very powerful effect of identity on vote choice, similar to the findings from the ANES. Immigration and national identity have, until recently, been immune from strong partisan divisions. Republican presidents George H. W. and George W. Bush and especially Ronald Reagan were strong advocates for increased immigration and George W. Bush insisted after the September 11 attacks on airliners that Islam is "a religion of peace."

In the Theiss-Morse survey there is a single factor for ideology and spending levels for cities, education, aid to African Americans, and welfare, as well as for government assistance to single mothers, the unemployed, farmers, and African Americans and a measure of ideology for the 2000 presidential vote. The national identity index had a low loading with these measures. Spending on defense and whether foreign interests have too much power did not load on this factor. By 2016 the Republicans had moved to the right across a wide range of issues, especially on immigration and national identity.

A factor analysis of economic and social issues and national identity/immigration/race leads to just one factor across a wide range of issues. There is just one dimension, which includes

- Indicators of nationalism including the national identity factor scores; authoritarianism; whether we should be more tolerant of others' morality.
- Evaluations of out-groups, including feeling thermometers for African Americans, gays, Muslims, blacks, and supporters of the Black Lives Matter movement (although not for Hispanics); whether Muslims are patriotic or violent; whether progress for African Americans is still held down by the legacy of slavery; whether immigrants harm the majority culture; and whether immigration should be increased or decreased, Syrian refugees allowed to come to United States, and building a wall along the border with Mexico should be supported.

- Issues of morality: whether abortion should be permitted; increased gun control.
- Issues of government spending on welfare, child care, health care, and assistance to the poor.
- Environmental policy: spending on the environment, whether to permit fracking.
- Foreign policy: fighting ISIS with troops; permitting torture of terrorists.
- Ideology measured on a left-right scale.

Before 2016, national identity had become linked with attitudes on race, religion, social policy, and economic policy. Politics in other countries had become multidimensional (see especially Inglehart and Norris, 2018; Simonsen and Bonikowski, 2020; and Vasilopoulou, 2018). Parties on the right on issues of identity and nationalism are often in favor of a more leftist orientation toward the economy. Political conflict in the United States has become unidimensional. In almost every way, American politics has become "us" against "them." In 2016 identity became the dominant theme in voters' choices for president. Identity continued to be important afterward but not as critical as in Trump's initial victory. After 2016, immigration outpaced identity as the major factor in voting decisions, but identity still was effective as a determinant of identity.

The rest of the story about how immigration became the major issue shaping voters' choice between parties and how it relates to identity is as follows.

The 2020 American Values Survey of PRRI (Public Religion Research Institute) shows that the major determinant of the intended presidential vote was immigration. I estimated an instrumental variable probit (see Table 2.4). The measure for immigration is a factor score of whether immigrants destroy culture; immigration is an important issue; it is acceptable for immigrants to be separated from parents; illegal immigrants may become citizens; immigrants threaten national culture; and immigrants are a burden on society. This measure overwhelms all others in the main equation for vote choice. Also significant, although less important, are policy liberalism (a factor score of positions on Medicare for all, free college tuition, gay marriage, abortion, banning the Confederate flag, abortion rights), as well as whether Trump encourages racism; being white; and the age of the respondent (see Tables 2.4 and 2.5).

Table 2.4 Instrumental Variable Probit of Presidential Voting in 2020: PRRI American Values Survey

First Equation: Intended Vote Choice

Variable	Coefficient	Std. Error	z
Immigration factor	.358****	.050	7.13
Trump encourages racism	.001*	.001	1.66
Policy liberalism	−.095****	.028	−.3.4
Age	.001*	.001	1.66
Income	−.001	.004	−.11
Education	−.008	.009	−.77
White	−.125****	.030	−4.13
Constant	.877****	.119	7.37

Immigration factor: Immigrants destroy culture; immigration an important issue; acceptable for immigrants to be separated from parents; illegal immigrants may become citizens; immigrants threaten national culture; immigrants are a burden on society.

Policy liberalism: positions on Medicare for all; free college tuition; gay marriage; abortion;, banning the Confederate flag; abortion rights.

Table 2.5 Presidential Vote from 2020 Pre-Election Survey from ANES

Variable	Coefficient	z Score	Coefficient
Party ID 3 point	−.524****	−4.72	−.110
Immigration factor	1.130****	11.12	.655
Direction of country	−.947****	−4.95	−.100
Abortion	.323**	.079	.094
Self-identification on issues	−.288**	.142	−.076
Important speaking English	.198	.083	.050
Born again identification	−.447**	.079	−.038
Age	.009**	.056	.049
Education	.055	.047	.032
Gender	−.257*	.163	−.021
Income	−.014	.015	−.025
Constant	.796*	1.31	

$N = 1058$ −2*; Log likelihood factor = .578; RMSE = 3159.16; * $p < .10$;** $p < .05$; *** $p < .01$; **** $p < .0001$. Immigration factor includes: party better on immigration, how government handles illegal immigrants, does one favor border wall, and how strongly one favors the wall. Self-factor: positions on government spending, medical care, aid to the poor.

Table 2.6 Correlations of Attitudes by Party of People Saying that Illegal Immigration Is the Most Important Issue in Their Intended Vote Choice, 2002–2020

Variable	Date	Date w/o 2007	Date w/o 2020	Percentage Saying Immigration Most Important Problem	Differences in Democrat and Republican Percentages Saying Immigration Most Important Problem
Percentage Saying Immigration Most Important Problem	.247	−.102	−.094		−.131
Percentage Republicans Saying Immigration Most Important Problem	.332	.090	.309	−.093	−.830
Percentage Democrats Saying Immigration Most Important Problem	.269	.140	−.903	.090	.505
Difference in Democrat and Republican Percentages Saying Immigration Most Important Problem	−.137	.250	.441	.131	

From Gallup, used with its permission.

Immigration became increasingly important for Americans who identified as either Democrats or Republicans, according to surveys by the Gallup organization (Table 2.6). Over time, from 2002 to 2020, the share of Americans saying that immigration was the important problem facing the country increased slightly, more for Republican identifers than for people calling themselves Democrats. Democrats and Republicans were becoming more polarized on this issue and the differences between the parties in saying that immigration was the most critical fell.

In the 2018 PRRI survey, the variable representing what it means to be a true American remains a highly potent factor in shaping attitudes toward support for the admission of illegal immigrants to the United States. For admitting more immigrants, the most important variable is party

Table 2.7 Voting Model for American Values Survey 2018 Dependent Variable Support Admission for Illegal Immigrants Support Admission for Illegal Immigrants Model

Variable	Coefficient	Std. Error	t
True American Factor	.215****	.020	10.960
Party ID 3 point	.007	.017	.039
Ideology factor	.802****	.022	36.760
Trump approval	.802	−.927	.017
Black	−.028	.056	.620
Gender	−.035	.027	.071
Age	.013	.013	.980
Constant	.2.227	.083	27.250

$N = 2500$; R2 = .578; RMSE = .655.

$* p < .10; ** p < .05; *** p < .01; **** p < .0001.$

Ideology factor includes: self-proclaimed ideology, minimum wage, protecting preexisting conditions for health insurance, gun control, changing the Constitution to prevent children born in the United States from being deported.

Table 2.8 Voting Model for American Values Survey 2018 Dependent Variable Vote for Congress (Second Equation Instrumental Variable Probit True American Factor Model)

Variable	Coefficient	Std. Error	z
Have gay friends	.066****	.012	5.880
Favor diversity	.120	.014	8.360
Trump approval	−.111	.019	−5.940
Party ID 3	.023	.021	1.070
Ideology factor	−.047	.025	−.193
Christian nation	.089****	.005	17.230
Age	.041**.	.014	2.960
Constant	−.672****	.098	−6.890

$N = 1886$; RMSE = 3917.4.

$* p < .10; ** p < .05; *** p < .01; ****; p < .0001.$

identification, but the approval of President Trump, the true American factor (being a Christian, born in the United States, and having Western European heritage), and gender are also significant (see Tables 2.8 and 2.9).

Table 2.9 Instrumental Variable Probit for 2018 Congressional Vote and National Identity from More in Common Survey

Variable	Coefficient	Std. Error	z
First Stage			
Party identification	−1.445****	.075	−19.39
Identity factor	−.223****	.067	−3.35
Age	.004	.004	.09
Gender	−.459****	1.390	3.30
Income	−.002	.020	−.10
Constant	2.284****	.284	8.04
Second Stage			
Identity factor	.164****	.047	−3.47
Immigration factor	.152****	.035	4.28
Feelings factor	.125	.029	4.46
Age	.003	.003	1.07
Gender	.364****	.098	3.71
Income	−.163	.047	−3.47
Black	−.115	.055	−2.07
Education	.016	.013	1.20
Constant	1.438****	.177	8.13

$N = 1732$ −2;*LLR = 1872.1; *$p < .10$ **; $p < .05$ ***; $p < .01$; **** $p < .0001$.

Immigration factor includes for immigration: overall impact, use of welfare benefits, sharing information with federal authorities, mayors enforcing the law more strictly, drawing on tax resources, building a wall against Mexicans, how many immigrants there are, do immigrants make a contribution to American society, and an overall feeling thermometer toward immigrants.

Feelings thermometer includes attitudes about how people feel about the country: angry, scared, trust fellow citizens, disillusioned, excited, or confident for the nation's future mayors.

The only other variable that is significant in predicting support for illegal immigrants is a factor score on ideology (including self-proclaimed ideology, minimum wage, protecting preexisting conditions for health insurance, gun control, changing the Constitution to prevent children born in the United States from being deported).

I also estimated an instrumental variable probit for vote choice and admission of illegal immigrants. In the support for immigrants model, the true American factor and the ideology factor were the only significant predictors. So what constitutes being a true American is very important for attitudes on immigration, and generally the parties are divided. For vote choice for

Table 2.10 Presidential Vote from 2020 Pre-Election Survey from ANES

Variable	Coefficient	z Score	Coefficient
Party ID 3 point	–.524****	–4.72	–.110
Immigration factor	1.130****	11.12	.655
Direction of country	–.947****	–4.95	–.100
Abortion	.323**	.079	.094
Self-identification on issues	–.288**	.142	–.076
Important speaking English	.198	.083	–.050
Born again identification	–.447**	.079	–.038
Age	.009**	.056	.049
Education	.055	.047	.032
Gender	–.257*	.163	–.021
Income	–.014	.015	–.025
Constant	.796*	1.31	

N = 1058 –2*Log Likelihood factor = .578 RMSE = 3159.16; * p < .10 **; p < .05 ***; p < .01 ****; p < .0001. Immigration factor includes: party better on immigration, how government handles illegal immigrants, does one favor border wall, and how strongly one favors the wall. Self-factor: positions on government spending, medical care, aid to the poor.

Congress, what constitutes being a true American is significant, though the effect is not as powerful as it was in the presidential models from the ANES in 2016. As usual, party identification, approval of the president, ideology, and race are significant predictors (Table 2.7).

From the More in Common survey in 2018, I estimated an instrumental variable probit of the Congressional vote in 2018. Consistent with the ANES results, American identity was a significant determinant of both vote choice and party identification, although less critical than it had been in 2016. Party identification overwhelmed the sense of identity in vote choice, and both altitudes toward immigration and feelings toward the country were stronger predictors of party identification than was identity. Yet identity remained significant in both estimations. (See Table 2.10).

I also estimated a model of vote choice from the 2020 ANES Pre-Election Survey, and the results show continued polarization between Democrats and Republicans on social and cultural issues. There were no questions on American identity but the social divisions in the 2016 remain salient. The most important determinant of vote choice was a set of beliefs on immigration (party better on immigration, how government handles illegal immigrants, does one favor border wall, and how strongly one favors the

Table 2.11 Differences between Most Democratic Positions and Most Republican Positions on Immigration Policies Cooperative Election Survey 2020

Variable	Most Democratic	Most Republican
Grant legal status to illegal immigrants	.94	.41
Increase number of border patrols	.21	.95
No federal funds for local police enforcement	.08	.79
Increase border security spending $25 billion	.04	.70
Immigration factor	−.78	.93

Most Democratic positions: Respondent identifies as a Democrat and a liberal and is represented by a Democrat in the House of Representatives.

Most Republican Positions: Respondent identifies as a Republican and a conservative and is represented by a Republican in the House of Representatives.

wall). The divisions that shaped the Trump-Clinton contest remained salient four years later in the Trump-Biden election. Identification as born again, positions on some issues on spending (aid to the poor, medical care, and overall spending), attitudes on abortion, and party identification were also significant, thus showing the persistent polarization of the electorate (see Table 2.11).

According to the Pew Research Center (2019, 18), immigration became the most important national problem for conservative Republicans but not for independents or Democrats. Conservative Republicans are particularly worried that whites will become a minority of America's population within the next three decades. The report (Pew Research Center, 2019, 18) states: "Over the past three years, the share of Republicans who say that this population change would be a bad thing has decreased from 39 percent to 21 percent, while the share saying that it would be neither good nor bad increased from 57 percent to 73 percent. Among Democrats, 33 percent now say that this population change is a good thing, up from 23 percent in 2016.

Trump supporters were the strongest opponents of illegal immigration: 87 percent favored building a wall at the Mexican border to keep illegal immigrants out and almost 60 percent believe that immigrants refuse to abide by American laws (Parker, 2018). Hopkins (2010, 56) argues: "immigration rises in national salience as the size of the immigrant population reaches a critical mass, as immigration's opponents become organized and vocal, and as political elites sense an opportunity."

I also obtained data from Gallup on how important illegal immigration was to people in elections from 2001 to 2020 by party identification. My argument on the importance of immigrating is tied into my larger claim that identity politics has become more important over time, especially to supporters of the Republican party. And the results largely confirm this: In 2001–2004 almost no Republican identifiers said that illegal immigration was their most important problem, but in 2018 the share rose to 29 percent before falling back to 13 percent in 2019 (and even 1 percent in 2020).

For Democrats, the share has always been minimal. The correlation with the most important problem share for each party and time is modest (about .3), even controlling for the 2007 outlier but larger when accounting for the 2020 outlier ($r = -.903$ for the Democrats) and .441 for the difference between the two parties (see Table 2.6). The story is that illegal immigration has become a more critical issue for Republicans than for Democrats and that overall positions on immigration were strong predictors of the expected 2020 vote. Cultural factors have become increasingly salient in American politics (see Table 2.12).

In the 2020 ANES pilot survey there were strong correlations between party identification and immigration policy. Overall the mean feeling thermometer for illegal immigrant is 56 (on a 0–100 scale) for Democrats and 27 for Republicans ($r = .407$, $N = 3075$). Twenty three percent of Republicans

Table 2.12 Probit Analysis of Presidential Vote 2020 from Congressional Cooperative Election Study (CCES)

Variable	Coefficient	Standard Error	Difference in Probabilities
Immigration factor	−.806****	.,025	−.191
Party identification 3 point	−.758****	.025	−.131
Ideology	−.239****	−9.97	−.065
Abortion	.280****	.024	−.047
Gun control	−.435****	−.026	−.059
Police factor 1	−.317****	.026	.066
Police factor 2	−.059**	.027	−.011
Health care	.648****	.027	.135
State of national economy	.297****	.016	−.011
Attend religious services	−.036	.011	.087
Constant	.967****	.107	

favor overall increases in immigration compared to 44 percent of Democrats ($r = .276$). Twenty-nine percent of Republicans oppose a pathway to citizenship for unauthorized immigrants compared to 9 percent of Democrats ($r = .287$), and three quarters of Republicans but just a third of Democrats want unauthorized immigrants to be forced to go back to their native countries ($r = .419$).

The correlations are similar for voting intentions. For the feeling thermometer, the correlation between the expected vote in 2020 for Trump or Joe Biden is .459; for increasing the number of immigrants it is .263; for peroxiding a pathway to citizenship it is .326; and for returning unauthorized to their home countries it is .486.

The Public Religion Research Institute (2020) reported similar findings about the 2020 electorate: Majorities of Republicans hold mostly negative views of immigrants, including 72 percent who agree that immigrants are a burden to local communities, 64 percent who agree that they compete with Americans for jobs, and 63 percent who agree that immigrants increase crime in local communities . . . and Democrats are notably less likely than Republicans to say that immigrants are a burden to local communities (31 percent) . . . , that they compete with Americans for jobs (and 50 percent), or that immigrants increase crime in local communities (21 percent).

Republicans (40 percent) are significantly more likely than Democrats (19 percent) to believe that immigrants increase disease in local communities . . . Fifty-seven percent of Republicans . . . agree that "immigrants are invading our country and replacing our cultural and ethnic background," significantly down from 36 percent in 2019 . . . compared to 15 percent of Democrats . . . apart, people expressed more . . . and anti-immigrant sentiment after Trump's victory than they had before . . . respondents are more likely to write offensive things about Mexicans after being exposed to Trump's prejudiced quote targeting that group . . . Trump's strongest opponents were already very unlikely to strongly agree with the statement about immigrants before the election (4 percent), and little changed for that group after the election (3 percent) . . . Trump supporters agreed with sexist and anti-immigrant statements more after Trump's victory than they had before.

This is confirmed in the 2020 Cooperative Congressional Election Study, in which 90 percent of Democrats favored granting legal status to immigrants who have held jobs compared to 46 percent of Republicans (tau–c = .37), 35 percent of Democrats favored increasing the number of border patrols on the US-Mexican borders compared to 91 percent of Republicans (tau–b

= −.43), and 66 percent of Republicans favored reducing immigration by half over the next 10 years compared to 19 percent of Democrats (tau-b = −.370).

The above model for vote choice from the 2020 American Values Survey of PRRI shows that the major factors shaping support for a more inclusive immigration policy are personal ideology and religiosity as well as party identification and beliefs about immigrants (do they work hard and have strong family values).

The religiosity factor includes measures such as identity as a secular Christian right, a religious progressive, a secular person, or as religious, while the personal ideology dimension includes progressive, feminist, environmentalist, and position on left-right spectrum. These results are consistent with the research cited on earlier elections in the United States and on the Brexit vote in the United Kingdom—attitudes on immigration and race are now essential to the partisan divisions in many Western countries.

Eighty percent of Republican identifiers believe that immigrants pose a cultural threat to America, compared to just 28 percent of Democrats. Forty-seven percent of Democrats in the public believe that immigrants have strong family values compared to just 15 percent of Republicans. Fifty-five percent of Democrats see immigrants as hard working but just 19 percent of Republican identifiers agree. And two-thirds of Republicans see immigrants as leading to increased crime while just 20 percent of Democratic identifiers agree. Almost all Republicans favor building the wall on the Mexican border (86 percent) while just 13 percent of Democrats agree. On allowing the children of illegal immigrants to remain in the United States, the division is 61 percent favorable to 24 percent.

The correlation of the 2020 vote intentions with the immigration measures (notably the overall factor and whether immigrants lead to an attack on American culture or threaten American culture) are higher than any of people's positions on the policy liberalism dimension. The only policy position that comes close to the immigration measures in terms of a zero-order correlation is Medicare for all. The simple correlation between the immigration factor and vote intention is .653.

A Pew survey in April 2021 shows that immigration is still dividing the parties. More than any other issue, except the coronavirus and gun control, the parties are separated with respect to their concern about immigration as the most important issue. Of the 13 issues in the Pew survey, 72 percent of Republicans compared to 28 percent of Democrats consider immigration to be the most important. This led to a difference of 42 percent on the most important issue question, while almost all of the traditional domestic and international issues had gaps of less than 30 percent.

Immigration is still a key dividing issue between the parties (Pew Research Center, 2021). A survey conducted by the Associated Press and the National Opinion Research Center in March, 2021 with data provided to me by AP-NORC) showed a difference of 31 percent between Democrats and Republicans favoring increased legal immigration (by 51 to 20 percent), a difference of 45 percent for permitting the children of illegal immigrants to remain in the country (by 78 to 35 percent), a gap of 24 percent in how great a priority it is to let illegal immigrants remain in the country (by 17 to 50 percent), and a range of 59 percent on the priority of permitting the children of illegal immigrants stay here (by 66 to 19 percent).

The Congressional Cooperative Election Study's (CCES) survey of potential voters in 2020 confirmed that immigration was the key issue dividing Democratic and Republican identifiers, liberals and conservatives. I created factor scores for the immigration measures and other policy positions from the survey. The immigration factor includes granting legal status to illegal immigrants, increasing the number of border patrols, denying federal funds for local police enforcement, and increasing spending for border security by $25 billion.

The model also includes party identification, ideology, and factor scores for positions on abortion, gun control, two measures of police conduct, and health care policy, as well as views on the national economy and the frequency of attending religious services. (The demographic variables of income, education, and gender were not significant and there was not a variable for age).

I estimated the model only for whites (see Table 2.11). The results show that positions on immigration had the greatest effect on vote choice in 2020: The most liberal positions on immigration led to almost a 20 percent increase in voting for Biden over Trump, compared to differences of 13–14 percent for health care values and party identification. Other issues and the state of the national economy as well as overall ideology and attendance at religious services led to changes of less than 10 percent either way.

Immigration was the major force shaping voting in 2020. On the specific immigration questions (see Table 2.12). Ninety-four percent of the most Democratic voters—people who identified with the Democratic party, called themselves liberals, and were represented by a Democrat in the House of Representatives—favored granting legal status to illegal immigrants, but just 4 percent wanted a major increase in spending on border security, 8 percent wanted to deny federal funds for police enforcement, and 21 percent favored expanding the number of border patrols.

The most Republican members—GOP identifiers who called themselves conservatives and were represented by a Republican in the House—favored increasing the number of border patrols by 95 percent, 79 percent wanted to deny federal funds for local police, 70 percent favored more border security, and only 41 percent agreed that illegal immigrants should be granted legal status.

The gap in the level of concern for deporting illegal immigrants was a difference of 33 percent (by 17 to 50 percent). This division is greater than for any other policy (coronavirus, 21; Russia, 21; China, 12; North Korea, 11; extremism, 100—except for the priority on climate change (59). Supporters of each party are not so polarized on the importance of most issues, except for climate change and immigration. Democrats and Republicans remain polarized on an issue that separates "them" from "us."

The survey of potential voters in 2020 confirmed that immigration was the key issue dividing Democratic and Republican identifiers, liberals and conservatives. I created factor scores for the immigration measures and other policy positions from the survey. The immigration factor includes granting legal status to illegal immigrants, increasing the number of border patrols, denying federal funds for local police enforcement, and increasing spending for border security by $25 billion (see Table 2.13). The model also includes party identification, ideology, and factor scores for positions on abortion, gun control, two measures of police conduct, and health care policy, as well as views on the national economy, and the frequency of attending religious services. (The demographic variables of income, education, and gender were not significant and there was not a variable for age).

This division was reflected in the policies each party followed. In May 2021 President Biden reversed Trump's policy by making it easier for immigrants to enter the United States. His proposal was aimed primarily at highly skilled immigrants but also would make it easier for refugees to enter the country legally (Shear and Kanno-Youngs, 2021).

In 2021 two conservative Republicans proposed an America First Caucus in the House of Representatives. The caucus would be based upon the following ideas:

America's legal immigration system should be curtailed to those that can contribute not only economically, but have demonstrated respect for this

Table 2.13 Presidential Vote from 2020 Pre-Election Survey from ANES

Variable	Coefficient	z score	Coefficient
Party ID 3 point	–.524****	–4.72	–.110
Immigration factor	1.130****	11.12	.655
Direction of country	–.947****	–4.95	–.100
Abortion	.323**	.079	.094
Self identification on issues	–.288**	.142	–.076
Important speaking English	.198	.083	.050
Born again identification	–.447**	.079	–.038
Age	.009**	.056	.049
Education	.055	.047	.032
Gender	–.257*	.163	–.021
Income	–.014	.015	–.025
Constant	.796*	1.31	

N = 1058 -2*Log Likelihood factor = .578 RMSE = 3159.16 * p < .10 ** p < .05 *** p < .01 ****
p < .0001 Immigration factor inludes: party better on immigration, how government handles illegal
immigrants, does one favor border wall, and how strongly one favors the wall. Self factor: positions
on government spending, medical care, aid to the poor.

nation's culture and rule of law . . . America's borders must be defended, and illegal immigration must be stopped without exception . . . An important distinction between post-1965 immigrants and previous waves of settlers is that previous cohorts were more educated, earned higher wages, and did not have an expansive welfare state to fall back on when they could not make it in America and thus did not stay in the country at the expense of the native-born. . . .

The America First Caucus will work toward an infrastructure that reflects the architectural, engineering, and aesthetic value that befits the progeny of European architecture, whereby public infrastructure must be utilitarian as well as stunningly, classically beautiful, befitting a world power and source of freedom. (America First Caucus, 2021)

The House party leadership prevailed upon members Marjorie Taylor-Greene (GA) and Paul Gosar (AZ) not to form the caucus because it feared a backlash from the general public over charges of racism.

Minority Leader Kevin McCarthy (CA) said of the proposed caucus: "The Republican Party is the party of Lincoln & the party of more opportunity for all Americans—not nativist dog whistles" (CNN Politics, 2021). Even afterward, Greene persisted in starting a national campaign tour based upon the theme "America First." She was joined by Florida Representative Matt Gaetz, another conservative extremist who was also facing federal charges for sex trafficking. This was an action that would disrupt the Republican party.

The Republican Lieutenant Governor of Texas, Dan Patrick, has referred to the rise of undocumented immigrants as "a silent invasion [that] is imperiling our safety" (Fernandez and Montgomery, 2019). The Rockland County (New York) Republican party presented a video advertisement calling an Orthodox Jewish legislator's plan to build a housing development for his community as "plotting a takeover [that] threatens our way of life" (Iati, 2019).

The Virginia Republican party initially refused to change the date of is 2021 primary election from a Saturday because holding the vote on the Jewish Sabbath would have meant that Orthodox Jews could not participate (Vozella, 2021). Hersch and Royden (2021) find that on the right, there is a strong connection between evangelicalism and anti-Semitism, since Jews do not accept Jesus as a savior. Evangelicals support Israel because the formation of the nation is essential for the return of Jesus to the earth, yet they are far more likely to believe that Jews are more loyal to Israel than to the United States and that Jews have too much power in the United States.

The CCES survey of potential voters in 2020 confirmed that immigration was the key issue dividing Democratic and Republican identifiers, liberals, and conservatives. I created factor scores for the immigration measures and other policy positions from the survey. The immigration factor includes granting legal status to illegal immigrants., increasing the number of border patrols, increasing the number of border patrols, increasing the number of border patrols, denying federal funds for local police enforcement, and increasing spending for border security by $25 billion.

The model also includes party identification, ideology, and factor scores for positions on abortion, gun control, two measures of police conduct, and health care policy, as well as views on the national economy, and the frequency of attending religious services. (The demographic variables of income, education, and gender were not significant and there was not a variable for age).

When the Democrats won the White House in 2020, they overturned most of Trump's positions on issues of national security. Supporters of each party actively disliked backers of the other party. People became upset about the possibility of their children marrying supporters of opposition parties and an overall measure of in-group favoritism on the intelligence of opposition supporters increased from .06 in 1960 to .48 in 2008 on a scale from zero to one (Iyengar et al., 2018; Iyengar and Yelkes. 2012). Although they argue that personal attachments are only weakly connected to ideology, Abramowitz and Webster (2018) hold that ideology and personal feeling are part of a larger syndrome of "negative partisanship."

In the more homogenous societies (especially in Europe), the parties had moved away from polarization. Noury and Roland (2020, 429) state that the "ideological convergence of existing mainstream parties created room for new parties to gain support using anti-globalization, anti-immigration, and anti-austerity platforms." In Central and Eastern Europe, dominant parties have adopted nationalist positions on immigration and culture, but left-wing policies on social welfare. The issue is one of who is "deserving" of government assistance. Nationalist parties in the former Communist countries seek to exclude non-Christian immigrants, but they also cater to their lower-income supporters by generous social welfare programs (Santora, 2019). Noury and Roland (2020, 429) argue that the competition for jobs with natives is part of the reaction against mainstream parties and support for nationalist fringe movements.

While there were differences between the mainstream parties on issues of identity, they had been reduced. On issues of identity, fringe parties arose and forced the major parties to adopt their positions. The result is that elections won't lead to major changes in policies on immigration and other identity issues since the major parties have become captives of the fringes.

More recently in the United States, conservative whites worry that they will be "replaced by immigrants" (Cox, 2019). They worry about the "cultural and ethnic replacement of Americans and . . . the foreign influx endangering our way of life" (deParle, 2019). In the Pew American Values survey in 2020, only immigration and climate change strongly divided Democratic and Republican party identifiers as the most important issues in the campaign compared to race, the coronavirus, the deficit, terrorism, health care, unemployment, and crime. Seeing immigration as the most important issue in the election had the strongest impact on vote choice between Trump and Biden, even more so than race or the virus: 80 percent of Republican identifiers saw immigration as the most important issue in the campaign compared to 36 percent of Democratic partisans. The only other issue with a similar divide was climate change (91 percent to 36 percent). The ANES post-election survey also showed that immigration was among the most important issues, just behind overall ideology and party identification (see Table 2.13).

In the 2020 ANES post-election survey, policy liberalism and party identification continued to be the strongest determinants of vote choice, but national identity and especially attitudes toward illegal immigration also were important. A sense of national identity (whether people were born in the United States, have European ancestry, and follow American customs) were largely shaped by attitudes toward minority groups, favoring separating the children of undocumented immigrants, beliefs that illegal immigrants increase crime, and feeling thermometers toward liberals on the one hand and fundamentalists on the other.

The cleavages of 2016 carried through to 2020. The post-election survey did not have enough cases to estimate a full model, but it did show that 80 percent of Democratic identifiers favored increasing immigration levels, while just 20 percent of Republican supporters took this position (tau-b = .421, gamma = .631, N = 4261) for the three point party ID scale and a dummy variable for the level of immigration).

Negativity toward people who were not white Christians with European ancestry separated partisans, as did feelings that children should obey and respect their parents and have good manners rather than be independent. Policy views were significant but were again strongly correlated with issues of identity. The polarization of the American electorate seen in 2016 continued four years later, and the Republicans became even more focused on cultural issues, especially evangelical identification and how often one attends religious services. (See Table 2.14.)

From Donald Trump's campaign in the United States to Brexit in the United Kingdom to Marine Le Pen in France and to AfD in Germany, political movements in Western countries have made inroads in electoral politics in Western societies. They have either scored major victories or established themselves as major forces in the politics of their countries. These movements have all stressed the primacy of national identities—what makes someone an American, a Brit, a Frenchman/Frenchwoman, a German—and why this matters for public policy.

In 2021 two conservative Republicans proposed an America First Caucus in the House of Representatives. The caucus would be based upon the following ideas (America First Caucus, 2021):

Table 2.14 Instrumental Variable Probit of Presidential Vote in 2020 from Pew American Values Survey Main Equation for Vote: Biden versus Trump

Biden versus Trump

Variable	Coefficient	Std. Error	z
Ideology (instrumented)	.497****	.030	16.60
Party ID 3 point	.109****	.022	4.90
Satisfaction with country	.003**	.002	1.76
Feel proud about country	−.067***	.023	−2.89
Born again	.062****	.022	2.81
Attend services often	−.034****	.006	−5.29
Gender	.020	.019	1.10
Black	.104****	.031	3.41
Constant	−.874****	.068	−12.72

N = 3298 R2 = .491 RMSE = .706

* p < .10 **; p < .05 ***; p < .01 ****; p < .001.

Second Equation: Ideology

Variable	Coefficient	Std. Error	z
Immigration factor	.353****	.025	14.08
Satisfaction with country	−.006**	.003	−2.01
Feel country proud	−.041	.040	1.01
Party ID	.159****	.021	7.60
Climate change (MIP)	−.201****	.020	−9.98
Unemployment (MIP)	−.051**	.024	−1.70
Crime (MIP)	.099****	.044	4.05
Born again	−.199****	.035	−5.65
Religious services often	.058****	.058	4.11
Gender	−.058**	.032	−1.77
Black	.091**	.053	1.71
Constant	2.546****	.090	28.40

R2 = .330 RMSE = .408

* p < .10; ** p < .05 ***; p < .01 ****; p < .001.

America's legal immigration system should be curtailed to those that can contribute not only economically, but have demonstrated respect for this nation's culture and rule of law . . . America's borders must be defended, and illegal immigration must be stopped without exception. An important distinction between post-1965 immigrants and previous waves of settlers is that previous cohorts were more educated, earned higher wages, and did not have an expansive welfare state to fall back on when they could not make it in America and thus they did not stay in the country at the expense of the native-born. The America First Caucus will work toward an infrastructure that reflects the architectural, engineering, and aesthetic value that befits the progeny of European architecture, whereby public infrastructure must be utilitarian as well as stunningly, classically beautiful, befitting a world power and source of freedom . . .

The leader of the Republicans in the Senate decided that the party should stress the issues of immigration and race, as well as social concerns for groups that are not part of the party's base. He argued: "There are a lot of exotic notions about what are the most important points in American history." Senator Rick Scott (R, Florida), who has decided to run for president in 2024, agreed: "Now what I talk about every day is do we want open borders? No. Do we want to shut down our schools? No. Do we want men playing in women's sports? No." And the head of the GOP in Iowa, Jeff Kaufmann, even believes that emphasizing such issues might expand the party's base (Hulse, 2021).

The post-election survey of the American National Election Study found that 92 percent of Republican identifiers saw their party as better on immigration while 85 percent of Democrats preferred their party's position. The overall correlation between party preferred on immigration is about equal to that with ideology.

This condemnation did not stop Taylor-Greene. Several weeks later she compared the decision by some businesses to require that patrons wear masks to "the Nazi practice of labeling Jews with Star of David badges . . . Vaccinated employees get a logo just like the Nazi's forced Jewish people to wear a gold star," Greene tweeted early on a Tuesday morning, linking her tweet to a news story on a Tennessee supermarket chain's decision to include a special logo on the name badges of vaccinated employees (DeBonis and Wagner, 2021, A7).

She was denounced by leaders of both parties, and one member threatened to file a motion to expel her from the House. Yet she defended her remarks, attacked two Jewish journalists who criticized her, and is still raising huge amounts of money for her reelection. She claims that her position represents a substantial share of the Republican party. Even as some Republicans such as Minority Leader Kevin McCarthy (California) backed away from Taylor-Greene and her far-right colleagues, they embraced attacks on Democrats.

McCarthy even "joked" that it would be hard for him not to use the Speaker's gavel to attack Nancy Pelosi if he were to take control of the Speaker's gavel (Diaz, Roberson, and Duster, 2021).

A survey from the Public Relations Research Institute supported her view: 23 percent of Republican identifiers compared to just 12 percent of Independents and only 1 percent of Democrats agreed that " [t]here is a storm coming soon that will sweep away the elites in power and restore the rightful leaders" (Public Religion Research Institute, 2011). Gabriel and Goldstein (2021) write in the New York Times that "Conservatives and even some liberals have said that discussions of race are crowding out the traditional curriculum and are encouraging students and teachers to see themselves less as individuals and more as members of identity groups."

You-Gov for CBS News found in July 2021 that an overwhelming share of supporters of Trump did not see the insurrection as a threat to democracy, while most Biden backers did see such a danger. Only 16 percent of Trump supporters but 61 percent of Biden voters saw the insurrection as threatening (You-Gov, 2021).

In Washington, 39 Republican senators called history education that focuses on systemic racism a form of "activist indoctrination . . . And across the country, Republican-led legislatures have passed bills recently to ban or limit schools from teaching that racism is infused in American institutions. From school boards to the halls of Congress, Republicans are mounting an energetic campaign aiming to dictate how historical and modern racism in America are taught, meeting pushback from Democrats and educators in a politically thorny clash that has deep ramifications for how children learn about their country.

Many conservatives portray critical race theory and invocations of systemic racism as a gauntlet thrown down to accuse white Americans of being individually racist. Republicans accuse the left of trying to indoctrinate children with the belief that the United States is "inherently wicked" (Meckler and Natanson, 2021).

3

The United Kingdom

Ford and Goodwin (2010) argued that the issues of immigration and membership in the European Union were inexpiably connected because immigrants threatened the security of Britain's own public services. The pro-Brexit vote was strongest among lower-income and less-educated whites living in communities and who held socially authoritarian and very conservative values. The number of immigrants in a community did not shape voters on Brexit, but how segregated areas were did—when people chose to live in all-white communities, they were showing hostility to foreigners (Finney and Simpson, 2009; Kaufman, 2017, 60; Uslaner, 2012, ch. 5).

The Conservative Party has been split on the issue of immigration for many decades. In 1968, Tory MP "Enoch Powell (a member of the Conservative shadow cabinet) gave his famous 'rivers of blood' speech in Birmingham, in which he articulated in inflammatory rhetoric a doomsday scenario for Britain's multiracial future. He believed that Commonwealth immigrants would not integrate into British society and that the Race Relations Bill would entrench this problem" (Barry and Landler, 2019).

The government of Prime Minister Edward Heath enacted a restrictive immigration law in 1971 limiting the admission of residents of former colonies to people who had at least one grandparent born in the United Kingdom (Givens, 2003, 6). While Labour leader Gordon Brown held that immigration was beneficial to Great Britain, his Conservative successor David Cameron warned that "multiculturalism has failed, because it has encouraged different cultures to live separate lives, apart from each other and the mainstream" (Barry and Landler, 2019).

This position was endorsed by his successor, Theresa May, who insisted that immigrants take a British citizenship test as a "patriotic guide." The test would include questions such as "the obligation to obey the law, who built the Tower of London, British territory, national parks, William Shakespeare, a British Paralympian, Christmas and the Battle of Britain" (Holtug, 2021, 5).

National Identity and Partisan Polarization. Eric M. Uslaner, Oxford University Press. © Oxford University Press 2022.
DOI: 10.1093/oso/9780197633946.003.0003

The Labour Party remained opposed to such limitations, but the UKIP (United Kingdom Independence) party was founded in 1993 and the next year won almost 10 percent of the vote for the British Parliament and almost 20 percent of the vote for the European Parliament. UKIP voters said that immigration was the most important reason for supporting this party (Givens, 2003, 7). People who had lived in Britain most of their lives saw immigrants "not only as a threat to their own position but also as beneficiaries of preferential treatment over their own relatives" (Eatwell and Goodwin, 2018, xix).

When people do choose to live in more diverse communities, they are signaling that they are more willing to welcome immigrants. But when there is a large increase in immigration in previously all-white communities, support for immigration restrictions for backing UKIP increases (Kaufmann, 2017; Uslaner, 2012), a tendency that also arose in France and the United States that revolved around "us" versus "them."

The 2017 election in Britain pitted Conservative Prime Minister Theresa May against Labour party leader Jeremy Corbyn, who ran as an old style socialist. A key issue in the background was Britain's departure from the European Union (Figure 3.1), although none of the three leaders had a clear position on withdrawal ("Brexit"). Corbyn wanted to restrict freedom of movement (immigration) to the United Kingdom. May was a reluctant

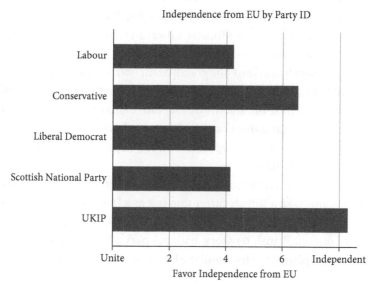

Figure 3.1 Share of Votes by Political Parties in the United Kingdom

convert to Brexit but seemed to embrace it after her predecessor David Cameron had strongly opposed it (and resigned after the referendum had passed).

The Liberal Democrats led by Tim Farron were strongly opposed to Brexit. The Conservatives won 42.4 percent of the vote in 2017 (losing their majority), Labour won 40percent, the Liberal Democrats fell to 7.4 percent. The main party opposing Brexit and immigration in general was UKIP, which received only 1.8 percent of the vote, a loss of 10.8 percent from the 2015 election (https://www.bbc.com/news/election/2017/results). By 2019 it had risen to 31 percent of the vote under Nigel Farage's leadership (Norman and Fiddler, 2019).

Immigration had long been a controversial issue in Britain. When Theresa May was Home Secretary, immigrants had to prove their identity to get a job, open a bank account, or even enroll their children in school, even as they had initially been encouraged to migrate to the United Kingdom from its former colonies.

Such demands indicate that the immigrants were not considered "true Brits." Many immigrants came from the Caribbean territory of Windrush, who could come to Britain since they had lived in a colony. But more recently, they had been forced to show proof of their identity, as people told them they were not wanted because of their race and the Conservative government had forced them to produce documents about their heritage. As late as the 1960s, a Windrush refugee saw signs displaying "No Irish, no dogs, no blacks" (de Freytas-Tamura, 2018).

Sobolewska and Ford (2019, 143–144) argued that

> Immigration played a prominent part in the EU referendum debate, and the desire for greater immigration control was strongly associated with support for leaving the EU. Public concern about immigration had been high since the early 2000s, and the Conservatives' failure to deliver on an election pledge drastically to reduce immigration collapsed public trust in the party. Voters . . . saw the free movement of labour from the newer members of the European Union as a primary reason why governments could not deliver migration control. By the time of the referendum campaign, views about immigration and about the EU were already closely linked, with many over migration.

UKIP supporters look very much like Trump voters in the United States. They believe that many people who get benefits from the state "don't really deserve any help" and "ordinary people do not get their fair share of the nation's wealth" (Curtice, n.d., 1).

However, UKIP supporters and opponents of immigration were a small share of the British electorate. Even as late as 2014 more people had a positive view of the impact of immigration than held a negative view (Ford and Lymperopoulo, 2017). Most people did not see either Christianity or being white as essential characteristics for immigrants. Applebaum (2019, 86) argued that "there was a racial undertone to this kind of English nationalism ... there can be no black 'Englishmen,' even if there can be black Britons. The concept of 'Englishness' also excluded the British Irish of Belfast . . . , Scots, and everyone else of the Gaelic fringe."

Even as Conservative Prime Minister Margaret Thatcher was a strong critic of immigration, the main parties refrained from taking positions opposing immigration. The two major parties were initially less polarized on a wide variety of policies including immigration (Adams et al., 2012). As more people of minority backgrounds came to live in Britain, both major parties adopted increasingly restrictive immigration policy, with the Tories being more willing to adopt policies favorable to nationalistic forces, including UKIP, while Labour initially had supported more liberal policies until 2002 (Carvahallo et al.). Thatcher had come to argue that who believed that the working class "need[ed] to be reassured rather than patronised" on the subject since "between 1997 and 2004, non-EU immigration more than doubled, from 166,000 per annum to 370,000, annual EU immigration rose from 66,000 to 269,000 by 2015."

Just as had happened in the late 1960s and early 1970s, public concern over immigration rose in unison with immigration levels. Whereas prior to 1999, the percentage of Britons who were concerned enough about immigration to list it as one of their top three issues was never higher than 5 percent, by 2006 it had overtaken health and defense as the issue about which the United Kingdom was most concerned (Goodwin and Dennison, 2018).

By the time of the referendum many voters believed that both major parties had failed to take strong enough positions on immigration so that leaving the EU was the only solution to restoring trust in the government. While the overall level of racial resentment was much lower in Britain than in the United States, "Leave" supporters believed that immigrants were consuming too many resources that they were not paying for. These concerns ultimately split the Labour party and shifted the Conservatives to support Brexit (Sobolewska and Ford, 2019, 143–153).

The two major parties were becoming polarized on issues of race and immigration, as has membership in society based upon formal criteria happened in the United States. Anti-immigrant positions were held only by the far right, the National Front, the British National Party, and the UKIP.

The major parties mostly shied away from racist abutments such as those made by Trump, or British Conservative Party leader Boris Johnson, who in 2017 "likened Muslim women wearing burkas to letterboxes, and who experienced a significant backlash from his own party" (Sobolewska and Ford, 2019. 152). The Brexit referendum in the United Kingdom was also based upon this distinction. People's recall of their votes was not strongly related to either their partisan predisposition or their sense of national identity (the correlation between the reported Brexit vote and national identity was –.28). There is not a strong relationship between attitudes on "independence" from the European Union and partisan identity in the United Kingdom—except for supporters of UKIP.

As with American supporters of Trump, pro-Brexit voters hoped for the "return of the United Kingdom to global power and influence. Britons would venture forth across the globe in the spirit of the buccaneers of the time of Elizabeth I," making England "great again" on its own (Wilson, 2017). A majority of people in England believed that membership in the European Union had "eroded British sovereignty" and did not see themselves as European (Clarke et al., 2017a, 448, 458, 460).

I estimated a model from the YouGov survey of voting for Brexit by whites (see Table 3-2). The four cultural factors were all strong predictors of voting for Brexit. The strongest effect, as measured by the difference in probabilities of voting for Brexit, was for identifying as English, where the people who most strongly connected to England were more than .5 likely to support leaving. The trait factor was almost as important at .3. The English identity dimension and the makes identity factor were also significant. UKIP identification and ideology also strongly shaped the Brexit vote.

For UKIP voting itself, I estimated a model showing that all of the factors related to culture, social equality, inequality, and distrust of government shaped people's attitudes (see Table 3-3). The strongest effects are for attitudes

Table 3.2 Effects of Factors on UK Brexit Vote in 2017 for Whites

Variable	Coefficient	Standard Error	Diff Probabilities
Trait factor	.200****	.023	.325
Makes identity factor	−.040*	.026	−.051
England identity factor	.054**	.022	.074
Identify English factor	.557****	19.41	.531
Belonging factor	−.030	.021	−.042
UKIP supporter	−1.458****	−7.45	−.360
Ideology	−.271****	.012	−.529
Constant	1.021****	.051	

* p < .10 ** p < .05 *** p < .01 **** p < .001, all tests one tailed

−2*Log Likelihood Ratio = 7598.592 McKelvey-Zavoina R2 = .400 N = 6994 Percent predicted correctly: .73

Table 3.3 Instrumental Variable Regression of Likelihood of Voting for UKIP from the Drivers of Populist Radical Right Support in Britain 2017–2018 Party Preference equation

Variable	Coefficient	Std. Error	t
Factor on radical Islam	−.498****	.039	−12.85
Immigration most important issue	−.954****	.063	−15.07
Vote for Brexit	−.364****	.038	−.95
Like contact with minorities	−.063****	.016	−.39
Globalization good for economic growth	.061****	.018	.340
Officials care about ordinary citizens	.212****	.021	10.14
Ordinary citizens can affect government	.058***	.019	3.00
Accept alternative lifestyles	.123****	.021	5.94
Government should reduce inequality	.097****	.018	3.40
Ideology	−.078****	.012	.61
Age	3.743****	.209	17.89

N = 3048 R2 = .369 RMSE = 1.456 * p < .10 ** p < .05 *** p < .01 **** p < .0001

Main equation for support for UKIP in tables on voting preferences.. Variables included in immigration factor: Islam is an archaic religion; Islam is democratic; Islam promotes violence

Table 3.4 Instrumental Variable Regression of Likelihood of Voting for UKIP from the Drivers of Populist Radical Right Support in Britain, UKIP from the Drivers of Populist Radical Right Support in Britain, 2017–2018 (Urban Constituency survey institute). Main voting equation

Variable	Coefficient	Std. Error	t
Immigrants much welfare	−.978****	.082	−11.87
Vote for Brexit	.395****	..090	4.39
Approve of alternative lifestyles	−.051	.046	.113
Ideology	.223****	.028	8.01
Officials care	.207	.046	−1.13
Can Affect Govt	.172****	.040	.032
Age	−.035****	.003	10.20
Constant	5.937****	.494	12.03

N = 3048 R2 = .085 RMSE = 2.987 * p < .10 ** p < .05 *** p < .01 **** p < .0001

Equation for support for Deservingness in Divergringness Tables.

on immigrants and Islam, followed bv whether government cares for ordinary citizens. Feelings about inequality were also important.

The second UKIP model presents results that replicate the first (see Table 3-4). Attitudes toward immigrants were the most significant in the survey by the Urban Constituency Institute, followed by ideology.

Overall, voting in the United Kingdom is now more than ever shaped by nationalistic sentiments. The Brexit vote is but a reflection of the overall level of polarization in British political and social life (Sobolewska and Ford, 2019).

I estimated a model of Brexit referendum voting from a You-Gov BBC survey in 2017 provided by Douglas Rivers of You-Gov. The survey did not include the measures of identity I use here but had a wide variety of other measures that relate to feelings of British identity that could play a role in the Brexit referendum. They include

1. Traits that make someone English, including having a good sense of humor, a sense of fair play, good manners, tolerance, being welcoming, friendliness, generosity, having a "stiff upper lip," being "outward looking," being loud, being liberal, being traditional, and being plain

speaking. I entered these traits into a factor analysis to produce a single dimension of British traits.

2. How one describes England: having a bright future, great, a country that has always stood alone, has led the world in innovation, is at ease with itself, is modern and ambitious; has a distinctive and important history, has a diverse population, and has many rural villages. A single factor, "the England factor," emerges.

3. What makes someone English. These measures are closer to the standard questions on what makes someone a "real" British person. They include living in the countryside rather than suburbs or a city; following the country's Christian traditions; having a social life with diverse friendships; following English history, sports, dance, and music; considering oneself to be English rather than British, Scottish, Welsh, or European; being born in England; speaking with an English accent; having one or two English parents; and how long one has lived in England. A factor analysis of these measures produced a unidimensional "males, English" factor (cf. McLaren, 2015).

Kenny (2015, 31) has argued: "Englishness needs greater recognition, and some form of institutional expression . . . England is often depicted as a haven for such values as pragmatism, tolerance and the whiggish merits of incremental change . . . and creativity [is] associated with its peoples given particular accent" but that the working class is "beleaguered, indigenous tribe . . . abandoned by an indifferent state, [left behind by] political parties and liberal public authorities."

4. Why people identify with England: simply identifying as English rather than as British; being born outside the country; where one lives, where one was born, and where one grew up. A single factor emerged as the "identify English" factor. The stronger someone has a sense of English, as opposed to British, identity, the more likely that person would be to support the Brexit referendum.

People who are more proud of British history and advances in science, culture, rural culture, Christianity, and personal traits that make someone distinctly English (plain speaking, loud, traditional, welcoming, friendliness, having a sense of humor, being plain speaking), the more likely they would be to vote for the "Leave" option. If you were born outside England, have one or two parents not born in England, have not lived in England very long or were not born there, you would be more likely to vote to "Remain" in the European Union. These finding are consistent with Kenny's (2016) argument. He found that most people who voted to leave the EU strongly identify with England rather than with Britain as a whole.

4

The Case of France

In France, Bennhold (2005) wrote about a young man named Walid:

"We are French, but we also feel like foreigners compared to the real French," said Mamadou, whose father came to France from Mali decades ago and married his mother, a French woman. Who, according to him, are the "real" French? The answer comes without hesitation and to vigorous nodding by a group of his friends: "Those with white skin and blue eyes." (Bennhold, 2005)

A French-Arab woman once said that her son was asked about his religious faith by a police officer. He said that he is a Muslim. The officer replied, "You are a French Muslim," but the young man's family wonder if they ever will be considered French. (Onishi and Méheut, 2020a)

France is technically blind to differences of race and religion. The theme of French society is "as laïcité," often inadequately translated as secularism, is embraced by a majority of French people. They or their forebears became French in this way. No politician here would utter the words "In God we trust." The Roman Catholic Church was removed more than a century ago from French public life (R. Cohen, 2020).

The state enacted legislation in 1905 that requires the state to be neutral with respect to religion. While the United States is officially neutral toward all religions, France is different. McAuley (2020d) wrote: "Catholicism . . . is largely understood as the freedom from oppressive religious authority. At the turn of the century, it was predominantly Catholic, with a small Protestant minority and an even smaller Jewish population."

Yet the Church has persisted as part of French culture. While the public display of religious objects is banned by law, an exception is made for Catholic symbols, but not for those of Judaism or Islam. The French Republic is seen as a fight against "militant Islamists" and both Muslims and Jews were denied citizenship rights during World War II (R. Cohen, 2020). The irony is that the privileged position of the Catholic Church was presumably ended in

National Identity and Partisan Polarization. Eric M. Uslaner, Oxford University Press. © Oxford University Press 2022.
DOI: 10.1093/oso/9780197633946.003.0004

formal law but permitted in government funding. Yet today only 8 percent of the public practice religion (Onishi and Breeden, 2020b); a church that most people ignore is still given special status to guard against faiths that more non-Christians practice.

French identity is officially neutral with respect to religion, but there is agreement on French lineage. France is seen as the center of European society, acting in defense of its heritage against foreign influences. The idea of France is a mixture of inclusive and exclusive identity. It is inclusive in the sense that people who come to France should be accepted as French if they adapt to a European way of life. As a former colonial power, people of French heritage see themselves with a special responsibility to assist residents of their former colonies whom they exploited before independence (Frankema, 2011). Yet inclusivity is "tempered" by their rejection of both the American model of complete assimilation and the continental European and Canadian model of multiculturalism. Under assimilation, all races and religions are accepted and subsumed, since there is no common heritage (everyone except Native Americans are immigrants, voluntarily or not). Under multiculturalism, all races and religions are expected to maintain their former traditions and are equally valued. The French people see their own culture as superior and new residents are expected to adapt themselves to their new home. White people have no reciprocal responsibility.

A substantial number of French people do not see Jews or Muslims "as French as other French people" and do not consider either as full citizens (Mayer, 2012). Jews are seen as more loyal to Israel than to France (Simmons, 1996, 121) and even linked rising fuel prices to the government's relationship with Israel. The mayor of a French city "demanded that schools should not provide Kosher or Halal meals to save money" (Hainsworth and Mitchell, 2000).

Francis Kalifat, the president of CRIF (Conseil Représentatif des Institutions juives de France), the council uniting France's Jewish institutions: "Anti-Semitism creates bridges between the far right and the far left: They have such a hatred in common that they come together." In France and other Western societies, the proliferation of new political forces that challenge the established liberal order—from both the right and the left—has revived old patterns of vilifying the Jews as the embodiment of the corrupt elites supposedly responsible for society's ills" (Trofimov, 2019).

The French writer Renaud Camus expressed the views of many when he expressed concern about a "great replacement" of France's original population by newer arrivals, mostly from Africa—mostly from France's former colonies in the Maghreb and in sub-Saharan Africa—who didn't come "as friends." Instead, he declared, they came as conquerors and colonizers, filled with hatred and a desire to punish France. He singled out Muslims for "not wanting to integrate" into French society (Onishi, 2019). Even the moderate President Emmanuel Macron stated: "Secularism is the cement of a united France," he said, calling radical Islam both an "ideology" and a "project" that sought to indoctrinate children, undermine France's values—especially gender equality—and create a "counter-society" that sometimes laid the groundwork for Islamist terrorism.

Macron also recognized that France bore responsibility for letting that ideology spread uncontested (Onishi and Breeden, 2019). The French debate whether they have faced "ensauvagement," an idea according to Stanford University historian Cécile Alduy that the nation's unresolved colonial legacy has left it "an underlying imaginary world, with savages on one side and civilized humanity on the other" (Onishi and Méheut, 2020a). Some of his opponents accuse Macron of forsaking his national identity to become a major figure on the world stage. "Macron speaks poorly about France when he's abroad. He's giving the country away. And why does he speak English all the time? General de Gaulle only spoke French. Macron's a globalist. We need someone to restore French grandeur and sovereignty," while another citizen said: "The climate in France today, he says, reminds him of the U.S. five years ago on the eve of Donald Trump's election" (Beardsley, 2021).

After an attack by extremists on the satirical magazine *Charlie Hebdo* that ran cartoons with caricatures of the Prophet Muhammed, counter-demonstrators marched with signs stating, "*Je suis Charlie*" ("I am Charlie") to protest against Muslims' very presence in France (Onishi and Méhuet, 2020d). Marcus (1995, 73, 105) linked the rise of the new National Front party with its anti-immigrant message as a "a simple confrontation of opposites: good ranged against evil, order against disorder, national identity favoured over internationalism . . . and civilisation over barbarism." Its founder, Jean-Marie Le Pen argued that "a plurality of cultures must be preserved but clearly not in France. He rejects the Anglo-Saxon and American models of integration—"multiculturalism" and the "politics of the melting pot." A restriction of immigration by both Jews and Muslims is necessary, he believed, to "protect French identity" (Marcus, 1995, 106). Libraries were required to have a balance of left and right wing books and magazines (Hainsworth and Mitchell, 2000). He believes that the FN will "bring back the 'good old days' of empire, when French grandeur was at its peak" and foresees "a united Europe of Nations [to counter both Communism and American influence] . . . with each one guarding its identity and integrity" (Davies, 2002, 137, 139).

Prior to the establishment of the FN, nativist movements in France were led by veterans' mass organizations. They were established to guard the nation from enemies, including Jews, Protestants, Masons, and foreigners. Many of its leaders had cooperated with the Nazis during the Vichy regime of World War II. France has struggled with nativism for much of its history. As Minkenberg (2018, 251) remarked: "[the increase in ethnocentrism is] not a reaction to actual immigration but reflects a politicization of immigration and must . . . be seen as an agenda-setting effect of FN mobilization."

The basis for the new party, the Front National, was in the words of Hainsworth and Mitchell (2000, 445): "the concept serves to underwrite the party's view of the nation. The nation and national identity are supreme values. The nation, moreover, is a 'rooted', historic, traditional, ethnically-inspired entity that can easily be undermined by (allegedly) alien values, groups, culture and influences."

After the war, the FN was established to form a "counter revolution" and reestablish the values of family, religion, and hard work (Mayer, 2018,. 434–437). The FN also sought to restrict the intrusion of the government sector into people's lives by limiting public spending and controlling immigration. Yet by 1982 the share of immigrants from North Africa had increased to over 40 percent of all migrants. The FN emphasized "difference," "identity," and "exclusion" (Stockemer, 2015, 11, 14).

McLaren (2015, 31) wrote of how French people, especially FN supporters, view the country: "French nationalism was initially perceived as essentially civil and territorial: 'To belong to the French nation, individuals did not need to be born in France, but could be assimilated into it . . . during the revolutionary years the key definition of citizenship was ethnic, being a 'Frenchman born of a French father.'" For Le Pen, "it is entirely natural to live among one's own kind. As he regularly says, "I prefer my daughters to my cousins, my cousins to my neighbors, my neighbors to those I don't known and those I don't know to my enemies" (Marcus, 1995, 105). Le Pen rejects the idea of complete integration, believing that immigrants must adapt to French society.

The biggest threat to French society, according to the FN, was the immigration of Muslims from North Africa. The FN denounced Muslim's celebration of the holy month of Ramadan as "a perversion of Lent" and as a pathology that "leads to over consumption and taxes the French health care system." The party also feared immigration from Western Europe, believing that people came to France to live off the generosity of the state, to engage in criminal activity, and to subvert the country's sovereignty so that a unified Europe could dominate the French people. It was not just poor immigrants who threatened the French Republic, but international bankers who sought to take over the country's economy (Stovkemer, 2017, 27, 34, 38).

The wealthy in France were acting in conspiracy with European business executives to sap the country's treasury and thus lead to greater inequality. The losers were the working class, which constituted a large share of the FN's xenophobic constituency (Goodman, 2019; Stockemer, 2015, 88). As with many nationalist movements, the FN favored generous spending on social security and health care, but only for French natives (Lefkoridi and Michel, 2017, 256). The FN is not hard right. The share of its supporters who identify on the right fell from 77 percent to 50 percent from 1994 to 1997 (Rydgren, 2004). FN voters are less concerned with economic issues than with law and order and immigration, so they do not fall into a simple left-right continuum: 22 percent of the party's voters say that law and order ranks first among all issues while 48 percent choose immigration (Schain, 1987).

The white French public has been consistently moving to the right. The party of Charles de Gaulle, which typified the conservative center—opposed to the Soviet Union but wary of American power—has fallen into the status of a minority party. The Socialist opposition has also faded into minority status, with a center-left movement of Macron replacing it. On the right, the Front National has displayed the Rally pour la Republique of de Gaulle and his successors.

The sharp change in the French political landscape is marked by the collapse of the main parties on both the center right and the center left. Macron has become the heir to the supporters of the French center left and the FN found it critical to unseat Jean-Marie Le Pen as its leader because he was too closely aligned with anti-Semitic forces. He ultimately was replaced by his daughter, Marine Le Pen, who continued to oppose immigration from Muslim countries but courted Jewish voters. Macron has been pushed to the right on issues of immigration (see below). He has moved to the center left on economics, proposing generous social spending, especially on health care as well as social benefits such as women's rights (Charlemagne, 2021). The FN is explicitly anti-Muslim (though it claims to be pro-Israel).

The center left has also moved toward a nationalist position on identity as Macron sees himself in a "battle to force Islamic organizations into the mold of French secularism . . . his administration has ousted the leadership of a mosque after temporarily closing it and pouring over its finances. Another mosque gave up millions in subsidies after the government pressured local officials. A dozen other mosques have faced orders to close temporarily for safety or fire-code violations (Bisserbie and Meichtry, 2021). He has argued that radical Islam "indoctrinate[s] on our soil and corrupt[s] daily" (McAuley, 2018b).

The government has launched a drive to develop an "Islam of France" compatible with the nation's republican values. This Islam would be consistent with "[the s]ecularism [as] the cement of a united France," calling radical Islam both an 'ideology' and a 'project' that sought to indoctrinate children, undermine France's values—especially gender equality—and create a 'counter-society' that sometimes laid the groundwork for Islamist terrorism" (Onishi and Breeden, 2020b) It would be "an Islam in France that can be an Islam of the Enlightenment," as Macron put it, and would halt "repeated deviations from the values of the republic and which often result in the creation of a counter-society" McAuley, 2020d).

Macron is promising an unconditional fight against Islamic terrorism and separatism in France and abroad (Cohen, 2021). Legislation enacted in 2020 would create a new crime of "separatism" that involves any threat to a public official or civil servant or contractors such as bus drivers (R. Cohen, 2020). Almost 70 percent of natives believe that Muslims are not making sufficient efforts to integrate into French society (Betz, 2018).

Eighty percent believe that immigrants come to the country simply to gain benefits and that this is especially true for Muslims who come to France (Mayer, 2012), and an identical share believe that "Islamism is at war with France." The government has also taken action to prohibit the teaching of Islamic doctrine in home schools (*The Economist*, 2021). The government also would have the power to monitor Internet browsing to check for radicalism (Novack, 2021). France would also work with Austria to fight terrorism throughout the world—mostly in Europe and the Middle East (Panveski, 2020).

The government has banned the wearing of the *burqua* and the *niqab* in public as a violation of both French culture and women's rights in the country. The government has also tried to prohibit women from wearing a "birkini" (a variant on a swimsuit) on French beaches. McAuley (2018c) wrote: "Interior Minister Gérard Collomb was among the critics. 'We cannot let this be a sign of identitarian will, something that shows that one is different from French society,' he said on television. (In French, the precise word he used, *identitaire*, carries a strong nativist connotation, often associated with the far right.)" Doctors would be prohibited from issuing virginity certificates to Muslim women prior to getting married (The Economist, 2021).

The FN has been boosted by a rebellion against the policies of the Macron presidency. Protesters called the Yellow Vests have taken to the streets to organize against the reelection of Macron because of rising fuel prices and his policies on immigration. The yellow vests have become a broad and sometimes violent movement demanding more social justice for low-skilled workers left behind by globalization, deregulation, and EU integration.

Although independent of parties and unions, the movement shares many of the Front National's demands: proportional representation in parliament, direct democracy through Swiss-style referendums, less European integration, and—above all—Macron's resignation (De Clercq, 2019). They have also destroyed monuments and shops in Paris (McAuley, 2020e). They are also a front on behalf of anti-Semites, arguing that Macron is a "whore of the Jews" and "a slave of the Rothschild's, a reference to the president's past employment with the investment bank, became a fixture of the demonstrations." They blamed a noted Jewish philosopher as head of an international "economic and social malaise," a "Zionist turd" who violates the movement's belief that "France is for us" (Trofimov, 2019). They linked their economic grievances with xenophobia.

The FN has now become the second political force in France, the only party capable of challenging Macron. It has become the center of support for voters who believe that there are too many North Africans in France—90 percent of its supporters hold this position. The core support of the FN is people who worry about immigration, the security of the country, and the need to "conquer Islam," including ensuring that women do not have to wear a headscarf in public (Brechon and Mitra, 1992, 70). The voters most opposed to immigration supported Le Pen over Macron by over 10 percent in 2017 (Mayer, 2018b, 683). Le Pen voters are more likely than Macron voters to overestimate the share of all immigrants and Muslim immigrants (by 10 percent) in the country (Mayer, n.d.).

To shore up support from potential FN voters, Macron and his party have developed an "integration contract: that must be signed by new immigrants to signal that they agree to uphold French values. As Radziemski (2021) writes, "The contract requires four days of civic education, yet what's taught is more akin to a government crash course in how to be French." And these values include the importance of gender equality and tolerance for gays and lesbians. One analyst of French society said that the purpose of the course is to make "a distinction between 'them' and 'us,' an 'us' that is equal, exemplary, and a 'them' that is inherently sexist."

Throughout Europe, the "threat" is from Muslim immigrants, who are ethnically and religiously distinct from the majority population, and who have less education and income, and are seen as lazy and not deserving of government benefits (Larsen, 2011, 351). Holtug (in press, ch. 3, 21) states: "if it is feared that immigration, not least of low-skilled labour and refugees, will be a net burden for the state, and therefore result in declining social services and/ or higher taxes, this may hamper solidarity with immigrants, at least to the extent such solidarity is based on norms of reciprocity or self-interest . . . extensive welfare regimes, and the Scandinavian countries in particular, tend to incur greater costs from immigration."

It is the threat to a country's national (specifically white Christian) culture, rather than the effects on its economy, that underlies opposition to immigration (Inglehart and Norris, 2019, 195; Bornschier, 2018, 222). Young people are especially likely to see France's culture threatened by non-white immigrants. They recall being stopped frequently by the police, and one young woman told reporters: "When you undergo an identity check nine times in two months because of the color of your skin, I don't think that's right, and I don't think it's a black sheep." They felt that they were under constant surveillance and white natives saw them as insufficiently committed to French customs. One black young man commented that "I'm in love with a republic that doesn't love me back" (Onishi and Méheut. 2021c).

The 2017 election was (as the 2016 election in the United States) largely shaped by national identity (factor score of the importance of birth in France and family origins, see Table 4.1). No other variable came close to predicting the final vote in 2017 (using data from the Centre des Etudes Europeannes provided by Nicholas Sauger of Sciences Po, Paris). National identity in turn

Table 4.1 Regression Predicting the Sense of Identity in France CSES Data 2017

Variable	Coefficient	Std. Error	t Score
Authoritarianism	.111**	.048	2.33
Importance of Religion	−.056**	.024	−3.27
Rating of Jews	.047*	.028	1.66
Rating of Muslims	.069**	.029	2.36
Education	−.011**	.006	−1.83
Ideology	−.006	.015	−.043
Constant	−.158	−1.04	1.04

$N = 492$; R2 = .062; MSE = .480

was shaped by opposition to free trade in the European Union and calls to reduce immigration. The overall level of polarization was lower in France than in the United States (not surprising since Macron ran as a centrist on economic issues). Attitudes on social issues (gay marriage, gay adoption, abortion) and an overall measure of ideology were moderately associated with vote choice and less strident positions on national identity.

5

Germany and Austria

Germany

The AfD is a descendant of the Nazi party. Cantoni. Hagemeister, and Westcott (2017) argue: "municipalities that, in the 1920s and 30s, expressed strong support for the Nazi party (the NSDAP) now have a stronger vote base for the AfD." One key difference is that the AfD (Alternatif für Deutschland) has rejected anti-Semitism and expressed strong support for Israel.

But it is strongly anti-immigrant, especially with respect to Muslims. More than half of Germans believe that Turks behave differently from other Germans and only 18 percent agree that Muslims accept German values (Abali, 2009). Yet the AfD still argues that Germany should no longer have to apologize for its past (Stanley, 2018). Even the head of the Christian Social Union, the Bavarian partner of the governing Christian Democratic Union (CDU), argued that "Islam doesn't belong in Germany" (Witte and Beck, 2018). Merkl's more center-left position has caused a split in the party's Bavaria affiliate, the Christian Social Union. The party is so badly divided by its own nativist instincts and the demand that it support its federal partner, the CDU, that the beneficiary has become the AfD (Pancevski, 2019).

In Germany, "Alternative for Germany's 100-page program states that, 'Islam does not belong to Bavaria,' and warns that the religion's spread endangers 'the internal peace, our legal and value systems, as well as our cultural identity' (Bennhold, 2018a). The Christian Social Party in the state felt pressured by the AfD to argue: "We tell about Islam all the time and don't realize how insecure we are about own roots . . . In Bavaria we stand up for our values." He promised, under AfD pressure, to stand up for Christian values in the state (Bennhold, 2018a).

In Austria and Germany, national identity has played a powerful role in shaping the vote shares of nationalist parties. Using data from the fifth module of the Comparative Study of Electoral System's fifth module made available to me, I show that support for the two "nationalist" parties in Austria

National Identity and Partisan Polarization. Eric M. Uslaner, Oxford University Press. © Oxford University Press 2022. DOI: 10.1093/oso/9780197633946.003.0005

(the Freedom Nationalist Party and the Pliz Nationalist party) were shaped mostly by the beliefs that one must be born in the country, have Austrian ancestry, and follow the customs of the country.

A combined measure of these three variables (a factor score) overwhelmed all other factors in shaping the vote for nationalist parties. This sense of national identity itself reflects the beliefs that minorities insist upon keeping their own traditions, that elites are rich and powerful, that immigration should be reduced, and also a measure of ideology (with nationalism parties strongly rightist). In Germany, support for the ultranationalism Alternative für Deutschland, or Alternative for Germany) party is almost exclusively determined by the belief that immigrants must follow German traditions. This nationalist doctrine in turn ins shaped by the belief that minorities *do not* adapt to German culture.

I estimated an instrumental probit model of voting for the AfD from the CSES survey in Table (5.2). The dependent variable for the first stage is voting for the AfD in national elections and the most significant predictor was the belief that immigrants must follow German traditions. Being born in Germany was not a significant predictor of AfD support in the first state or even as shaping the importance of following traditions in the second stage. Perhaps surprising is that spending more on welfare benefits predicted neither support for the AfD nor whether immigrants must follow German traditions. People who were conservative or who saw the AfD as a right-wing party were more likely to vote for the AfD, but not to say that immigrants must follow German traditions.

I also estimated an instrumental probit model of the Freedom Party of Austria, or FPO (*Freiheitlich Partei Österrich*, FPÖ) voting for the Austrian lower house in Table 5.1. The importance of Austrian identity was critical to FPO support—but it was far more based upon whether one was born in the country and had Austrian ancestry than in Germany. The identity factor stressing Austrian background was by far the most critical factor shaping support for the nationalist party. The belief that elites are rich and powerful also shaped support for the FPO as did the perception that this party was conservative. The sense of identity was shaped most strongly by attitudes toward immigrants (although the direction of causality likely goes both ways) as well as the belief that immigrants should not maintain their traditions, the idea that elites are powerful, one's personal ideology as well as the belief that the FPO is a right-wing party, and satisfaction with the state of the economy.

Table 5.1 Influence of Identity and Immigration on Support for the FPO in Austria from CSES Data

Importance Factor	1.641****	.046	35.31
Elites Rich and Powerful	.097**	.036	2.66
State of Economy Better	.042	.064	.076
Is the FPO Right Wing	.125****	.035	3.58
Constant	−2.020****	.334	−6.05
Second Stage IV Regression			
Elites Rich and Powerful	−.079****	.018	−.4.29
State of Economy Better	.070	.026	2.68
Minorities Keep; Their Own Traditions	−.098****	.929	−4.96
Ideology	.076****	.011	6.86
Live in Rural Area	.002	.020	.010
Immigration Factor	−.188****	.026	−7.31
Constant	.990****	.191	5.19

$N = 934 - 2{*}LLR = 2270.10; * p < .10; ** p < .05; *** p < .01; **** p < .0001.$

Importance factor variables: Important for immigrants to be born in country; importance for immigrants to have Austrian ancestry; importance for immigrants to follow Austrian culture. Immigration factor variables: immigrants good for economy; Austria's culture is generally harmed by immigrants; immigrants increase crime rates in Austria.

FPO supporters are thus strong right-wing nationalists with little faith in the country's leaders.

Austria has long been associated with Germany. It was once part of the German empire and the German dictator Adolph Hitler was born there (and conquered the country in World War II). Its people consider themselves part of German culture. Its newer nationalist party, the FPO, Heinrich, Werner, and Habersack (2020, 169) write,

> stresses the importance and need to defend specific Austrian values. Command of the German language is defined as a condition for entrance into the education and social systems whereas Austrian cultural identity was emphasized for protecting Austrian media . . . and guarding against the cultural influence of Islam. Such sentiments feature heavily in the speeches of [its] leaders, who claim immigration reduces the quality of life for Austrians, leads to crime ('parallel societies') and introduces an alien

Muslim population incompatible with Austrian society. National sovereignty claims also concern 'Austrian interests' with respect to broader institutional influences.

As with the Nazis in Germany, The FPO worries about the influence of foreigners ("Auslanders") and aliens ("Fremden") as "unwanted" members of society (Boreus, 2013, 298–299). The FPO wants to ensure the purity of the German bloodline and seeks to reunify Austria with Germany (Chianteram and Andreas. 2003, 7). It is particularly wary of migrants from Islamic countries (Heinrich, Werner, and Habersack, 2020, 169). Also in common with the Nazis, it is worried about the influence of *any* non-German values, including those held by members of European Community countries. The party sees Austria as a country that other European nations have exploited since the signing of the Treaty of Maastrict that established the European currency union in 1992 (Chianteram and Andreas. 2003, 7).

Austria and Germany do differ from each other in two related ways. First, the extent of anti-foreigner sentiment is much greater in Austria .than in Germany. Second, the nativist movement is stronger politically in Austria than in Germany. The FPO became the largest party in Austria following its 26 percent of the national vote in 2017, while the AfD remains a minor force in German politics. In the European Social Survey, Austrians were among the least likely of all European countries (including Germany) to favor the immigration of people from outside of Europe to their country, especially those from different racial or ethnic backgrounds—and to expect the state to provide these migrants with governmental benefits.

The other major forces shaping this sense of identity were two sets of factor scores.

People who opposed immigration or who identified with what are often called "populist" attitudes were considerably more likely to say that people who came to Germany must follow the country's culture. The populism factor variables include: "Compromise in politics is selling out on one's principles," the people, not politicians, should make most important policies; politicians follow will of people; there are differences between elites and people; rather be represented by citizens than elites; politicians talk too much and take little action; politicians don't care about people; most politicians are trustworthy; politicians are the main problem in Germany; I want strong leader even if he bends the rules; politicians care only about the interests of the rich; political issues difficult to understand; I have confidence to take an active role

Table 5.2 Influence of Identity and Immigration on Support for the AfD in Germany from CSES Data

First Stage IV Probit

Variable	Coefficient	Standard Error	z
Important to follow traditions as identity	2.068****	.083	24.79
Important to be born here as identity	−.124*	.089	−.14
Ideology	.051**	.024	2.12
State of economy better	.043	.051	.08
Government should spend more on welfare	.087**	.043	.20
Is the AfD right wing	−.044**	.048	−2.12
Age	−.009****	.002	−3.94
Constant	−1.867****	.334	−.60

Second stage IV Probit

Important to be born here as identity	.035	.031	2.21
Minorities must adapt to German culture	−.068****	.012	−5.50
Factor sore for immigration attitudes	−.161****	.016	−9.68
Factor score for populism attitudes (see items bellow)	−.030****	.0il	−2.74
Is the AfD right wing	.004	.007	.062
Ideology	−.008	.007	.027
Government should spend more on welfare benefits	−.009	.015	−.06
Age	.001**	.001	2.05
Constant	.619****	.115	5.37

$N = 1732 - 2\text{*LLR} = 1872.1; * p < .10; ** p < .05; *** p < .01; **** p < .0001.$

Populism factor variables: 'Compromise' in politics is selling out on one's principles. The people, not politicians, should make most important policies; politicians follow will of people; there are differences between elites and people; rather be represented by citizens than elites; politicians talk too much and take little action; politicians don't care about people; most politicians are trustworthy; politicians are the main problem in Germany; want strong leader even if he bends the rules; politicians care only about the interests of the rich; political issues difficult to understand; confidence to take an active role in politics; politicians care about what people think; politicians cannot solve problems.

Immigration factor variables: immigrants good for economy; Germany's culture is generally harmed by immigrants; Immigrants increase crime rates in Germany; immigrants should be obliged to assimilate into the German culture; immigration should be reduced.

in politics; politicians care about what people think; and politicians cannot solve problems.

The immigration factor variables are migrants are good for the economy; Germany's culture is generally harmed by immigrants; immigrants increase crime rates in Germany; immigrants should be obliged to assimilate into the German culture; immigration should be reduced. The AfD is thus a strongly conservative party whose supporters have little faith in immigrants or in the politicians of the major parties (see Table 5.2).

6

Sweden

Sweden stands out as distinctive because it violates the argument that institutions matter, because it has adopted universalistic benefits for immigrants and refugees as well as all people, and because its parties are less polarized than most other nations. Becker argued: "Under the grand, egalitarian idea of the 'folkhemmet,' or people's home, in which the country is a family and its citizens take care of one another."

If institutions shaped attitudes on either belongingness or deservingness, Sweden should be the most polarized country among those I consider. Sweden has a parliamentary electoral system rather than a Presidential one and the parties directly choose the candidates for every district. Not only do people choose between parties but not candidates in the national elections, but local voting patterns closely follows those in national elections. This basis of elections, according to Duverger, should lead to strongly divided parties.

Yet in Sweden, there is general agreement between the center-left and center-right on both universalistic benefits and migration policies (Alund and Schierup, 1991, 9). Swedish national identity is shaped by a commitment to egalitarianism (Alund and Schierup, 1991, 19). It is also based upon an inclusivist sense of identity. Sweden is one of the most homogenous countries in the world. The largest share of immigrants who were not born in Sweden comes from Finland and a large share of Swedes have family in the neighboring Nordic country (Lodefalk, N.D.). In recent years, the country has accepted refugees from the Middle East and the former Communist countries of Central and Eastern Europe.

Yet almost 80 percent of Swedes were born in the country (Pancevski, 2019). As a homogenous nation, one might expect Swedes to have a more exclusivist identity. Yet they are among the most generous in accepting people from conflict-ridden countries. Given Sweden's Parliamentary electoral system and the homogeneity of its population, the country would be expected to have strong partisan divisions—especially compared to the more diverse United States with its first-past-the-post federal electoral system. Yet precisely the opposite holds. Boreus (2013, 304) writes: "Swedish nationalism

National Identity and Partisan Polarization. Eric M. Uslaner, Oxford University Press. © Oxford University Press 2022.
DOI: 10.1093/oso/9780197633946.003.0006

has been characterized a taking pride in opposing the kind of nationalism that is ethnocentric and oppressive if minorities."

Even when Sweden had an unequal distribution of income, it was considered wrong to consider one's self superior to others. Therborn et al. (1978) write: "the situation of the lower classes in nineteenth century Sweden, grim and miserable as it was, was rather better than in most of the more advanced countries . . . In the first decade for which European comparable data are available, the 1840s, Sweden is on a par with the most developed nations. By the time industrialization takes off in Sweden, Swedish infants are entering a considerably less cruel and dangerous world than their brothers and sisters in the societies of more advanced capitalism."

In Sweden, social equality has a long history. When I visited the University of Uppsala in 2004 to present some lecturers, I was given a tour of the university's museum by its director. In the last room I saw a picture of the king and his court—which included the landed gentry and the clergy, as one would expect. Yet it also included the peasants, and it turned out that even the king had once been a farmer. This was unheard of in any other kingdom back in the 14th century.

This is reflected in the Danish idea of "Jante Law," which holds that every person is as worthy as everyone else. This concept is accepted throughout the Nordic countries and is embodied in the policy that each person, regardless of ethnic origin, race, or gender is entitled to a decent standard of life. Its foundation lies in the early spread of education, which the Danish leader (Paldam, 1991; Akestalo et al. 2009) enacted when he abolished feudalism.

The first reform leading to a more egalitarian country came when Sweden enacted universal education (Uslaner, 2021, 64–-65).

Education is central to producing an egalitarian society. Education provides young people with opportunities to make their own way in the world and to free them from domination by economic masters. In many parts of the world—including Sweden, the United States, and the miracle economies of Asia, reform of the education system was a key element in overall economic redistribution (Uslaner, 2018). As Therborn et al. (1978, 41) argues, the lower classes in Sweden had a key asset—"that was much more scarce in other countries . . . literacy . . . that had been established by Lutheran clergymen" before the state had funded widespread learning. By the mid-19th century, literacy was universal.

In Sweden, support for the Sweden Democrats is *not* strongly shaped by criteria for being Swedish, despite the party's slogans. But it *is* determined by attitudes that immigrant are bad for the Swedish economy, that they harm Swedish culture, and that they increase crime. Supporters of the Sweden Democrats are especially concerned that immigrants are less hardworking and consume more welfare than native Swedes (Milne, 2018a).

Most Swedes do accept the view that immigrants can adapt to Swedish culture (Becker, 2019; see also Oscarrson and Holmberg, 2016). Swedes rank as the most tolerant people in Europe (Mudde, 2010). Even the Swedish Democrats accept the argument that "One can become a member of the Swedish nation either by being born into it or later in life by actively choosing to become part of it" (Jungar, 2015). Even the nationalist New Democracy party in Sweden insists that "immigrants, including temporary foreign workers and refugees, be allowed to work in Sweden" (Betz, 1993, 419).

The inclusive Swedish identity is based upon the principle that everyone residing in the country "belongs" to the society. Prior to the admission of many refugees and immigrants of Middle Eastern origin, everyone was expected to identify as Swedish. By the mid-1960s, large scale immigration led the country to adopt multiculturalism, since the new immigrants were not fully integrated into the Swedish culture. The adoption of this policy was based upon the acceptance of cultural diversity so that new immigrants could maintain their "distinct cultural identities" (Bovesi, 2013, 317).

By the 1980s Swedish authorities revised the policy of multiculturalism because it "risked jeopardizing their swift and successful integration into the Swedish labor market and mainstream society: [Swedish policies toward immigrants] .. were designed to promote a long-term, cautious and natural adaptation' to the larger society." In 1997 the government changed what had been called an "immigrant and minority policy" to a policy of integration since immigrants and refugees were expected to become full members of Swedish society (Borevi, 2014).

The absorption of people of different background was a sign that Sweden was becoming a society of egalitarianism and high trust among fellow citizens and for the country's institutions (Goossen et al., 2020, 133). In a cross-national analysis of both egalitarianism and trust (Uslaner, 2018) I found that Sweden (as well as other Nordic countries such as Norway, Finland, and Denmark) had the highest levels of both trust and egalitarianism of any country in the world. And this laid the foundation for the Nordic policies on universalism.

Sweden long had conflict between management and labor with strong class divisions. In the late 19th and early 20th centuries, Sweden was marked by sharp voting cleavages by class (Oskarson and Demker, 2015, 629). To keep the peace in the early 20th century, labor and workers joined together to enact a series of economic and social reforms (Schlemp, 1993, 114). The guild system was abolished and wages were made more equal and the country established greater equality between men and women (Rothstein, 2021, 81–82).

Most Swedes had positive views of immigrants. Among Europeans, they were the most supportive of refugees and the country admitted more immigrants than any other nation in Europe. The dominant views of Swedes were that "immigration 'makes their country a better place,' that immigrants 'enrich the cultural life of their country' and that 'immigration is good for the economy'" (Hjorth, 2016, 13). Swedes scored highest among Europeans for being a "non-nationalist nation," with more than three-quarters judged as tolerant compared to an average for the European Union of 60 percent (Mudde, 2010).

More than any other Europeans, Swedes were the most willing to accept Muslims as friends, neighbors, or family members. They were also the most likely to deny that one had to be born in the country to "belong" to it or to insist that their culture was superior to that of other traditions. Yet they worry that immigrants are not becoming sufficiently attached to Swedish values or doing enough to integrate into the larger society (Berman, 2018) or that Muslim immigrants do not accept the gender equality that is central to Swedish identity (Mudde, 2010).

Yet some Swedes ultimately realized that refugees and immigrants from poor countries were *not* becoming integrated into the economy or society. They were not supposed to view refugees as "unwanted . . . not belonging to Swedish society" (Boreus, 2013, 298–299). They saw the immigrants as "an assault on 'Swedish culture' and 'heritage,'" as lazy and unwilling to work and a drain on the country's treasury. Goodman (2019) writes: "People are quite open to showing solidarity for people who are like themselves," says Carl Melin, policy director at Futurion, a research institution in Stockholm. "They don't show solidarity for people who are different" (cf. Dal Bo et al., 2019). Such people were more likely to support assistance to immigrants of Western European background than those from Eastern Europe or the Middle East (Hjorth, 2016, 18).

These were the supporters of the Sweden Democratic Party. Although it was a small fringe party it had an outsized role in shaping immigration policy. It pushed the mainstream parties to the right on immigration policy and ran just behind the opposition Moderate Party in 2014 (Anderson and Erlanger, 2018). The Sweden Democratic Party stressed that immigrants segregated themselves into poor ethnic neighborhoods and made no attempt to integrate into the larger society (Bittner, 2018). This pushed the long dominant Sweden Democrats to move away from their support of multiculturalism and to return to their traditional slogan of "Keep Sweden Swedish," reflecting a nostalgia for a mythical country of the 1950s (Erlanger, 2017).

The fringe SDP is racist and includes members who formerly were Nazis. The party program refers to "the 'homogenous composition of the population' as an 'invaluable asset' to Sweden, and argues that immigration of non-Europeans should be very restrictive" (Widfeldt, 2002). Its slogan is similar to Donald Trump's in the United States: "Make Sweden Great Again" and it charges that the country is under threat of Islamic law from the refugees (AFP and Snell, 2018). The party's roots laid in Swedish fascism; it did not renounce any Nazi connections until 1996. Yet it still saw immigrants as threats to national identity and sources of crime and unemployment as well as abusers of the welfare state (Rydgren and Ruth, 2011).

Using data from the 2019 CSES, I estimated a model of support for the Sweden Democrats in Table 6.1. Consistent with the argument that Sweden is a more inclusive society than most others, the only criterion for being a "true Swede" that shapes support for the Sweden Democrats is the demand that immigrants follow Swedish customs. Neither being born in the country, having Swedish ancestry, nor speaking Swedish shapes liking for the Swedish Democrats. Views of immigrants *are* critical. When people believe that migrants harm Swedish culture or increase crime, they will be more likely to view the Swedish Democrats. Especially important are the beliefs that immigrants must adapt to Swedish culture, but the feeling that immigrants are good people leads to less support for this party. Neither age, education, or rural residence shapes support for this nationalist party is right-wing.

I also estimated a model of party preference for the Sweden Democrats using the 2017 European Values Survey. The significant predictors of Swedish Democratic support were the demand that immigrants follow Swedish customs, and three measures of out-group attitudes: whether they need to follow the majority rather than their own customs, whether they harm Swedish

Table 6.1 Support for the Sweden Democrats: CSES 2018

Variable	Coefficient	Standard Error	t
Need to be born in country	−.144	.129	−1.12
Need to have Swedish ancestry	−.031	.138	−.023
Need to speak Swedish	.092	.124	.740
Need to follow customs	−.250**	.108	−.231
Out-group majority opinion more important than minority rights	−.277****	.066	−4.16
Out-group immigrants good	.657****	.078	8.45
Out-groups harm culture	−.559****	.089	−6.29
Out-group immigrants boost crime	−.412****	.073	−5.61
Education	−.064	.050	−1.29
Live in rural area	.215	.220	.098
Age	−.004	.044	−.09
Constant	7.205****	.611	11.8

$* p < .10; ** p < .05; *** p < .01; **** p < .001; N = 1073; R2 = .221;$ RMSE = 2.436.
Like Swedish Democrats: Strongly 17%, Moderately 12%; Dislike: Moderately 23%, Strongly 11%.

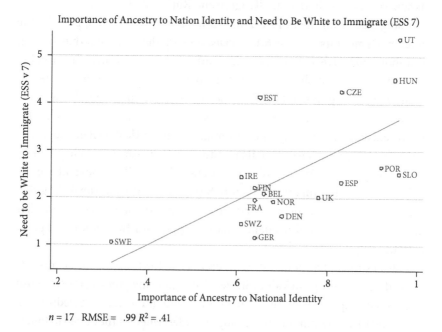

$n = 17$ RMSE = .99 $R^2 = .41$

Figure 6.1 Importance of Ancestry to National Identity and Need to Be White to Immigrate

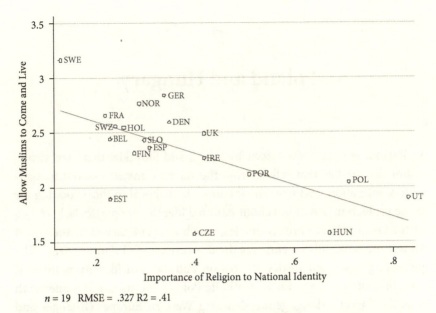

n = 19   RMSE = .327 R2 = .41

Figure 6.2 Allow Muslims to Come and Live, by Importance of Religion Identity

culture, and whether they increase crime in the country (see Table 6.1). Other measures such as the need to be born in Sweden, to have Swedish ancestry, or to speak Swedish are not significant predictors of support for the party. Demographics such as education, age, and where one lives were also not significant. Swedes generally believe in an inclusive view of human nature.

7

Poland and Hungary

In Poland, Hungary, the Czech Republic, and Slovakia, there are strong nationalist parties that reflect "ride the wave of anxiety—about globalization, migration, and new phenomena—and appeal to those looking for some protection. Anxieties about national identity are particularly strong in the former Communist countries, which were subjugated by the Soviet Union and have only recently regained sovereignty" (Erlanger, 2017). The governing "Law and Justice thrives on cultural and identity politics. It has contrasted a conservative, Catholic Poland and its family values with a godless, freethinking, gender-bending Western Europe" (Erlanger and Santora, 2018).

In Hungary "the government changed the Constitution to make it illegal to 'settle foreign populations' in Hungary, a rebuke of attempts by the European Union to encourage Hungary to admit small numbers of refugees who had been living in other European countries. [The Prime Minister] believes the laws are necessary to maintain Europe's Christian identity." (Kingsley, 2018). The government began to construct a fence along Hungary's borders with Serbia and Croatia, essentially halting immigration to the country. Der Spiegel declared him "the political victor" of the immigration crisis, and, since then, each new terrorist attack at a Christmas market in Berlin or Strasbourg seems to bolster his standing (Zerofsky, 2019). Even in Germany and Sweden, we see emerging parties focusing on identity.

Sides, Tesler, and Vavreck (2018) also argue that identity was a critical to Trump's victory in 2016: They emphasize the central role of race—negativity toward African-Americans (as well as Latinos and Muslims)—in Trump's victory. Racial attitudes emerged as a fundamental fault line between the two parties. By 2016, negative attitudes toward African-Americans had become a central dividing line in American politics: Republican identifiers came to believe that minorities were not deserving of governmental assistance and that government policies discriminated against whites (Sides, Tesler, and Vavreck, 81, 88–89). I agree with their analysis, but see the issue of identity as more encompassing.

National Identity and Partisan Polarization. Eric M. Uslaner, Oxford University Press. © Oxford University Press 2022. DOI: 10.1093/oso/9780197633946.003.0007

While it is tempting to explain the polarization on identity to Trump's campaign emphasizing "American First," his demand to cut immigration, his demonization of Muslims, and his insistence on building a wall on the border with Mexico, Bartels (2018) argues convincingly that Trump exploited divisions between the parties that had preceded his ascendance in the Republican party (see also Bonikowski, 2017).

Identifiers of the two parties were further apart on issues of cultural conservatism (which included "ethnic nationalism, traditional morality, including respect for the American flag, the English language, and our national borders, antipathy toward Muslims, immigrants, atheists, and gays and lesbians, and racial resentment, and concerns about discrimination against whites" (Bartels, 2018, 7). This "cultural conservatism" to a large extent "defined" Republicans—it was 10 times as important to Republican identification as it was to Democratic affiliation and was especially strong among supporters of Trump. But the attitudes of Republican identifiers on these issues did not stem from Trump's campaign, but rather the Republican nominee rode the wave of Republican "cultural conservatism." This is consistent with the argument of Tesler (2016b), Tesler and Sears (2010), Citrin and Sears (2014), and Mason (in press), as well as the analysis below.

Both cases point to cultural divides between supporters and opponents of populist parties and these divisions are not purely (or even predominantly) racial. Jones (2016) argues that Christian identity has become more salient in the United States as white Christians are no longer a majority. In the 2016 Voter Study Group survey in the United States, 40 percent of respondents said that being Christian was either very or fairly important to American identity. Of the seven options given in the survey, the importance of being a Christian had the highest zero-order correlation with the 2016 Presidential vote.($r = -.339$).

The concern that Christianity is becoming a minority religion is also a worry about what is happening to American culture. The evangelical church's "most successful leaders are considered apostles and prophets, including some with followings in the hundreds of thousands, publishing empires, TV shows, vast prayer networks, podcasts, spiritual academies, and branding in the form of T-shirts, bumper stickers and even flags. It is a world in which demons are real, miracles are real, and the ultimate mission is not just transforming individual lives but also turning civilization itself into their version of God's Kingdom: one with two genders, no abortion, a free-market economy, Bible-based education, church-based social programs and laws such as the ones curtailing LGBTQ rights now moving through statehouses around the country."

Evangelicals also saw the Charlottesville rioters and the January 6, 2021 insurrection as "a Christian populist uprising," leading many who stormed the Capitol to believe they were taking back the country for God. They believed that the protesters, the insurrectionists, and those who refused to take the anti-Covid vaccine as doing God's work in defense of Donald Trump (McCrummen, 2021). Only 27 percent of Republicans saw the insurrection as a threat to democracy compared to 68 percent who did not, while the figures for Democrats are 93 percent to 4 percent (YouGov America, 2021). Throughout the West, and especially in the United States, Christian fundamentalism has emerged as "the quintessential radical right force" (Minkenberg, 2018). Not only do evangelicals see gays and lesbians as the enemies but they associate them with the Democratic party and believe that a third of all Democrats are gay, lesbian, bisexual, or transgender (Finkel et al., 2020).

In the insurrection on January 6, 2021, hundreds of Trump supporters stormed the Capitol, threatened the lives of members of Congress as well as Vice President Michael Pence, and wounded almost 150 members of the Capitol Police; over 50 insurrectionists have been charged with major crimes. Yet in July, Trump still insisted that "The crowd was unbelievable and I mentioned the word 'love,' the love in the air, I've never seen anything like it . . . That's why they went to Washington . . . Too much spirit and faith and love, there was such love at that rally, you had over a million people," which was not true.

Thirty-seven percent of Trump voters support mandatory vaccination against COVID-19 compared to 85 percent of Democrats (DeBaumont, 2021). People who vote Republican have become full supporters of a nationalist and socially right-wing agenda and this trend started well before Trump became the GOP nominee.

Republicans in the United States see multiple minorities—African-Americans, Muslims, and Latinos—as less deserving than whites (although legal Hispanic immigrants are not viewed so negatively, at least on feeling thermometers). Bias in Europe is reserved for Muslims—there are hardly any blacks or Hispanics. If the roots of nations are similar across countries, they must rest on claims that are more directly comparable. National identity is a more generalizable foundation– and the objects of people's concerns include anyone who is not like themselves—no matter what they look like.

Cramer (2016, 2017) argues that "rural resentment" extends beyond racial minorities to people who live in big cities among people from different backgrounds—as well as to public employees who do not do manual labor–much as European populists dislike government bureaucrats (especially those who work for the European Union). People in rural areas are less likely to be minorities than those in urban areas, to have less income, and see urbanites as different from themselves, culturally and politically (Parker et al., 2018). Residents of rural areas were especially likely to see themselves as hurt by Democratic policies that led to greater globalization and to rewarding people in urban areas at their expense (Brewer, 2016; Porter, 2017).

The polarization of American politics extended to national identity in 2016—with the Republicans and Democrats strongly divided on a wide range of issues as well as identity. As American parties have become more polarized in recent decades, European parties have become less ideologically distinct. The French party system became more polarized on issues of identity in 2017 as the National Front displaced the Republicans as the main right-wing opposition. But the immigration issue in Europe was not as strongly linked to other issues facing the electorate. In most of Europe anti-immigrant right-wing parties are often supportive of more government spending (Ivarsflaten, 2008).

In Central and Eastern Europe, anti-immigrant parties govern in Hungary and Poland, but favor high levels of social welfare spending for "true" Hungarians/Poles, but not for immigrants (Table 7.1, Table 7.2). They were not ideologically consistent on issues of government spending––favoring substantial benefits for their own supporters and opposing subsidies for immigrants. Issues of identity and welfare spending were not linked.

For both Hungary and Poland the major factors shaping support for the nationalist parties are having an inclusive sense of identity (sharing national customs) and being Christian for Poland, as well as authoritarian tendencies for both nations and low levels of interpersonal trust for Hungary.

The American divisions are different from the worries in Europe, where leaders such as Hungary's Orban express fears that Islam will overtake Christianity as the dominant religion. American and Europeans do share a common fear: that their own identity is under threat, so it is critical to fight to maintain the dominance of one's own culture—in Trump's words to fight to ensure an "American First" agenda or the Sweden Democrats' insistence on "keep[ing] Sweden Swedish" (see below). Minkenberg (2018) argues: "the East European radical right has stood for a merger of religion

Table 7.1 Party Preferences for Hungarians European Values Survey

	Coefficient	Std. Error	z	Diff in Probabilities
Immigrants Share Culture	−.135****	.032	4.3	.14
Important Shared Culture	−.313	1.53	-.2	-.04
Important European Culture	−.107	.081	-.1	-.04
Authoritarianism Tolerance	−.398	2.21	-1.8	.06
Authoritarian Obedience	.490***	2.01	.2	.08
Income (Adjusted)	−.075*	.046	-1.6	-.09
Education	−.062**	.030	3.1	-.10
Gender	.230*	1.35	1.7	.03
Constant	−.987**	-.426	-2.1	

N = 947 McKelvey Zavoina R2 = .746 -2*LLR = 435.22
* p < .10 ** p < .05 *** p < .01 **** p < .0001
Variable

Table 7.2 Support for the Jobbik Party in Poland: European Values Survey

Variable	Coefficient	Std. Error	z	Diff in Probabilities
Important share culture	−.842**	.384	−.2	−.253
Important being Christian	−.825****	.114	−7.3	−.296
Authoritarianism independence	−.547****	.126	−4.4	−.183
Trust	−.443****	.129	−3.4	−.147
Age	.006*	.003	1.8	.173
Income (adjusted)	.057	.057	1.0	.223
Education	−.098**	.044	−2.2	−.312
Gender	.010	.113	.1	−.374
Constant	1.114**	.463	2.4	

N = 583; McKelvey Zavoina R2 = .290 -2*LLR = 680.96.
* p < .10; ** p < .05; *** p < .01; **** p < .0001.

and ultra-nationalist platforms since it appeared on the political scene in the1990s. Most notably, the Polish radical right professes an ultra-Catholicism that recycles the anti-liberal, anti-Semitic, and anti-Western doctrines of [an] interwar ideologue."

In Europe the fringe parties have pushed both the right and left main-stream parties to more restrictions on immigration. It is thus less likely that a change in government in Europe (especially Western Europe) will lead to a significant shift in immigration policy. The weaker polarization between the major parties on issues of national identity in Europe gives greater power to the fringe parties. *The fringe parties have in essence taken the major parties as hostage on the issue of immigration They push the major parties to the right on immigration, but they may not have clear positions on the issues that divide the major parties.* A shift in which major party controls the government may lead to policy changes on economic or social issues, but is less likely to lead to big changes in immigration policy.

Bojan Pancevski (2019) wrote in the *Washington Post*, "The Sweden Democrats' proposals—a moratorium on new asylum seekers, faster deportations of illegal immigrants, tighter rules on granting Swedish cit-izenship—have become more mainstream as other parties have sought to respond to the mounting popular sentiment" and quoted Swedish political scientist Patrick Ohberg: "By effectively performing a U-turn on immigra-tion policy, the mainstream parties managed to stop the bleeding of votes to the Sweden Democrats." Policy shifts on issues of immigration (and the cri-teria for receiving benefits provided by the state) are thus less likely in Europe since the minority populist parties constitute an electoral threat to main-stream parties of the right and the left.

The nationalist Sweden Democrats have a slogan promising to "Keep Sweden Swedish," akin to Trump's promise of "America First" and they were advised by Trump's former aide Steve Bannon. One Sweden Democratic MP argued that Jews and Samis were "not Swedish" (Milne, 2018a). He also said to the League's leader: "You are the first guys who can really break the left and right paradigm. You can show that populism is the new organizing prin-ciple." Ironically, Trump's Republican party has done far more to polarize politics than have parties in Europe.

I consider how national identity is shaped by and shapes a sense of tol-erance (generalized trust), attitudes toward immigration (who should be allowed to immigrate and whether immigration inevitably leads to conflicts), attitudes toward minorities (Muslims and Jews), and support for "anti-estab-lishment" parties–and whether such parties in Europe are evidence of either anti-immigrant / anti-Muslim sentiment or whether they may be less conse-quential– and not contributing to political polarization.

National identity has become important in shaping politics in the United States and Europe. But studies of vote choice and partisan identification have largely focused on other factors such as attitudes toward immigrants, minorities (especially Muslims), authoritarianism, and economic vulnerability. Each of these factors is important, not so much independently but more as they reinforce a sense of national identity. I shall focus on why national identity is important, how to measure identity, and the roots and consequences of identity to politics.

The least divided society is Sweden, where identity is more inclusive, the immigration and deservingness policies are comprehensive, and there is widespread agreement on social and economic policy. There is concern that some immigrants do not have employment and may be using the universal welfare system at the expense of the larger community.

Other Western European countries I study (Austria, France, Germany) have traditionally been centrist on most policies. In recent years, fringe parties have become dominant in Austria and France on identity and immigration policies (even as they have been more centrist on economic and social policies). In Germany there has been a rise of a fringe party (the AfD) which has pushed the Christian Democrats to the right on immigration policy, if not on identity.

In Central and Eastern Europe, right-wing parties have become dominant on issues of identity and immigration Although they are center left on economic issues for people of their own religion and race, they are conservative on social issues such as gay rights and abortion. The European Union has started legal action against Hungary and Poland for violating the rights of gays and lesbians. Erlanger and Pronczuk (2015) have written: "Poland's Law and Justice party is similarly using issues of identity, nationalism and resistance to a more liberal European Union elite to prop itself up against growing opposition to its long rule." Hungary has been more willing to accept European court rulings than Poland, while the latter country is contemplating leaving the Union to protest its actions.

Social and economic issues do not divide the parties so deeply in Taiwan and Israel. In both countries identity and security are the central issues dividing the parties. So overall, the most polarized system is in the United States.

The politics of national identity has long been an issue in the United States, with its diverse population and openness to immigration. It is a more recent development in Europe, with populist parties gaining support in the 1980s with the rise of immigration (Mudde and Kaltwasser, 2013, 497).

As a country becomes more diverse, tensions arise over what constitutes "legitimate membership in the nation" (Bonikowski, 2017, S187–S188). For many, the criteria were "the appropriate immutable, or at least highly persistent, traits, such as national ancestry, native birth, majority religion, dominant racial group membership, or deeply ingrained dominant cultural traits,, Beliefs about the nation's meaning—shaped in part by particular perceptions of the nation's past and visions for its future—are central to people's sense of self and their connections to others around them. At the dawn of nation-state formation in the eighteenth and nineteenth centuries, nationalist leaders explicitly articulated these ideas as an imperative for political self-governance by ostensibly homogeneous cultural communities."

Nationalism rests on ethnocentrism: "Members of in-groups (until they prove otherwise) are assumed to be virtuous: friendly, cooperative, trustworthy, safe, and more. Members of out-groups (until they prove otherwise) are assumed to be the opposite: unfriendly, uncooperative, unworthy of trust, dangerous, and more" (Kinder and Kam, 2010, 8).

The rise of nationalism in Europe involved "a struggle over the nation's meaning" that is broader than "nationalism, authoritarianism, [or] conservatism" (Bonikowski, 2017, S187–S189). The search for national identity is also a glorification of the "common man" or "common woman," in contrast to the elite. The elite is a catch-all term, including intellectuals, political leaders, and especially institutions that cross national boundaries. The latter challenge the idea of a "true" American (German, Brit, etc.)—they were the object of scorn for Trump's "America First" campaign and the negativity of populist parties toward the European Union: Brexit was "Britain first." Elites are seen as holding privileged positions that give them power and wealth and put "internationalism ahead of the nation" and favor "supranational entities such as the European Union . . . and multinational corporations . . . [that] foster universalization and homogenization" that weaken national identity (Rydgren, 2004, 244).

Even as nationalists took aim at transnational governance and local elites, their wrath was strongest for Muslim immigrants, whom they saw as hostile to their own identity. Hungarian President Viktor Orban said: "the Islamic religion and culture do not blend with Christian religion and culture; it is a different way of life (Pew Research Center on Religion and Public Life, 2017). The right-wing AfD party in Germany issued a manifesto stating: "Islam is not a part of Germany" (Henley, Bengtsson, and Barr, 2016). Hungary's Prime Minister Viktor Orban ordered the construction of a fence on the country's southern border to keep immigrants out, warning of the "Muslim invasion" to come in "Christian Europe" (Witte, 2018).

My focus is on the connection of national identity with other issues that form a polarized political environment. The story is simplest in the United States, where the parties have become increasingly polarized on both social and economic issues over the past 30 years. Issues of identity were not strongly linked to other views until 2016, when Trump's "America First" campaign brought national identity to the center of a conservative ideology.

The story was not as simple in Europe. Views on immigration and national identity had long been associated with more conservative parties, but the differences were not always stark. As immigration rose to prominence in political debates, parties in many European countries became more polarized on national identity and ideology. Nationalism has been mostly linked with radical right-wing politics in Europe. But these radical right parties were almost exclusively at the fringe where they received 20 percent of the vote or less.

The major parties were divided over immigration, but the differences were not great.

France was a notable exception—where the National Front displaced the Republicans as the main right-wing party and there was substantial polarization across a wide range of issues. Other exceptions were parties in Central and Eastern Europe—notably Hungary and Poland, where nationalists took strong stands against immigration and Muslims but favored substantial spending for their white working-class voters.

Eisenmann, Mounck, and Guitchin (2017, 4, 8) argue that "Parties like Poland's Law and Justice (PiS) party and Hungary's Fidesz tend to emphasize a nationalism based on soil, blood, or culture; take a hard line against immigration; and have, especially in Poland and Hungary, quickly started to dismantle key democratic institutions like the free media and an independent judiciary . . . these parties have waged campaigns for fiscal sovereignty, advocated for stronger fiscal transfers within the European Union, and promised to expand the welfare state."

"Some of these parties have increasingly taken a nationalist turn: rooted in notions of economic sovereignty and self-determination, rather than in direct appeals to ethnic ancestry, this form of nationalism has allowed left-populists to exploit issues of immigration and rail against foreign economic influence." Minkenberg (2018) writes about Poland: "the Polish radical right professes an ultra-Catholicism that recycles the anti-liberal, anti-Semitic, and anti-Western doctrines of [an] interwar ideologue."

What constitutes a "true" member of a society? And why does it matter? I examine how national identity shapes vote choice in national elections—or when vote choice is not available in a survey, one's partisan affiliation. Party choice is in almost all cases an indication of left-right ideology. A strong effect of national identity on vote choice (or partisan affiliation) indicates that the major parties are polarized on identity. There are moderate levels of polarization on identity in Western Europe (but not the United Kingdom. In Central and Eastern Europe, the major parties place defending traditional culture (Christianity) as essential. The strongest evidence of polarization on issues of identity comes in the 2016 election in the United States.

What distinguishes the sets of counties I examine is how identity is related to political choice and to polarization. The United States has become distinctive in that (1) the sense of national identity has become "exclusivist" for the Republican Party in recent elections but remains inclusivist for the Democrats. So the parties are polarized on the issue of national identity; and (2) this polarization is also linked to strong divisions among partisan leaders and supporters on a wide range of other issues, social, moral, and economic.

In contrast to a long history of moderation of American parties, where commentators and politicians emphasized the fundamental similarities between the positions of the two parties, currently there is a high level of polarization among both leaders and supporters across a wide range of issues, including national identity. Such polarization across a wide range of issues does *not* occur in most other countries.

8

Taiwan and Israel

I have also examined the sources of political support in Taiwan and Israel. In both countries, identification with the majority population has become increasingly salient (see Table 8.1).

In Israel, the right-wing party of Prime Minister Binyamin Netanyahu has become preoccupied with giving Jewish citizens priority for citizenship and benefits over others, even including Druze who have served in the Israeli army despite not being Jewish. Netanyahu has made this distinction an important part of his policy and campaign agendas.

Since its founding, Israel has been preoccupied with determining who "belongs" as a citizen. The country was founded as a refuge for victims of Naziism in Europe and discrimination in the Arab world. In the war of independence in 1948, Israel fought the Palestinians and many of the latter fled to the West Bank, to Jordan, or elsewhere. But large numbers stayed and remained under Israeli rule. The Druze, a Muslim minority, even participated fully in Israeli society and joined the military.

Pedazhur (2012, 29) wrote: "There is not and has never been a separation of religion and state in Israel." When the nation was founded, there was considerable debate as to whether the priority should be the establishment of a Jewish nation first and foremost or a democratic country. This shaped the longer-term arguments as to the divisions between religious and secular authorities, between religious and secular political parties (Pedazhur, 2012, 29).

Lewin (2016, 67) summarizes the debate between a democratic and a religious Israel as one of an inclusive society and one "of a Jewish state in the Land of Israel, where all the Jews will gather and sustain their eternal historic continuity as a national community" that "under a constant and everlasting threat of extinction. . . .[such that] inherent Jewish strength enabled the nation to overcome its enemies by virtue of courage, diligence, ingenuity, and above all—moral superiority."

The pre-state Zionists debated what Israel should be. Chief Rabbi Isaac Halevi Herzog (1936–1959) believed that the entire legal system of the State

National Identity and Partisan Polarization. Eric M. Uslaner, Oxford University Press. © Oxford University Press 2022.
DOI: 10.1093/oso/9780197633946.003.0008

Table 8.1 Left-Right Voting Probit from Pew Israel Study 2016

Vote for Parties on Left-Right Continuum

Variable	Coefficient	Std. Err.	z	Chg. Probabilities
Jewish ancestry	12.78*	.095	1.34	.022
Jews preferred treatment	.338****	.054	.054	.194
Israel more Jewish state	−.195*	.110	−.176	−.033
Favor settlements	.412****	.057	.722	.155
Ideology	−1.100****	.059	−18.51	−.981
Constant	2.177****	.303	.719	

McKelvey Zavoina R2 = .775 −2 * LLR = 896.51 N =1560.

* $p < .10$; ** $p < .05$; *** $p < .01$; $p < .001$.

of Israel should be based on *halacha*—"even when it applied to non-Jews."
He denigrated the British and Ottoman legal systems as inferior to Jewish
law. But other religious leaders Rabbi Shlomo Gorontchik (Chief Rabbi
from 1972 to 1985) favored a democratic constitution with rabbinic courts
only serving religious functions (Lockshin, 2021). When Israel became independent, the conflict between leaders who stressed democracy and those
who wanted a stronger connection between the rabbinzte and the government meant that the founders did not try to enact a Constitution (Smooha,
2019, 675).

In a fundamental way, religion always stood at the forefront of Israeli identity. The nation was founded as a Jewish state.

While Arabic is an official language, all government operations are
conducted in Hebrew, the official calendar is a Jewish one, and Jews are favored by the Law of Return: Anyone with a Jewish grandparent is granted automatic citizenship upon arrival. Jews everywhere would have an immediate
right to settle in Israel since they are all connected to "the land of ancient
Israel" (Zawdu and Willen, 2021). Non-Jews must go through a more difficult system of immigration comparable to what one finds in other countries
and Palestinians are excluded altogether (Smooha, 2019, 676).

There were three separate lines of cleavage in Israeli politics. The overriding issue has been national security—whether to seek peace with the
Palestinians and other Arab states or to emphasize the defense of the country.
Second was the more traditional left-right division on social issues: whether
the government or the private sector would control benefits such as health

care, transportation, and welfare. Third was the religious-secular divide. How much would the state contribute to religious schools run by the ultra-Orthodox (*haredi*) population, whether ultra-Orthodox men would have to serve in the army or even be required to work rather than spend their years studying religious texts. These three issues defined the political life of the country. Security and social issues split the country ideologically, with the right opposing Palestinian statehood, peace agreements with the Arab countries, and government involvement in the economy and the left taking the opposite positions. When Prime Minister Menachim Begin signed a peace treaty with Egypt in 1979, the right became less confrontational on some issues of security.

The religious-secular divide is more complicated and now has become the central focus of Israeli politics. When the country was founded, the first Prime Minister David Ben-Gurion of the Labour Party, favored a democratic system but also agreed that the country needed to recognize its Jewish character. Stores and businesses would be closed on the Sabbath (Saturday), there would be a five-day work week (ending Friday afternoon and resuming on Sunday morning), there were initial disputes over whether radio or sports events would be allowed on the Sabbath, but agreement that the food served at all institutions run by the government (offices and universities) must be kosher and the sale of pork would be prohibited if not enforced (Halbfinger, 2019).

Ben-Gurion agreed with these provisions for two reasons. He accepted the Jewish character of the state and he also relied upon the support of ultra-Orthodox parties to keep his own party in power. Ben-Gurion and future Prime Ministers let the Orthodox community set the religious policies for the country because they saw Israel as a Jewish state and " by assiduously observing the religious commandments. . . they earn divine grace to avert the decrees planned by the government" (Sharon, 2011). Although *haredim* constitute less than 15 percent of the Israeli public, they control religious life and have gained support for their own institutions from the public treasury by aligning themselves with Netanyahu and his coalition partners (Bergman, 2021).

For many years, the religious parties took no strong stands on issues of security or social policy as long as they received government subsidies for their own religious schools. Yet, one by one, they fell away from alliances with Labour and its more-left wing and even center allies as these parties became more supportive of less strict forms of Judaism and even secular marriage. First, the Zionist National Religious Party deserted the left to support the right. Then the Sephardic (of North African and Asian Jews) *Shas* party allied with the right, followed by the Ashkenazi (European) ultra-Orthodox United Torah Judaism bloc and its predecessor Agudat Israel, which was often skeptical of the idea of a Jewish state. Most *haredim* have their primary identity as Jewish rather than Israeli (Hanson, 2014, 41). At first there was a strong alignment of voters' positions on all three dimensions. Security, social welfare, and religious commitment were all part of a single dimension.

By the time Binyamin Netanyahu became Prime Minister in 1996, social and security issues had become secondary and the major dividing line in Israeli politics was religious. He took the right in Israel into nativism, where it had feared to go in the past. The party had focused on security and economic issues and was supported by both Ashkenazis and Sephardim. It won the votes of migrants from the Middle East on the basis of cultural issues, even as one might have expected them to support a more generous Labour party that would help them economically. In contrast to European political systems, the poor supported the right and the wealthy were more likely to back the left on economic issues. Netanyahu's Likud established centers for poor Mizrahim to socialize and find work and new homes. They believed that the left, specifically the Labour party, represented only am old European elite, as showing "a mentality of Vienna concerts" while the Mizrahim were the true Israeli "masses" (Halbfinger, 2019).

Netanyahu realized that nationalism would cement his role as a leader and that he should represent himself as a defender of the religious order in the country (Perliger and Pedazhur, 2018, 8). To maintain his coalition with the ultra-Orthodox, he allowed them to worship at a specific religious site— Mount Meron. He permitted them to avoid having vaccine certifications in their national documentation certificates (Hendrix et al., 2021). These actions won the support of the overwhelming share of religious Jews who became a bulwark of the right (Cohen, 2021, 163).

This division along religious lines is now predominant in Israeli political life. The conflict was stirred by two key events—the rise of a centrist party, *Shinui*, stressing secular values and the fall of the Soviet Union. When Communism fell, large numbers of Soviet citizens, some of whom had only remote connections to Judaism and few of whom were very religious, emigrated to Israel (Shafir and Peled, 2002, 154) They had three major influences on the country. First, they were opposed to legislation that enforced religious restrictions. These views were shared by the majority of Israelis who supported the separation of religion and state and civil marriage (Shafir and Peled, 2002, 150).

Second, many did not look kindly on Israelis of different backgrounds, and third many fared very well financially since they had strong technical skills. Many of these immigrants worked on highly technical areas, such as the computer industry, and the influx of such skilled people boosted the country's economy.

At the same time, there was an influx of immigrants from Ethiopia. These immigrants were not well educated. They were poor, they were black, their religious heritage was in question by the ultra-Orthodox authorities (since it was unclear how far back they could trace their Jewish roots), and they faced much discrimination. As the country became wealthier, Israelis became less willing to work as laborers, so many foreign workers and asylum seekers took their places. The 1987 Palestinian uprising (the *intifida*) led to the refusal of many Arab citizens to lose their positions as workers in the country and this also contributed to the influx of foreign workers. Many wanted to stay but were not generally welcomed, especially by the right-wing parties. Netanyahu worried that widespread immigration by foreign workers might lead to "fake conversions that could enter the country" and the "collapse" of the Jewish state as he number of foreign workers would grow significantly (Harkov, 2021).

Canetti-Nissim and Pedazhur (2003, 310) write: "People who had immigrated from Europe only a few years, or at most a generation, before, treated the North African Jews with suspicion. They considered themselves to be descendants of superior cultures." The wealthier Askenazi Jews also had negative views of Sephardic Jews who had been in the country for many years and the two major ethnic groups rarely worshipped or lived together.

The Druze and other Arabs, the Bedouin, have faced both social and economic discrimination. Rasgon (2021) writes that the Bedouin consider themselves second-class citizens with high unemployment and poverty rates with much of their land confiscated, "a clash between a traditional society that values its independence and a modern nation-state that seeks to extend its control."

As these three dimensions became joined, racial attitudes hardened. Both Ashkenazic and Sephardic Jews were increasingly prone to say that Israeli Arabs were not full members of the society—and want to drive the Jews out of the country. Canetti-Nissin and Pedazhur (2003, 310) report that 40 percent of Israeli Arabs see their Arab identity as primary. They primarily speak Arabic and rarely interact with Israelis.

Israelis see both Palestinians in the country and foreign workers as a threat to their existence. They do see Russian immigrants as part of the nation. The negative feelings, as reflected in a survey conducted by Nissim-Canetti and Pedazhur (2003), are shaped not only by race but also by political affiliation. Ashkenazis and especially right-wing supporters have the most xenophobic attitudes toward Palestinians and foreign workers. Ariely's (2011) survey in 2011 found that white Israelis strongly endorsed the exclusion of cultural and political rights of both non-Jewish immigrants and Palestinians. Over half of Ashkenazis said that Palestinians pose a threat to security. Threat perceptions were shaped most by political ideology (right versus left) but also by how religious people are.

He argues: "Privileged dominant group members identify their values and ways of life as defining the essence of citizenship. This is especially true in Israel which has defined itself as a Jewish state and which is based on the ethno-national Zionist ideology." The most religious see the greatest threats on issues of security, symbolism, and economic competition.

As the positions hardened, the Netanyahu government first proposed and then enacted a law in 2018 that would deny full citizenship to Israeli Arabs—including the Druze who had been so loyal. The law was enacted in 2003 as a response to the Palestinian uprisings and it even prevented them from obtaining a driver's license or to work in the country (Rubin and Hendrix, 2021). The purpose of the law was to "an exclusive right to 'self-determination' within Israel." Its message was: "[the] establish[ment of] two classes of Israeli citizens: Jews and non-Jews, (who constitute 25 per cent of Israel's population . . .) Only Jewish citizens of Israel have the right to determine the kind of state they live under; non-Jewish citizens of Israel don't have that same right. If non-Jews do not accept Israeli sovereignty, they should not be able to claim citizenry (Berger, 2018). The law sends an unequivocal message to Israel's non-Jewish citizens—the state is not yours and does not belong to you" (Waxman and Peleg, 2019).

Netanyahu and the Likud saw themselves as part of the worldwide "populist insurgencies whose successes are now a notable feature of political life across the democratic world." The law was especially popular with young voters (64 percent of those aged 18-34) and other leaders throughout the world, including President Trump (Spyer, 2019). It did not prevent other Arab leaders from establishing diplomatic relations with Israel. Israelis have become polarized on the issue of national identity. A 2021 survey by the newspaper *Maariv* found that one-third of Israelis on the left "hated" people on the right and the same share on the right "hated" people on the left (Lieber and Jones, 2021).

Yet the Israeli Supreme Court overturned this law in 2021 by an overwhelming vote since it violates "the state's democratic identity that are anchored in the other Basic Laws and constitutional principles that institute the legal system in Israel" (*Jerusalem Post* Staff, 2021). The court was responding to criticism by human rights groups as well as Druze organizations to the provisions that reserved citizenship and benefits to Jewish Israelis (Jeremy Bob, 2020). Ultimately the voters recoiled from this action when they defeated Netanyahu and replaced him with Naftali Bennett, whose party (Yamina) representing Russian Jews was based on the secular identity that Likud had tried to suppress. People finally decided that the monopoly held by the ultra-Orthodox over daily life in Israel and the country's social mores was too severe.

The Pew Survey (see Table 8.1) documents that in 2016 giving Jews preferential treatment for both citizenship and government, having Jewish ancestry, and seeing Israel as more of a Jewish state than a democracy were central even to left-right voting. Favoring building settlements in the West Bank and ideology also shaped voting, but deservingness was highly significant according to all three of these indicators. The issues of belonging and deservingness also shaped voting for centrist and religious parties, but their effects were not as powerful as they were for left-right voting.

In Taiwan, the issue of identity with the island or mainland China has emerged as the major issue distinguishing the support bases of the dominant parties. Increasingly residents of Taiwan identify themselves as Taiwanese rather than Chinese and this has led to the rise of the DPP (Democratic Progressive Party) as the governing party, replacing the Kuomintang, which still sees Taiwan as part of China. In Figure 8.1, taken

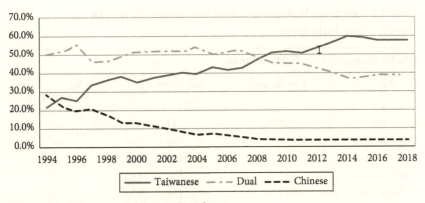

Figure 8.1 Taiwanese/Chinese identification

from Wang (2017), a majority of people in Taiwan identified as Taiwanese and just 10 percent as Chinese by 2014. By 2009, majorities of every ethnic group identified as either purely Taiwanese or mixed Taiwanese/Chinese rather than as purely Chinese (Wang, 2017, 55). Ethnicity is related to political divisions. These finding are based on the 2016 Asian Barometer Survey.

Ethnic Chinese are the most likely to back the KMT while indigenous groups and Taiwanese expatriates are supportive of the DPP and its acceptance of Taiwanese autonomy (Achen and Wang, 2017). I present the results of a probit for major party voting from the Asian Barometer in 2016 in Table 8.2.

Three measures of ethnicity were the key to vote preference between the KMT and the DPP. Overall Taiwanese ethnic identification and the necessity of being born on the island both led to increases in the probability of support for the nationalist party by approximately 30 percent. The need to feel Taiwanese produced a 20 percent boost in DPP support and the gain for this party was strongest among the young and people who felt that the KMT was comprised of too many members of the old traditional elite.

I also found similar results for the TEDS 2016 data and the third wave of the Asia Barometer (2013)—in which ethnic identification was the dominant determinant of voting for major parties.

Ethnicity has generally been the major factor shaping voting for the dominant parties (but inequality and personal finances also matter). Unlike most

Table 8.2 Taiwanese Voting from Asian Barometer 4th Wave Dependent Variable Major Party Support

Vote for Parties on Left-Right Continum

Variable	Coefficient	Std. Error	z	Chg. Probabilities
Ethnic ID	.772****	.144	5.34	.194
China negative	.329****	.056	5.94	.137
Proud Taiwan	.185**	.104	1.78	.422
Trust executive	.793****	.100	8.03	.137
Media biased	.703****	.128	5.51	.182
Economy fair	.199**	.109	1.82	.146
Gender	.114	.124	−.017	.624
Age	-.005	.027	−.017	−.010
Constant	3.682	54.815	.07	

McKelvey Zavoina R2 = .604 -2 * LLR = 540.76 N =.634

$*p<.10; **p<.05; ***p<.01; p<.001.$

other countries, voting for the dominant parties is not based upon ideology since few in Taiwan see the world as a battle between the left and the right. The strongest determinant of voting for the KMT versus the DPP in 2016 is whether one identifies as Chinese or Taiwanese: A Taiwanese identifier is almost 70 percent more likely to vote for the DPP than is someone who sees him/herself as Chinese. The only other variables that predict voting behavior are one's position on Taiwan independence and whether one needs to be born on the island to be recognized as Taiwanese. Neither ideology nor approval of the political system matters. Vote choice in the country is unidimensional: National identity overwhelms every other factor.

Hsaio et al. (2017, 199–201, 208) argue:

> In Taiwan, however, left-right language is simply not used to describe the current party system—not by ordinary people, not by journalists, not by politicians, and not by Taiwan scholars. Asking them about it is like asking them about sharia law or dancing the flamenco—cultural concepts that are prominent elsewhere but not in Taiwan . . . conventional left-right issues do not consistently differentiate the two main Taiwan parties . . . elite politics in Taiwan is organized differently than in most. Western countries, and the

parties have little incentive to use left-right language in explaining themselves to voters . . . party competition in Taiwan is structured by the "China factor," especially on the "independence vs. reunification with China" issue, but this is clearly not a conventional left-right dimension. About half the citizens could not respond when asked where they placed themselves on the left-right dimension. (see Table 8.3).

Table 8.3 Feelings Toward Pro-Taiwan Parties in 2016 Taiwan Election Probit Analysis TEDS Data

Variable	Coefficient	Standard Error	Diff Probabilitires
Overall ethnic identifiction	.452****	.062	.689
Need to be born in Taiwan	.334***	.098	.276
Populism: People decide policy	.087	.067	.091
Independence Position	.132****	.031	.373
Constant	−2.926****	.315	

* p < .10 ** p < .05 *** p < .01 **** p < .0001
N = 446 McKelvey Zavoina R2 = .541 -2*LLR = 407.21

9

Deservingness

I turn now to the concept of deservingness. It is a stronger measure of identity than simply belonging because it involves the expenditure of resources for people who may not be of the same background (religion, ethnicity, where one or one's parents were born, or race) than the majority population. How do measures of belongingness and attitudes toward immigrants shape attitudes about government spending for public assistance? In some countries, immigrants and minorities are entitled to government support regardless of their background or even their citizenship.

I estimated measures of deservingness for Austria, France, Germany, Sweden, Hungary, and Poland from the 2003 International Social Survey Programme where the dependent variable is whether the government spends too much money on immigrants; for the United Kingdom from the 2018 Urban Constituency Survey Institute; and for the United States from the 2016 American National Election Study and report the results in Tables 9.1 through 9.8. I also report on deservingness for Israel from a 2016 Pew survey in that country (Table 9.10) and Taiwan (from the 2003 ISSP, Table 9.11).

For the European countries, the method of estimation is probit analysis and the tables show the coefficients, standard errors, and difference in probabilities between the minimum and maximum values of the predictors. I use these rather than the mean since it is a superior method and allows estimation to occur holding all of the other variables to retain their actual values (see Hanmer and Kalkan, 2013).

I estimated factor scores for attitudes on immigration for culture and immigration for economic concerns. For culture, the measures are whether immigrants want to preserve their own traditions, preserve their own culture, bring new ideas to their host country, or increase crime. For economics, the measures are whether immigrants are good for the economy or take jobs from the country's citizens (see Table 9.1).

For the United States I estimated a regression equation from the 2016 ANES with the dependent variable as whether government spends too much on immigrants. The two variables with the greatest effect are the

National Identity and Partisan Polarization. Eric M. Uslaner, Oxford University Press. © Oxford University Press 2022.
DOI: 10.1093/oso/9780197633946.003.0009

Table 9.1 Deservingness Probit for All Nations

Government Spends Too Much on Immigrants

Variable	Coefficient	Standard Error	t
Identity with America	-.058****	.013	-3.55
Ideology	.076****	.006	11.94
Party identification 3 point	.033***	.013	2.52
Authoritarianism	.065****	.019	3.37
.Immigrations good for economy	.034**	.014	2.50
Thermometer for illegal immigrants	-.006****	.001	-9.57
Thermometer Muslims	-.001**	.006	-2.12
Thermometer Hispanics	.002**	.001	1.77
Thermometer Blacks	-.004***	.001	-3.92
Gender	.065**	.030	2.53
Age	-.004	.001	-.64
Income	.003	.009	.40
Education (years)	-.035***	.006	5.72

feeling thermometer for illegal immigrants and a general measure of left-right ideology. Also significant are the importance of identification as an American, feeling thermometers for Muslims, blacks, and Hispanics, authoritarianism, party identification (Democrats being more willing to spend on immigrants), whether immigrants help or hurt the economy, education, and gender.

These results show that attitudes on spending for immigrants follow the more general level of polarization in the country–far more so than in other countries analyzed. For 2020, attitudes toward illegal immigrants were again the strongest determinant of attitudes toward welfare spending from the ANES post-election study. Also significant were whether immigration helped the economy, feeling thermometers toward blacks, and overall ideology. More educated people were also more favorable toward greater welfare spending. So again, negativity toward out-groups largely shaped beliefs in deservingness (see Garand, Xu, and Davis, 2012 for similar results).

From the American Values Survey of PRRI in 2020 people who held restrictive views on immigration (see Table 9.2) were more likely to oppose spending government funds on programs that would help out-groups. Also important were party and personal ideology, but neither were as critical as attitudes about immigrants.

Table 9.2 Regression on Welfare Spending from 2016 ANES for USA

Variable	Government Spends Too Much on Immigrants		
	b	Standard Error	t
Identity with America	−.058****	.013	−3.55
Ideology	.076****	.006	11.94
Party identification 3 point	.033***	.013	2.52
Authoritarianism	.065****	.019	3.37
.Immigration good economy	.034**	.014	2.50
Thermometer illegal immigrants	−.006****	.001	−9.57
Thermometer Muslims	−.001**	.006	−2.12
Thermometer Hispanics	.002**	.001	1.77
Thermometer Blacks	−.004***	.001	−3.92

$R2 = ..253$; RMSE $= .6375$; $N =.2563$; $* p < .10$; $** p < .05$; $*** p < .01$; $**** p < .001$.

Concern for spending for people of different backgrounds currently shows a wide opinion gap between the Democratic parties. Democrats are more inclusive, Republicans more exclusive. But some say that this pattern didn't reflect the divisions in the Democratic party when Social Security and other major government benefits were adopted in the 1930s. The price Franklin D. Roosevelt paid to get Southern Democrats to back these policies was to ensure that the benefits went mostly to whites (Katznelson, 2013). Others argue that these programs always benefitted the vast majority of Americans, not just whites (Barry, 2014). The initial divide discussed by Katznelson was based upon gathering support from a party where the Senate members came from both the North and the South. Now that the Democrats no longer have more than a handful of Southern seats, the conflict has become more partisan.

In countries such as Germany, Austria, France, the United Kingdom, and Israel- the issue of welfare spending is not strongly linked to ideas of citizenship. In Sweden, these two domains are not linked at all, but in the United States there are powerful relationships between belongingness, deservingness, and ideology (including all sorts of spending and social issues) more generally.

For the United Kingdom, the dependent variable is estimated as the second equation in the belongingness instrumental regression discussed above. There are no questions in this survey on English/British identity

Table **9.3** Instrumental Variable Regression of Likelihood of Voting for UKIP from the Drivers of Populist Radical Right Support in Britain, 2017–2018 (Urban Constituency Survey Institute)

Variable	Deservingness equation		
	Coefficient	Standard Error	t
Factor on radical Islam	−.498****	.039	−12.85
Immigration most important issue	−.−954****	.063	−15.07
Vote for Brexit	−.364****	.038	−.95
Like contact with minorities	−.063****	.016	−.39
Globalization good economic growth	.061****	.018	.340
Officials care about ordinary citizens	.212****	.021	10.14
Ordinary citizens can affect government	.058***	.019	3.00
Accept alternative lifestyles	.123****	.021	5.94
Government should reduce inequality	.097****	.018	3.40
Ideology	−.078****	.012	.61
Age	3.743****	.209	17.89

$N = 3048$ $R2 = .369$ RMSE = 1.456.

$* p < .10; ** p < .05; *** p < .01; **** p < .0001.$

Main equation for support for UKIP in tables on voting preferences.

Variables included in immigration factor: Islam is an archaic religion; Islam is democratic; Islam promotes violence.

(see Table 9.3). The two variables with the greatest impact are related to the immigrant–the radical Islam factor and whether immigration is the most important issue, as well as whether officials care about ordinary citizens and whether people are willing to accept alternative lifestyles. Also significant are whether ordinary citizens can affect government and whether government should reduce inequality. Overall, cultural issues play a much larger role in shaping attitudes on welfare spending than do economic concerns.

In Austria (see Table 9.4), the only measure of identity that is critical for receiving government benefits is having Austrian ancestry. People of Austrian ancestry at .113 are more likely to support welfare spending on immigrants. Where one was born, respecting institutions, or feeling a member of Austrian society was not so critical. The most important determinants of deservingness were measures of immigration: a factor score of the effect of immigration on the country's culture and the economy and especially attitudes about

Table 9.4 Deservingness Probit from 2013 ISSP for France

Government Spends Too Much on Immigrants

Variable	Coefficient	Diff Probabilities
Important to be born here	.067	.019
Important to respect institutions	.415	.094
Important to feel member of society	.260	−.057
Important to have ancestry	−.039	.529
Factor scores for pride	−.006	−.007
Factor scores for immigration effects on culture	.730****	.750
factor scores for immigration effects on economy	.136**	.214
legal immigrants have rights	.116*	.109
Exclude illegal aliens	−.487****	−.499
Self placement on income scale	.029	.059
Kids born abroad	−.007	−.015
Kids born to alien parents.	.149	.045
Gender	.201	−.020
Age	−.001	−.020
Income	−.000	−.108
Education (years)	.029	−.008
Constant	−.019	

McKelvey Zavoina $R2 = ..656 −2 * LLR = 309.46 N = 387$

$* p < .10; ** p < .05; *** p < .01; p < .001.$

excluding illegal aliens (with differences of probability of .519 and .256). Ethnicity is a critical factor in being willing to share resources with people of different backgrounds and this is especially important in a country that had a Nazi past

In France (see Table 9.5) national identity plays no significant role in deservingness, but altitudes toward immigrants, both legal and illegal, are key. Most critical are factor scores for the immigration on culture and the economy and whether to exclude illegal immigrants. French respondents who are most worried about the effect of immigrants on culture are 75 percent less likely to endorse welfare spending, while those concerned about the effects on the economy are 21 percent less supportive. As in Austria and Germany, many people in France are worried that Muslim immigrants threaten the French culture of *laicité* (secularism) and people are less willing to share benefits with people who are different from themselves. Where

Table 9.5 Deservingness Probit from 2013 ISSP for Austria

Variable	Government Spends Too Much on Immigrants	
	Coefficient	Difference in Probabilities
Important to be born here	.036	.007
Important to respect institutions	−.517	−.101
Important to feel member of society	.038	.008
Important to have ancestry	.478**	.113
Factor scores for pride	−.075	−.079
Factor scores for immigration culture	.520**	.519
Factor scores for immigration economy	.427**	.256
Legal immigrants have rights	.137*	.122
Exclude illegal aliens	−.376***	−.407
Self-placement on income scale	.002	.004
Kids born abroad	.071	−.131
Kids born to alien parents	−.036	.060
Gender	−.243	−.050
Age	.001	−.002
Income	−.000	−.086
Education (years)	.002	−.110
Constant	1.338**	

McKelvey Zavoina R2 = .650 −2 * LLR = 266.14 N = 345; * $p < .10$; ** $p < .05$; *** $p < .01$; $p < .001$.

people are born or where their parents were born play little role in shaping the sharing of government benefits.

There are similar results for Germany, where Naziism began but now one of the leaders in accepting immigrants and refugees of diverse backgrounds. None of the measures of national identity are significant but attitudes on the effect of immigrants on German culture are the dominant factor in shaping attitudes toward giving benefits to people of diverse backgrounds–so that people are worried about the effect of immigration on culture are .82 less likely to support welfare spending.

This is especially notable since the AfD party has focused its campaign on the negative effects of Islam (notably Turkish immigrants) on German society. Where one was born or where your parents were born plays little role nor do attitude toward illegal immigrants (see Table 9.6). These results

Table 9.6 Deservingness Probit from 2013 ISSP for Germany

Government Spends Too Much on Immigrants

Variable	Coefficient	Diff Prob
Important to be born here	.222	.063
Important to Respect Institutions	−.189	−.051
Important to Feel Member of Society	.902	.266
Important to Have Ancestry	.144	.041
Factor scores for pride	−.030	−.041
Factor scores for Immigration Effects Culture	.777****	.820
Factor scores for Immigration Effects Economy	.222	.148
Legal Immigrants Have Rights	.076	.084
Exclude Illegal Aliens	.076	−.224
Self placement on income scale	−.190**	−.139
Kids Born Abroad	.131	−.121
Kids Born to Alien Parents	−.107	.141
Gender	−.179	−.050
Age	.005	.117
Income	.000**	−.631
Education (years)	−.070**	−.220
Constant	.358	

McKelvey Zavoina R2 = .509 -2 * LLR =405.72 N = 426
* p < .10 ** p < .05 *** p < .01 p < .001

are consistent with findings by Schmidt-Catran and Spies (2016, 257), who found that people are willing to grant welfare payments to immigrants only if they integrate into the national culture. They also support the findings of Seymyomov et al. (2004, 688) that most Germans see immigrants reliance on government benefits as a drain on the Treasury.

Sweden is perhaps the most generous country in the world in accepting immigrants and especially refugees from different backgrounds. So it is not surprising that measures of national identity play little role in shaping deservingness (see Table 9.7). The key factor is the effect of immigration on culture–not especially notable since Swedes are more likely to believe that anyone can become Swedish. Worrying that immigrants will not adapt to Swedish culture makes people almost completely unwilling to back welfare spending (by almost 91 percent). It is surprising that whether one is born to alien parents has a significant effect on deservingness and

Table 9.7   Deservingness Probit from 2013 ISSP for Sweden

Government Spends Too Much on Immigrants

Variable	Coefficient	Difference in Probabilities
Important to be born here	.199	.051
Important to Respect Institutions	−.033	−.008
Important to Feel Member of Society	.155	.039
Important to Have Ancestry	−.105	−.026
Factor scores for pride	.008	.098
Factor scores for Immigration Culture	1.013****	.906
Factor scores for Economy	.355**	.227
Legal Immigrants Have Rights	.113*	.117
Exclude illegal aliens	−.334****	−.329
Self-placement on income scale	.064	.142
Kids born abroad	−.156*	-.150
Kids Born to Alien Parents.	.158**	.165
Gender	.001	.000
Age	.011**	.179
Income	.000	.131
Education (years)	.012	.171
Constant	−.958*	

McKelvey Zavoina $R2 = .624$ $-2 * LLR = 394.76$ $N = 442$ $* p < .10 ** p < .05 *** p < .01 p < .001$

that excluding illegal aliens is so important in a country that has welcomed refugees.

In others, the criteria are more strict, especially in the former Communist countries of Hungary and Poland. There people favor generous spending on assistance programs for people of their own kind, while in most other countries minorities and even immigrants receive subsidies in the same manner as the majority population. But even here there are differences. As Fukuyama (2018, 151) argues, people living in the former Communist countries of Central and Eastern Europe "were less willing to accept culturally different newcomers than the original founding countries" since "they were not forced to wrestle with their nationalist pasts, nor did they make an effort to entrench liberal values in their citizens. They had virtually no experience with immigration and were among the least diverse societies in the developed world" (Fukuyama, 2018, 151).

Table 9.8 Deservingness Probit from 2013 ISSP for Hungary

Government Spends Too Much on Immigrants

Variable	Coefficient	Difference in Probabilities
Important to be born here	.222	.063
Important to respect institutions	−.189	−.050
Important to feel member of society	.144*	.266
Important to have ancestry	−.031	.045
Factor scores for pride	−.031	−.041
Factor scores for immigration culture	.777****	.820
Factor scores for immigrations economy	.221*	.139
Legal immigrants have rights	.078*	.085
Exclude Illegal aliens	−.190**	−.224
Self placement on income scale	−.055	−.139
Kids born abroad	−.107	−.121
Kids born to alien parents	.132*	.`141
Gender	−.179	-.050
Age	-.−005	.117
Income	−-.000**	−.631
Education (years)	−.069**	.220
Constant	.353	

McKelvey Zavoina R2 = .506 −2 * LLR = 405.72; N = 416; * p < .10; ** p < .05; *** < .01; p < .

In Hungary (see Table 9.8) and Poland (see Table 9.9) feeling a member of the society is significant. So are attitudes toward immigrants (notably the effect of immigrants on culture (the difference in probabilities is .820 for Hungary and .758 for Poland) and excluding illegal aliens (−.224 for Hungary but just .055 for Poland). In both countries right wing politicians have campaigned against Muslim immigrants as threats to the countries' Christian cultures.

In Hungary, there are also significant effects for the impact of illegal immigrants on the economy (the effect is .139). This is notable since the governing parties in both countries emphasize negativity toward immigrants of different backgrounds but great generosity toward the majority population. In Poland alone among the countries I analyzed using the ISSP people who have strong pride in their country are less willing to share government benefits with people of different backgrounds–and in both countries the

Table 9.9 Deservingness Probit from 2013 ISSP for Poland

Government Spends Too Much on Immigrants

Variable	Coefficient	Difference in Probabilities
Important to be born here	.248	.067
Important to respect institutions	−.060	−.017
Important to feel member of society	.846*	.200
Important to have ancestry	−.068	−.019
Factor scores for pride	−.346****	−.421
Factor scores for immigration effects culture	.816****	.758
Factor scores for Immigration economy	.009	.006
Legal immigrants have rights	.253****	.290
Exclude Illegal Aliens	−.322****	−.055
Self-placement on income scale	−.022	−.347
Kids born abroad	−.031	−.034
Kids born to alien parents	−.171**	−.177
Gender	.031	.137
Age	.006	.009
Income	−.000**	−.400
Education (years)	.000	.056
Constant	−1.012	

McKelvey Zavoina R2 = .495 −2 * LLR =489.1 N = 496; * p < .10; ** p < .05; **** p <

majority is less generous to children whose parents were born outside the country by 76 percent. Kupper and Zick (2010, 76) present data showing that more than a third of all Poles are willing to deny government benefits to people of different backgrounds *and* two-thirds believe that Catholicism is the only true religion.

I have also examined the sources of deservingness in Israel. Identification as Jews has become increasingly salient, both for voting and for deservingness.

In Israel, the right-wing party of Prime Minister Benjamin Netanyahu has become preoccupied with giving Jewish citizens priority for citizenship and benefits over others, even including Druze who have served in the Israeli army despite not being Jewish. Netanyahu has made this distinction an important part of his policy and campaign agendas.

The Pew Survey (see Table 9.10) documents that in 2016 giving Jews preferential treatment for both citizenship and government, having Jewish

Table 9.10 Support for Benefits Israel ISSP 2003 Survey

Variable	Coefficient	Standard. Error	z
Important factor	.058*	.038	2.30
Immigrants help economy	.064	.082	1.21
Immigrants help culture	.070**	.033	2.11
Proud of country	.049	.044	1.110
Constant	1.57****	.034	45.40

$N = 751$; $R2 = .0182$; RMS = .883.

ancestry, and seeing Israel as more of a Jewish state than a democracy were central even to left-right voting. Favoring building settlements in the West Bank and ideology also shaped voting, but deservingness was highly significant according to all three of these indicators.

The issues of belonging and deservingness also shaped voting for centrist and religious parties, but their effects were not as powerful as they were for left-right voting. In March 2021 the Israeli Supreme Court attacked the power of Orthodox Jews over religious observance by (as Kingsley, 2021, wrote): "grant[ing] the right to automatic citizenship to foreigners who convert within the state of Israel to Conservative, also known as Masorti, or Reform Judaism."

Who was considered a true Israeli—being born in the country, of Jewish parenting or grandparenting heritage, or sim is critical to deservingness, Believing that immigrants help the economy (especially those with the technical skills) or enrich the economy also lead to a greater willingness of Israelis to share benefits with the needy (see Table 9.10). For vote choice, both nationalism and ideology matter, much as like most European countries. For deservingness, nationalism is central and ideology is not significant.

Yet nationalism takes two forms. First, one's identity is central over and beyond ethnicity, so there is a clear distinction between Jewish and non-Jewish Israelis. Yet where one was born also matters. Russian immigrants are seen as more deserving than people from Ethiopia. Russian migrants have fared much better economically and their European heritage is more in line with Israeli culture than are the roots of Ethiopians who came to Israel. While the religious authorities have questioned both sets of immigrants, there is more concern among native (especially Ashkenazic) Israelis about Ethiopian refugees.

Table 9.11 Taiwanese Social Fairness

Support for Parties on Social Fairness

Variable	Coefficient	Standard Error	t
Immigration factor	.226****	.029	7.93
Society fair to poor	−.148****	.024	−5.77
Important to be rich	.071****	.019	3.66
Important that people be equal	.110****	.022	5.08
Most people can be trusted	−.021	.010	−2.71
People deserve equal treatment	−.024****	.021	5.08
Bottom 10 percent is treated well	−.002**	.026	−1.98
Justice system is fair	−.001	.005	−.0`0
Education system is fair	−.002	.004	.39
Constant	.291****	.162	18.00

$R2 = .175$; RMSE = .700; $N = 1320$.

$* p < .10; ** p < .05; *** p < .01; **** p < .001$.

Immigration factor: Allow immigrants from different ethnic group as majority; allow immigrants from different race group as majority; allow immigrants from poorer countries; immigration bad or good for country's economy; country's cultural life undermined or enriched by immigrants; immigrants make country worse or better place to live.

For Taiwan, some traditional measures of economic equality do matter for social benefits (see Table 9.11). Taiwanese believe that it is important that benefits be awarded to the poor rather than the rich, that equality is critical, and that the people deserve equal treatment, and that the poorest 10 percent of the country is treated well. Yet, the single most important factor shaping the provision of benefits is a factor score of who is permitted to immigrate to the country. There is a strong bias fir people who are of Chinese ancestry, who are believed to make life better for the full population and to enrich the nation's culture and to make life better for the poorest 10 percent (see Table 10.12 from the 2016 Asian Barometer Survey).

Taiwan and Israel thus stand out as countries where identity has become paramount for both vote choice and deservingness. The traditional left-right divide has faded for Israeli vote choice but has never been important in Taiwan. In that sense, these two countries are different from the ones in the United States, Great Britain, Western Europe, and the former Communist nations of Hungary and Poland. For these countries, the parties are polarized, both economically and culturally.

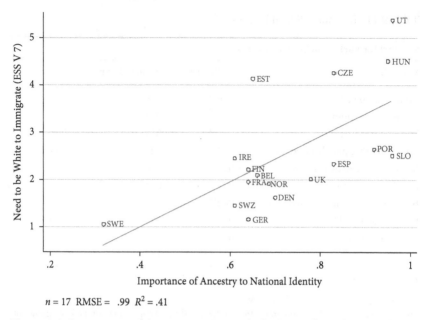

$n = 17$ RMSE = .99 $R^2 = .41$

Figure 9.1 Importance of Ancestry to National Identity and Need to Be White to Immigrate

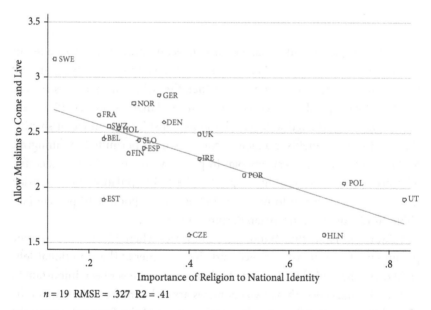

$n = 19$ RMSE = .327 $R2 = .41$

Figure 9.2 Allow Muslims to Come and Live, by Importance of Religion Identity
There is a strong aggregate relationship between Europeans' willingness to permit only whites to immigrate to their countries and their insistence that migrants be Christian, according to data I have aggregated from the European Social Survey.

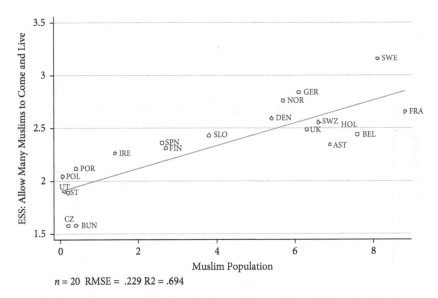

Figure 9.3 Factor for Immigrants Residence, by Bonikowski Populism Index
European countries with larger Muslim populations are more willing to admit new Islamic immigrants.

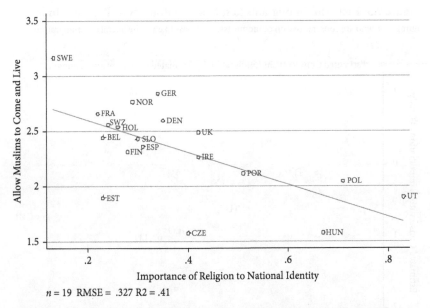

Figure 9.4 Estimated Conservatism Immigration, by Estimated Conservatism Economics
Europeans who strongly identify as Christians are less willing to admit new immigrants who are Muslims.

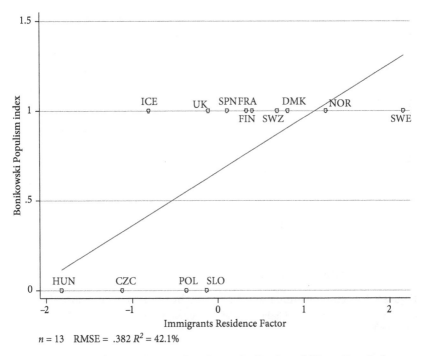

Figure 9.5 Factor for Immigrants Residence, by Bonkowski Populism Index

Europeans who are conservative on economic issues are less likely to be liberal on immigration.

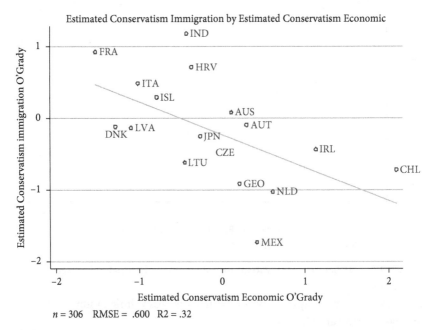

Figure 9.6 Estimated Conservatism Immigration, by Estimated Conservatism Economics

10

The Sources of Nationalism

What leads to nationalism in some countries but not others? Lucassen and Lubbers (2012, 548) explain the rationale for far-right parties: "The unique selling point of far-right parties is their anti-immigrant or anti-immigration standpoint . . . Unfavorable attitudes toward immigrants have therefore been demonstrated to be the most important predictors in explaining far-right-wing support . . . these unfavorable attitudes are induced by experiences of threats from immigrants, both economically and culturally."

While the total share of Muslims in a country does not shape support for right-wing parties in Europe, the fear that people of diverse backgrounds might threaten a country's culture is a powerful force shaping support for nationalist parties (Lucassen and Lubbers, 2012, 548).

Using the Pew Global 2016 survey I estimated probit analyses of support for right-wing nationalist parties for the full set of countries and for specific countries that I examine in more detail here (Germany, Hungary, Poland, Sweden, and the United Kingdom). I present the probit coefficients, their standard errors, and the difference in probabilities from the minimum and maximum values of two measures of national identity: insisting that someone be born in the country and sharing the dominant religion in Table 10.1.

The parties are the AfD in Germany, Jobbik in Hungary, Law and Justice in Hungary, the Sweden Democrats in Sweden, and the United Kingdom Independence Party in Britain). The results are straightforward: In the former Communist countries of Hungary and Poland, sharing the dominant religion is central, while being born in the country is more important in Germany, Sweden, and the United Kingdom. In both Hungary and Poland, leaders and citizens worry that Muslim immigrants threaten Christian culture. In the Western European countries, people are less fearful of a decline of Western civilization and more worried about sharing ethnicity. Across all countries, both factors shape support for right-wing nationalist parties.

Neither the level of immigration (legal or illegal) nor the share of Muslims in a country's population leads to the rise of nationalist (or extreme right)

National Identity and Partisan Polarization. Eric M. Uslaner, Oxford University Press. © Oxford University Press 2022.
DOI: 10.1093/oso/9780197633946.003.0010

Table 10.1 Support for Right-Wing Parties by Characteristics for Being a True Member of a Society

Variable	Coefficient	Standard Error	Diff Probabilities
All Countries			
True born in country	−.241****	−−11.95	−.163
True dominant religion	−.147****	−10.72	−.147
Germany			
True born in country	.370**	.147	.040
True dominant religion	−.121	−.077	−.011
Hungary			
True born in country	.016	.114	.006
True dominant religion	.545****	.096	.201
Poland			
True dominant religion	.353**	.135	.105
True dominant religion	.618****	.115	.182
True born in country	.493***	.136	.086
Sweden			
True born in country	.493****	.136	.086
True dominant religion	.034	.155	.005
United Kingdom			
True born in country	.502****	.103	.087
True dominant religion	.313***	.094	.051

For full sample: N = 1426 McKelvey-Zavoina R2 = .634 − 2LRR = 957.776; For Germany: N = 979 McKelvey-Zavoina R2 = .742 -2*LRR = 370.864

For Hungary: N = 989 McKelvey-Zavoina R2 = .120 −2*LRR = 1291.992

For Poland: N = 980 McKelvey-Zavoina R2 = .352. −2*LRR = 1093.496

parties—or for a sense of national identity emphasizing ancestry or religion (cf. Lucassen and Lubbers, 2012, 564, 567).

I examine these questions using aggregate levels of attitudes toward immigrants (legal and illegal) and Muslims using the European Social Survey (rounds 7 and 8), the ISSP, and the European Values Surveys:

- An index of the strength of anti-establishment parties, the Timbro Authoritarian Populism Index (Heino, 2016), provided by Andreas Johansson Heino.

- A survey from the Pew Research Center 2018 survey "Being Christian in Western Europe" (Pew Research Center, 2018). This survey, conducted in Europe in 2018, is includes questions about attitudes toward Muslims and Jews as well as to immigration and traits of immigrants such as being hardworking. I examine individual-level responses to these questions and to an index of national identity (parents or grandparents need to be born in this country). I aggregate the responses to these questions and examine whether they are related to the strength of anti-establishment parties and to attitudes toward what the criteria for immigration (need to be Christian, need to have ancestry of the country of residence).
- I examine linkages between (1) the strength of anti-establishment parties; (2) attitudes toward immigration and toward Muslims; and (3) people's criteria for being a "true" citizen with measures of ideology and positions on gay rights, whether people should share the same customs; whether the government should adopt policies that would equalize opportunities or income (from the CSES and ESS).

There is a strong relationship between national identity and the need to be white to immigrate (see Figure 10.1). There is a powerful relationship between allowing Muslims to come and the belief that only Christians should be allowed to immigrate (see Figure 10.2). Countries with the largest shares of Muslims have populations that are more willing to accept more Muslims (see Figure 10.3).There is at best a modest relationship between the strength of far right parties and attitudes toward Muslims (whether Muslims should be allowed to emigrate, $R2 = .141$) and whether religion is important for a sense of national identity ($R2 = .21$).

The single most dramatic result is the very strong relationship between the share of Muslims in a country and people's willingness to allow Muslims to emigrate to their country (see Figure 10.4). But this is not the story that ethnocentric leaders would have us believe.

National identity is the major factor in shaping attitudes toward immigration. Using the Bonkowski populism factor, I show that allowing Muslims to immigrate to the country, permitting any immigrants to enter the country, or to vote for right wing parties are all shaped by issues of identity (see Figure 10.5). The relationships for population and right wing voting are too sparse to graph). Identity is broader than being of the same descent or religion of the majority so it is more encompassing. It is the most comprehensive predictor

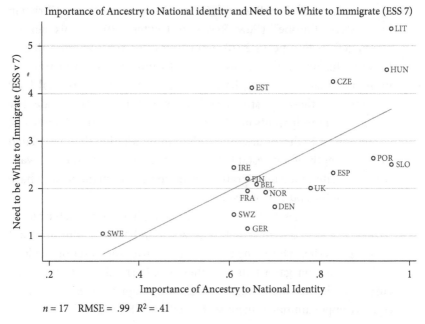

Importance of Ancestry to National identity and Need to be White to Immigrate (ESS 7)

n = 17   RMSE = .99   *R*² = .41

Figure 10.1 Need to Be White to Immigrate (ESS 7)

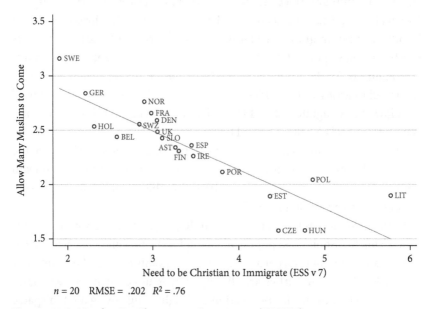

n = 20   RMSE = .202   *R*² = .76

Figure 10.2 Need to Be Christian to Immigrate (ESS V7)

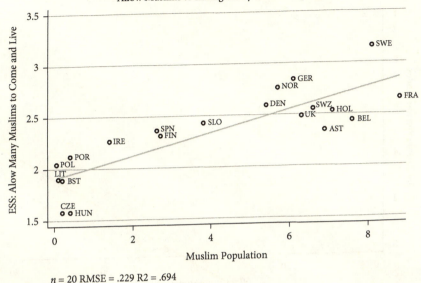

Figure 10.3 Importance of Ancestry to National Identity for Accepting Muslim Immigrants

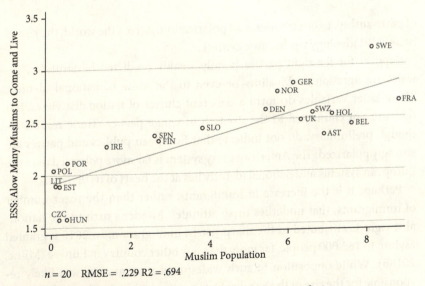

Figure 10.4 Allow Muslims to Immigrate by Muslim Population

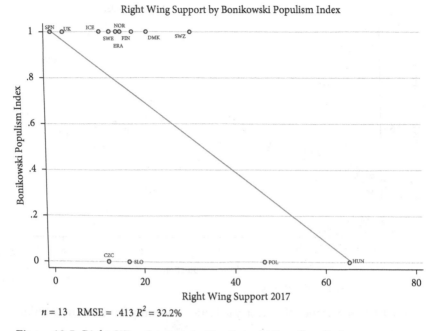

Right Wing Support by Bonikowski Populism Index

Figure 10.5 Right-Wing Support, by Bonikowski Populism Index

of partisanship, issue attitudes, and polarization. Across the world, the rise of nationalist ideology has become central..

Support for far right parties is only weakly predicted by attitudes, toward immigration or Muslims–or even to the sense of national identity. These latter variables do form a coherent cluster of nationalist views, but they are not connected to the strength of fringe parties. These results, although preliminary, do not indicate that European publics and parties are strongly polarized. The American party system is far more polarized than the European systems and national identity lies at the heart of its divisions.

Perhaps it is the increase in immigrants, rather than the sheer number of immigrants, that underlies these attitudes. Sweden's turn to the nationalist right is attributed to the sharp rise in immigration: In 2015 it granted asylum to 163.000 people, far more than any other country in Europe (Milne, 2018b). While opposition to such widespread immigration was likely responsible for the rise of the Sweden Democrats, neither the share of Muslims in a country's population in 2010 or 2016 from the Pew Center (2017, 31) nor the change in the share of a country's Muslim population led to greater support for right-wing authoritarian parties (using the Timbro indices) nor the beliefs that immigrants must be either whites or Christians (from version 7 of the European Social Survey).

The countries with the largest shares of Muslims or the greatest change in Muslim populations had the weakest right-wing parties and were the most welcoming to immigrants who are not white or Christian. It is not the share of Muslims that shapes attitudes about who can immigrate to one's country. Instead it is the exclusivity of one's sense of national identity: In countries where people are more likely to say that ancestry is an important part of their national identity, they are more likely to say that whites should have priority in immigrating. In countries where religion is important to national identity, people are *less* likely to say that Muslims should be allowed to live there (both R2 = .41, see the graphs below). For both measures of identity, Swedes are the least exclusive.

Religion is most important to identity in Central and Eastern Europe (especially Poland and Hungary), where right-wing nationalist parties have been most strident in opposing immigration by Muslims. The two measures of identity (ancestry and religion) are part of a general "syndrome" of exclusivity (r = .75 across 25 countries). Kupper and Zick (2010, 14, 49) find among Europeans that people who feel that Christianity is a major part of their identity are more opposed to immigration from non-Christian countries and are also more likely to be anti-Semitic and anti-Muslim.

In Figures 10.6 and 10.7 I show that cultural conservatism is more critical than economic conservatism in shaping public attitudes toward immigration. This is consistent with what I reported in the models for deservingness (see especially Sobolweska and Ford, 2020, 147, 179, 238–247, 335; and Kitschelt and McGann, 2018). The public opinion data come from (Caughey, O'Grady, and Warshaw, 2019, 678), who conducted surveys of people in Europe every biennium from 1981 to 2016 and asked about the size of government and its role in mitigating inequality (for the economic dimension), postmaterialism, gender equality, abortion, gay rights, environmental protection, and libertarianism versus authoritarianism for the social dimension, and national identity and admitting people into the country for the immigration measure).

The fit with attitudes on immigration for social attitudes is much stronger (R2 = .62) compared to that for economic concerns (R2 = .32), consistent with the results presented in the discussion of deservingness. At both the start and the end of the time series, the former Communist countries had the most conservative publics on immigration and social issues and the

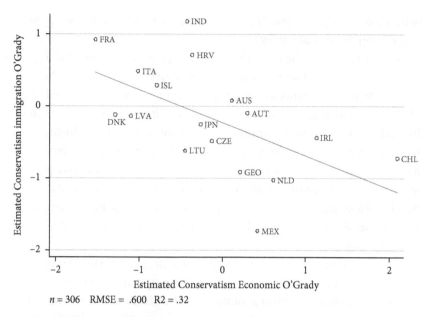

Figure 10.6 Estimated Conservatism Immigration, by Estimated Conservatism Economics

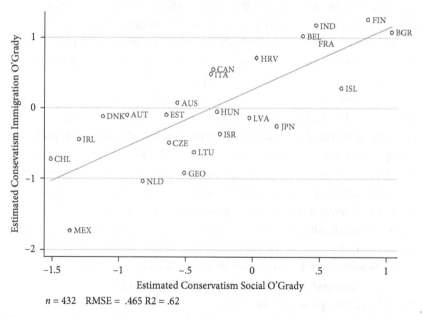

Figure 10.7 Estimated Conservatism Immigration, by Estimated Conservatism Social

Scandinavian nations (together with Belgium and the Netherlands the least). The importance of social conservatism for the support for right wing parties is consistent not only with the results above but also with the findings of Bonikowski (2017, S187) who stated:

Much of the identity-based discourse employed by the radical right is consistent with the definition of ethno-nationalism: the idea that legitimate membership in the nation is limited to those with the appropriate immutable, or at least highly persistent, traits, such as national ancestry, native birth, majority religion, dominant racial group membership, or deeply ingrained dominant cultural traits. For many individuals, that tension is experienced viscerally as an affront to their collective identity as the 'true' members of the national community, the tendencies need not be fully articulated.

Greven (2016, 5) writes: "For right-wing populists, immigration is not simply a question of economic competition but it constitutes a threat against the presumed (constructed) identity of the people and their traditional values . . . disaffection with the establishment—the other, fundamental construction of "us vs. them"—is a uniform feature of right-wing populism across Europe and the United States." See also Greven (2016), Geertje and Lubbers (2012), and Sniderman et al. (2004, 37), who claim about Dutch society:

increasingly, the strains over immigration in Western Europe are being cast in terms of a division between European majorities and Muslim minorities. Our findings lend support to a hypothesis of culture conflict. A perception that Dutch culture is threatened is the dominant factor in generating a negative reaction to immigrant minorities. And the issue of cultural integration, when it becomes salient, evokes proportionately just as strong a reaction from those who are least concerned about a threat to Dutch culture as from those who are most concerned about one.

Betz (2018, 98–99) states:

The radical right's nativist discourse on Islam has all the ingredients of a moral panic, designed to evoke anxieties and fears and thus reinforce already existing sentiments of cultural and symbolic insecurity and disorientation among the general public, reflected in the notion that one no longer feels at home in one's own community and country . . . Its central feature is the assertion of the right to the protection of cultural difference as a first step toward the reestablishment and reaffirmation of a strong sense of national identity. For only a strong sense of national identity allows a nation to assert its sovereignty.

These parties appeal to lower-income natives with generous social benefits targeted to them, not to immigrants.

Zick, Andreas, Thomas F. Pettigrew, and Ulrich Wagner (2008, 234) argue: "Many nations, such as Germany, regard the new immigration as a novel event and ignore that they have experienced immigration for centuries. This to explain the often-arbitrary categorization of European ethnicities . . . the children and grandchildren of the immigrants of the 1960s and 1970s are still often considered foreigners. This perception affects citizenship policy. In some nations, such as Germany, most immigrants and their progeny have never received citizenship, even if they were born and raised in the country. In other states, such as the United Kingdom and France, immigrants of the third generation still are often considered to be foreigners despite their citizenship."

Williams (2018, 319) argues: "East European parties tend to be caught in older ways of framing nationalism and xenophobia around fascism, with swastikas more commonly used as symbols and outright racial purity strands of racism rather than the newer anti-immigrant issue framing from the late 1980s seen among West European RRPs, which is premised upon immigrants as scapegoats for economic and social problems."

A recent study using the German General Social Survey of 1996 measured the actual immigrant proportion in small districts, the perceived immigrant proportion, the perceived threat from immigrants, and exclusionary attitudes toward immigrants. No relationship was uncovered between the actual immigrant proportion and either perceived threat or anti-immigrant attitudes. But perceived immigrant proportion did correlate with both perceived threat and exclusionary attitudes . . . the actual immigrant percentage in the area and the perceived percentage were essentially unrelated.

From the Pew Study of Christians in Europe in 2017, the levels of support for allowing non-Muslims to be white or to be Christians in former Communist countries. The same relationship holds for providing benefits to newer immigrants,, where the most restrictions occur in Hungary, the Czech Republic, and Estonia–especially compared to the more lenient Scandinavian countries, Luxembourg, and Switzerland. Here there is just one notable exception (Iceland).

Voting for nationalist parties and supporting welfare benefits for immigrants are especially high in former Communist countries. The electorates there are rebelling against left-wing governments by supporting right-wing parties. They do support increased spending for government programs, but only for people who are white and Christian (and of their own heritage).

In Central and Eastern European countries that had been under Communist rule, Bustikova (2018. 4) argues:

> radical right parties are left-leaning on the economy when compared to other parties in their respective political systems . . . Their policy platforms stand for protection against the volatility of markets, more social spending, and greater state control over the economy. Despite their overwhelming lean to the left, it does not follow that these parties have a clear social base among low-income   people . . . Dissatisfaction with policies under-taken during the process of   democratization, such as the expansion of ethnic and social minority rights, by politicians who are viewed as unac-countable is increasingly linked to anti-   democratic attitudes in Eastern Europe. . . In Eastern Europe, responsiveness to the demands of minorities and democracy are bundled together, so the backlash against establishment politicians and parties feeds off the intensity of an identity-based cleavage. Given the relatively higher levels of aggregate xenophobia in the East , attempts to modify ethnic relations, which are wrapped in populist calls for a more direct relationship between voters and leaders, can be interpreted as covert appeals to revisit inclusive democracy as a form of political repre-sentation. The ability of new liberal democracies to survive hinges on their ability to contain this backlash against the expansion of minority rights.

Overall, people are most willing to restrict immigration when they believe that the migrants are not as intelligent as natives or would increase crime. People are most fearful of refugees coming to their country who may not be as smart as they are when the migrants are of a different race or religion, especially if they are Muslim and are not believed to want to adapt to the mainstream of society or might even threaten them (see Table 10.2). Failure to adapt is critical everywhere, even in the most tolerant nation (Sweden). Worries about religious identity are strongest in West Germany, Hungary, and France, all of which have political parties that have fared well on nation-alist platforms. Natives are more willing to restrict immigration when they fear that immigrants would increase crime and this effect is strongest when people believe that religion is critical to their own belief system and that Muslims would not fit into their countries and might be prone to terrorism (see Table 10.3).

Table 10.2 Overall Importance of Citizenship Factors for Countries Examined in Depth from Pew Global Survey 2016

	Identity Born	Identity Religion	Ideology	Importance Religion	Diversity Good	Muslims Adapt	Muslims Terrorism
All Countries	.282****	.175****	.050****	.023****	.367****	−.312****	−.181****
France	.280****	.134*	.083***	.053*	.337****	−.360****	−.2340****
Germany (West)	.094*	.136**	.089****	.056**	.399***	−.218****	−.1734****
Hungary	.095	−.158*	.044**	.029	.141****	−.376****	.012
Poland	.183*	.033	.010	−.023	.079*	−.245****	.013
Sweden	.185****	.00*	.068	.041	.487****	−.314****	−.162****
UK	.204****	.071	.019	.014.	.521****	−.264****	−.188****

**** p < .001; *** p < .01; ** p < .05; * p < .10.
Bold entries for all countries are the most significant.

Table 10.3 Overall Importance of Citizenship Factors for Countries Examined in Depth from Pew Global Survey: Fear Immigrants Would Increase Crime

	Identity Born	Identity Religion	Ideology	Importance Religion	Diversity Good	Muslims Adapt	Muslims Terrorism
Country							
France	−.011	−.137*	.−.032*	.024	−.183****	..105***	.104****
Germany (West)	−.017	−.112*	−.075***	−.046*	−.222****	.256****	.244****
Hungary	−.263**	−.493**	−.022	−.058	−.058	.170**	.249****
Poland	−.044	.365**	−.007	.093*	.048	−.054	.153***
Sweden	−.076	−.178**	−.061***	−.011	−.267****	.323****	.160****
UK	−.144**	−.019	−.032*	−.032	.258****	.100*	.285****

**** p < .001; *** p < .01; ** p < .05; * p < .10
Bold entries for all countries are the most significant.

This sets them apart from the public in the United States and some European countries such as the United States, the United Kingdom, and France, where conservative parties favor reductions in spending for all citizens—and especially from northern European countries (notably Scandinavia as well as the Netherlands and Germany) where even conservative parties are willing to provide welfare to immigrants and where few voters support extremist right-wing parties.

Major change in nationalist policy can only occur when the parties are polarized on this and other issues. We see this in the United States and the United Kingdom. However, in Sweden and Germany the major parties are not polarized on immigration or other issues, while in the former Communist states there is widespread support for restrictions on immigration with less deep divisions over social issues. In Taiwan and Israel, nationalist issues are the central focus of partisan politics. The prospects for change in nationalist policy thus can only take place when the parties and the public are divided.

National identity has become an important force in politics across a range of nations. The impact is greatest in the United States, but that is attributable to the strong polarization on identity between the Democratic and Republican parties. The divisions between major parties on the left and right is not as strong in Western Europe—and weak in Central and Eastern Europe.

This is attributable to the presence of fringe nationalist parties in most Western European countries (with Britain and France being exception, though for different reasons) and the strong role of national identity for the dominant parties in the former Communist countries. There is little support for the argument that national identity or the support for right-wing parties can be traced to levels of immigration. Countries with the largest shares of immigrants or the largest share of Muslims have lower levels of national identity and less opposition to immigration (especially by Muslims).

A strong sense of national identity is a way of dividing the world into "us" and "them." It is more than a simple surrogate for racism, negative attitudes toward minorities more generally, or authoritarianism–although each is related to national identity and the aggregate relationships suggest that negative views of minorities underlie other attitudes and political choices.

What makes national identity an important determinant of vote choice (and partisan identification) is straightforward: Political leaders from Donald J. Trump to Marine Le Pen. Strong national identity reflects a bias against minorities (Muslims especially in Europe, minorities more generally in the United States), but it is more than that. National identity is all about perceptions of who is worthy of to be a "true" American, Brit, etc.—and it is more than denigration of "them." The issue is one of values, not of institutional structures. It is an assertion that "us" "matters" and that political and social life must place "us" first. Who we aren't depends upon who we think we are. Leaders follow the public, they don't determine what people think.

References

Abali, Oya S. 2009. "German Public Opinion on Immigration and Integration." Migration Policy Institute, Transatlantic Council of Migration, at http://www.migrationpolicy. org/research/german-public-opinion-immigration-and-integration

Abdelkader, Engy. 2017. "A Comparative Analysis of European Islamophobia: France, UK, Germany, Netherlands, and Sweden," *Journal of Islamic and Near Eastern Law*, 16: 31–63, at https://escholarship.org/uc/item/870099f4

Abrajano, Marisa, and Zoltan L. Hajnal. 2015. *White Backlash: Immigration, Race, and American Politics*. Princeton: Princeton University Press.

Abramowitz, Alan I. 2018. *The Great Alignment: Race, Party Transformation, and the Rise of Donald Trump*. New Haven: Yale University Press.

Abramowitz, Alan, and Steven Webster. 2018. "Negative Partisanship: Why Americans Dislike Parties But Behave Like Rabid Partisans," *Advances in Political Psychology*, 39: 119–135.

Achen, Christopher H., and T. Y, Wang. 2017. "The Taiwan Voter: An Introduction," in Christopher H. Achen and T. Y, Wang, eds., *The Taiwan Voter*. Ann Arbor: University of Michigan Press.

Adams, James, Jane Green, and Caitlin Milazzo. 2012. "Has the British Public Depolarized along with Political Elites? An American Perspective on British Public Opinion," *Comparative Political Studies*, 45: 507–530.

AFP and Kelsey Snell. 2018. "Make Sweden Great Again," https://dailymail.co.uk/Make-Sweden-Great-Swedish-anti-immigration=partyadopts-Trumps-slogan-ahead-elections.html

Agh, Attila. 2016. "The Decline of Democracy in East-Central Europe Hungary as the Worst-Case Scenario," *Problems of Post-Communism*, 63: 277–287.

Alderman, Liz, and Melissa Eddy. 2023. "Wearing a Head Scarf Can Be Grounds for Job Suspension, E.U.'s Top Court Rules," *New York Times* (July 15), at https://www.nytimes. com/2021/07/15/business/Europe-court-head-scarves.html

Alesina, Alberto, Elie Murard, and Hillel Rappoport. 2019. "Immigration and Preferences for Redistribution in Europe," IZA Discussion Paper 12130. Institute for Labor Economics, Bonn, Germany, at https://www.nber.org/papers/w25562

Alesina, Alberto, and Marco Tabellini. 2021. "The Political Effects of Immigration: Culture or Economics?" IZA (Institute of Labor Economics, Bonn Germany) DP No. 14354, http://ftp.iza.org/dp14354.pdf

Anderson, Cristina and Steven Erlanger. 2018. *"Sweden's Centrists Prevail Even as Far Right Has Its Best Showing Ever,"* New York Times, at https://www.nytimes.com/2018/09/09/ world/europe/sweden-elections.html

Applebaum, Anne. 2019. *Twilight of Democracy*. New York: Doubleday.

Applebaum, Lauren D. 2002. "Who Deserves Help? Students' Opinions About the Deservingness of Different Groups Living in Germany to Receive Aid," *Social Justice Research* 15: 201–225.

Applebaum, Lauren D. 2003. "The Influence of Perceived Deservingness on Policy Decisions Regarding Aid to the Poor," *Political Psychology*, 22:419–442, at https://doi.org/10.1111/0162-895X.00248

Ariely, Gal. 2011. "Political Culture and Israeli Politics," in R. Hazan., M. Hofnung., G. Rahat., and A. Dowty. The Oxford Handbook of Israeli Politics and Society. Oxford University Press.

Associated Press-NORC Center for Public Affairs Research. 2017. "The American Identity: Points of Pride, Conflicting Views, and a Distinct Culture," at http://www.apnorc.org/projects/Pages/points-of-pride-conflicting-views-and-a-distinct-culture.aspx

Backer, Susann. 2000 "Right Wing Extremism in Unified Germany," in Paul Hainsworth, ed., *The Politics of the Extreme Right*, 87–120. London: Pinter.

Backes, 2018, in Germany

Baker, Peter and Nicholas Fandos. 2019. "Hungary's Orban Gave Trump Harsh Analysis of Ukraine Before Key Meeting," *New York Times* (October 22), at https://www.nytimes.com/2019/10/22/us/politics/trump-ukraine-orban.html

Ballard, Jamie. What Americans Think of the US Flag in 2021, YouGov America, at https://today.yougov.com/topics/politics/articles-reports/2021/03/31/what-americans-think-american-flag-poll-data

Bar-On, in Hungary/Poland

Barry, Brian. 2014. *Culture and Equality: An Egalitarian Critique of Multiculturalism.* New York: John Wiley.

Barry, Ellen, and Mark Landler. 2019. "Brexit and the U.S. Shutdown: Two Governments in Paralysis," *New York Times* (January 12), at https://www.nytimes.com/2019/01/12/us/politics/brexit-shutdown-us-britain-trump.html

Bartels, Larry M. 2018. "Partisanship in the Trump Era," *Journal of Politics*, 80:1483–1494.

Bauback, Rainer. "Citizenship, Identities, and Solidarity in the EU," in Keith Banting and Will Kymlicka, eds., *The Strains of Commitment*, 80–106. Oxford: Oxford University Press.

Beardsley, Eleanor. 2021. "Presidential Race Looming, France's Regional Elections Will Show Status Of Parties," National Public Radio Saturday Weekend Edition (June 18), at https://www.npr.org/2021/06/18/1008196300/presidential-race-looming-frances-regional-elections-will-show-status-of-parties

Beauzamy, Brigitte. 2014. "The Rise of the Front National to National Prominance." In Ruth Wodak, Majid Khosragvinik, and Brigitte Mral, eds., *Right-Wing Populism in Europe*. London: Bloomsbury.

Becker, Jo. 2019. "The Global Machine Behind the Rise of Far-Right Nationalism," *New York Times* (August 11), at https://www.nytimes.com/2019/08/10/world/europe/sweden-immigration-nationalism.html

Bennhold, Katrin. 2021. "Germany Places Far-Right AfD Party Under Surveillance for Extremism," *New York Times* (March 4), A13, at https://www.nytimes.com/2021/03/03/world/europe/germany-afd-surveillance-extremism.html

Bennhold, Katrin. 2020a. "Merkel's Chosen Successor Steps Aside. The Far Right Cries Victory," *New York Times* (February 11), at https://www.nytimes.com/2020/02/10/world/europe/annegret-kramp-karrenbauer-resign.html?searchResultPosition=3

Bennhold, Katrin. 2020b. "Germany Dismisses Military Intelligence Official After Neo-Nazi Scandals," *New York Times* (October 4), at https://today.yougov.com/topics/politics/articles-reports/2021/03/31/what-americans-think-american-flag-poll-data

Bennhold, Katrin. 2020c. "QAnon Is Thriving in Germany. The Extreme Right Is Delighted," *New York Times* (October 11), A1, A16, at https://www.nytimes.com/2020/

10/11/world/europe/qanon-is-thriving-in-germany-the-extreme-right-is-delighted. htmlDelighted," *New York Times* (October 11), A1, A16

Bennhold, Katrin. 2020d, "German Fringe Finds in Trump a Cult Savior, *New York Times* (September 8), at https://www.nytimes.com/2020/09/07/world/europe/germany-trump-far-right.html

Bennhold, Katrin. . 2020e. "She Called Police Over a Neo-Nazi Threat. But the Neo-Nazis Were Inside the Police," *New York Times* (December 21), A1, A13, at https://www.nytimes.com/2020/12/21/world/europe/germany-far-right-neo-nazis-police.html

Bennhold, Katrin. 2019. "German Elections Reveal, and Deepen, a New East-West Divide," *New York Times* (August 31), at https://www.nytimes.com/2019/08/31/world/europe/east-germany-afd-elections-saxony-brandenburg-merkel.html

Bennhold, Katrin. 2018a. "Bavaria: Affluent, Picturesque —and Angry," *New York Times* (June 30), at https://www.nytimes.com/2018/06/30/world/europe/bavaria-immigration-afd-munich.html

Bennhold, Katrin. 2018b. "Migration and the Far Right Changed Europe. A German Vote Will Show How Much," *New York Times* (October 12), at https://www.nytimes.com/2018/10/12/world/europe/germany-bavaria-election.html

Bennhold, Katrin. 2018c. "Chemnitz Protests Show New Strength of Germany's Far Right," *New York Times* (August 30), at https://www.nytimes.com/2018/08/30/world/europe/germany-neo-nazi-protests-chemnitz.html

Bennhold, Katrin. 2018d . "Germany's Far Right Rebrands: Friendlier Face, Same Doctrine," *New York Times* (December 27), at https://www.nytimes.com/2018/12/27/world/europe/germany-far-right-generation-identity.html

Bennhold, Katrin. 2005. "'We're French,' But Not 'Real' French," *International Herald Tribune* (November 5-6), 1-4, available at http://www.nytimes.com/2005/11/04/world/europe/04iht-france.html

Bennhold, Katrin, and Melissa Eddy. 2019. "Election in Germany Helps Far Right Tighten Its Grip in the East," *New York Times* (October 27), at https://www.nytimes.com/2019/10/27/world/europe/germany-election-afd-thuringia.html?searchResultPosition=1

Bennhold, Katrin and Michael Schwartz. 2021. "Capitol Riot Puts Spotlight on 'Apocalyptically Minded' Global Far Right," *New York Times* (January 25), at https://www.nytimes.com/2021/01/24/world/europe/capitol-far-right-global.html

Berend, Nora. N.D. Magyar Myth Makers, History Today at https://www.historytoday.com/archive/magyarmyth-makers.

Berger, Miriam. 2018. "Israel's hugely controversial "nation-state" law, explained," Vox (July 31), at https://www.vox.com/world/2018/7/31/17623978/israel-jewish-nation-state-law-bill-explained-apartheid-netanyahu-democracy

Bergman, Ronen. 2021. "How the Pandemic Nearly Tore Israel Apart," *New York Times* (March 5), at https://www.nytimes.com/2021/02/25/magazine/how-the-pandemic-nearly-tore-israel-apart.html

Betz, Hans-George. 2018. "The Radical Right and Populism." In Jens Rydgren, ed., *The Oxford Handbook of the Radical Right*. Oxford: Oxford University Press, at DOI: 10.1093/oxfordhb/9780190274559.013.5

Betz, Hans-George. . 2015. "T he Revenge of the Ploucs: The Revival of Radical Populism under Marine Le Pen in France." In Hanspietr Kreisl and Takis S. Pappas., eds., European Populism in the Shadow of the Great Reception. Colchester, UK: ECPR Press.

Betz, Hans-George. 1993. "The New Politics of Resentment: Radical Right-Wing Populist Parties in Western Europe," *Comparative Politics*, 25:413–427.

Bilefsky, Dan. 2018. "Don't Burn Women: Warning to Immigrants Looms Over a Quebec Village," *New York Times* (April 12), at https://www.nytimes.com/2018/04/12/world/canada/canada-herouxville-immigration.html?rref=collection%2Fbyline%2Fdan-bilefsky

Bisserbie, Noemie, and Stacy Meichtry, 2021. "France's Macron Pushes Controls on Religion to Pressure Mosques," *Wall Street Journal* (June 22), at https://www.wsj.com/articles/frances-macron-pushes-controls-on-religion-to-pressure-mosques-11624385471

Bittner, Jochen. 2018. "How the Far Right Conquered Sweden," *New York Times* (September 6), at https://www.nytimes.com/2018/09/06/opinion/how-the-far-right-conquered-sweden.html

Bonikowski, Bart. 2017. "Ethno-nationalist Populism and the Mobilization of Collective Resentment," *British Journal of Sociology*, 68:S181–S213

Boreus, Kristina. 2013. "Nationalism and Discursive Discrimination against Immigration in Austria, Denmark, and Sweden." In Ruth Wodak, Majid Khosravinik, and Brigitte Mral, eds., *Right-Wing Populism in Europe*, pp. 277–308. London: Bloomsbury.

Borevi, Karin. 2014 "Multiculturalism and Welfare State Integration: Swedish Model Path Dependency," *Identities*, 21:6, 708–723, DOI: 10.1080/1070289X.2013.868351

Borevi, Karin. 2013. "The Political Dynamics of Multiculturalism in Sweden. In Raymond Taras, ed., *Challenging Multiculturalism*, 138–162.Edinbourgh, Scotland: Edinburgh University Press.

Bornschier, Simon. 2018. "Why a Right-Wing Nationalist Party Emerged in France But Not in Germany," *European Political Science Review*, 4:121–145.

Bovesi, Kristina. 2013. "Nationalism and Discursive Discrimination against Immigration in Austria, Denmark, and Sweden." In Ruth Wodak, Majik Khosravinik, and Brigitte Mral, eds., *Right-Wing Populism in Europe*, pp. 277–308. London: Bloomsbury.

Bréchon, Pierre, and Subrata Kumar Mitra. 1992. "The National Front in France: The Emergence of an Extreme Right Protest Movement." *Comparative Politics*, 25:63–82.

Brewer, Mark D. 2016. "Populism in American Politics," *The Forum*, 14:249–264.

Brockway, Mark, David Campbell, and Geoffrey Layman (2016). "Secular Voters Didn't Turn out for Clinton the Way White Evangelicals Did for Trump," *Washington Post* (November 18), at https://www.washingtonpost.com/news/monkey-cage/wp/2016/11/18/secular-voters-didn't-turn-out-for-clinton-the-way-white-evangelicals-did-for-trump/

Brooks, David. 2019. "The Coming G.O.P. Apocalypse," *New York Times* (June 3), at https://www.nytimes.com/2019/06/03/opinion/republicans-generation-gap.html

Burton, Taira Isabella. 2018. "The GOP Can't Rely on White Evangelicals Forever" (November 7), at https://www.vox.com/2018/11/7/18070630/white-evangelicals-turnout-midterms-trump-2020

Buštíková, Lenka. 2018. "The Radical Right in Eastern Europe." In Jens Rydgren, ed., *Oxford Handbook of the Radical Right in Eastern Europe*. Oxford: University Press, DOI: 10.1093/oxfordhb/9780190274559.013.28

Buštíková, Lenka, and Herbert Kitschelt. 2009. "The Radical Right in Post-communist Europe. Comparative Perspectives on Legacies and Party Competition," *Commuist and Post-Communist Studies*, 42:459–483.

Cantoni, Davide, Felix Hagemeister, and Mark Westcott. 2017. "Persistence and Activation of Right-Wing Political Ideology," at https://epub.ub.uni-muenchen.de/40424/1/cantoni.pdf

Carvalho, Jose, Roger Eatwell, Daniel Wunderlich. 2015. "The Politicization of Immigration in Britain." In Wouter van der Brug, Gianni D'Amato, Didier Ruedin, and Joost Berkhout, eds, *The Politicization of Migration*. New York: Routledge.

Casselman, Ben. 2017. "Stop Saying Trump's Win Had Nothing to Do with Economics," (January 9), at https://fivethirtyeight.com/features/stopsayingtrumpswinhadnothingt odowitheconomics/

Castles, Stephen, and Davidson, Alistair. 2020. *Citizenship and Migration*. New York: Routledge.

Caughey, Devin, Tom O'Grady, and Christopher Warshaw. 2019. "Policy Ideology in European Mass Publics, 1981–2016," *American Political Science Review*, 113:1981–2016.

Charlemagne. 2021. "Emmanuel Macron, Surreptitious Socialist," *The Economist* (July 21), 51 at https://www.economist.com/europe/2021/07/10/emmanuel-macron-surreptitious-socialist

Chianteram, Patricia and Peto Andreas. 2003. "Cultures of Populism and the Political Right in Central Europe," *Comparative Literature and Culture*, 5, at https://www.researchgate.net/publication/27238148_Cultures_of_Populism_and_the_Political_Right_in_Central_Europe

Chien, Amy Cheng and Amy Quinn. 2021. "With Pig Parades and Youth Camps, Taiwan's Ailing Kuomintang Tries a Revamp," New York Times (February 14), A4, at https://wwnytimes.2021/02/12/world-asia/taiwan-kumonintaing-china.html).

Christianity Daily. 2016. "More than 60 Percent of Evangelicals Voted in 2016, Says Baran Study" (December 6), at http://www.christianitydaily.com/articles/8710/20161206/faith-played-huge-role-election-2016-barna.htm

Churchwell, Sarah. 2018. "End of the American Dream? The Dark History of 'America First,'" *The Guardian*, at https://www.theguardian.com/books/2018/apr/21/end-of-the-american-dream-the-dark-history-of-america-first

Citrin, Jack, and David O. Sears. 2014 *The Politics of Multiculuralism*. New York: Cambridge University Press.

Citrin, Jack, and Matthew Wright. 2009. "Defining the Circle of We: American Identity and Immigration Policy," *The Forum*, 7, no. 32009, article 6.

Clarke, Harold D., Matthew Goodwin, and Paul Whiteley. 2017a. *Brexit: Why Britain Voted to Leave the European Union*. Cambridge: Cambridge Unversity Press.

Clarke, Harold D., Matthew Goodwin, and Paul Whiteley. 2017b. "Why Britain Voted for Brexit: An Individual-Level Analysis of the 2016 Referendum Vote," *Parliamentary Affairs*, 70: 439–464.

Cohen, David. 2021. "Trump on Jan. 6 Insurrection: 'These Were Great People,'" Politico (July 11), at https://www.politico.com/news/2021/07/11/trump-jan-6-insurrection-these-were-great-people-499165

Cohen, Roger. 2021. "Terrorism Fears Feed the Rise of France's Extreme Right," *New York Times* (April 25), A10, at https://www.nytimes.com/2021/04/24/world/europe/france-terrorism-far-right.html

Cohen, Roger. 2020. "France Takes on Islamist Extremism with New Bill," *New York Times* (December 10), A12, at https://www.nytimes.com/2020/12/09/world/europe/france-islamist-extremism-bill.html

Cox, Karen L. "What Changed in Charlottesville," *New York Times* (August 11), at https://www.nytimes.com/2019/08/11/opinion/confederate-monuments-charlottesville.html?searchResultPosition=2

Cramer, Katherine. 2017. "The Views of Nationalists: What Trump Voters' Perspectives and Perceptions of Trump Voters Tell Us About U.S. Democracy." Presented at the Annual Meeting of the American Political Science Association, San Francisco, August/September.

Cramer, Katherine. 2016. *The Politics of Resentment.* Chicago: University of Chicago Press.

Crepaz, Markus. 2006. " If You Are My Brother, I May Give You a Dime!' Public Opinion on Multiculturalism, Trust, and the Welfare State." In Keith Banting & Will Kymlicka (eds.), *Multiculturalism and the Welfare State: Recognition and Redistribution in Contemporary Democracies,* 92–120. Oxford: Oxford University Press.

Curtice, John. N.D."A Revolt on the Right? The Social and Political Attitudes of UKIP Supporters," *British Social Attitudes National Center for Social Research,* at http://www.bsa.natcen.ac.uk/media/38974/bsa32_ukip.pdfde

Dal Bo, Ernesto, Frederico Finan, Olle Folke, Torsten Persson, and Johanna Rickne. 2018. "Economic Losers and Political Winners: Sweden Is Radical Right," at http://perseus.iies.su.se/~tpers/papers/Draft180902.pdf

Davies, Peter. 2002. *The Extreme Right in France, 1789 to the Present,* London: Routledge.

deBaumont. 2021. "'Vaccine Passport' Language a Turnoff for Many Americans." *deBaumont Solutions for Healthier Communities* (June 6), at https://debeaumont.org/news/2021/vaccine-passports/

DeBonis, Mike, and John Wagner. 2021. "McCarthy, Other Congressional Leaders Condemn Greene for Comparing Coronavirus Masking Policies to the Holocaust," *Washington Post* (May 26), A19 at https://www.washingtonpost.com/powerpost/mccarthy-greene-holocaust-tweet/2021/05/25/d77bbb50-bd5f-11eb-9c90-731aff7d9a0d_story.html

De Clercq, Geert. 2019. "France's Le Pen Launches Eu Campaign with Appeal to 'Yellow Vests'," *Reuters* (January 13), at https://www.reuters.com/article/us-france-politics-farright/frances-le-pen-launches-eu-campaign-with-appeal-to-yellow-vests-idUSKCN1P70RO

Democracy Fund Voter Study Group. 2017. "Views of the Electorate Research Survey, December 2016. [Computer File] Release 1: August 28, 2017." Washington: Democracy Fund Voter Study Group, at https://www.voterstudygroup.org/.

DeParle, Jason. 2019. "What Makes an American?" *New York Times,* at https://www.nytimes.com/2019/08/09/sunday-review/immigration-assimilation-texas.html?searchResultPosition=1

Desjardins, Lisa. 2017. "How Trump Talks about Race," (August 22) at https://www.pbs.org/newshour/politics/every-moment-donald-trumps-long-complicated-history-race

Diehl, Jackson. 2019. " The Politics of the 1930s Are Still Playing out in Eastern Europe," *Washington Post* (November 10), at https://www.washingtonpost.com/opinions/global-opinions/the-politics-of-the-1930s-are-still-playing-out-in-eastern-europe/2019/11/10/42dbd666-0171-11ea-9518-1e76abc088b6_story.html

Dolezal, Matin, Marc Helbling, and Swen Hunter. 2010. "Debating Islam in Austria, Germany and Switzerland: Ethnic Citizenship, Church–State Relations and Right-Wing Populism," *West European Politics,* 33:171–190.

Duchesne. Sophie. 2016. "National Identity in France: A Blind Spot. In Robert Elgie, Emiliano Grossman, and Amy G. Mazur, *The Oxford Handbook of French Politics,* 483–503. Oxford: Oxford University Press.

Dunt, Ian. 2019. "Boris Johnson Will Do Anything for Brexit. Even Destroy His Own Party" (September 5), at https://www.washingtonpost.com/outlook/boris-johnson-will-do-anything-for-brexit-even-destroy-his-own-party/2019/09/05/6a64d96e-cff1-11e9-87fa-8501a456c003_story.html

Dustler, Chandelis, and Catberine Valentine. 2021. "Trump Allegedly Praised Hitler as Doing 'A Lot of Good Things,' New Book Claims" (July 7), at https://www.cnn.com/2021/07/07/politics/donald-trump-adolf-hitler-book-claims/index.html

Duverger, Maurice. 1954. *Political Parties*. New York: John Wiley.

Easton, Mark. 2018. "The English Question: What Is the Nation's Identity?" (June 3), at https://www.bbc.com/news/uk-44306737

Eatwell, Roger, and Matthew Goodwin. 2018. *National Populism: The Revolt against Liberal Democracy*. London: Pelican.

The Economist. 2021. Viktor Orban Seizes Control of Hungary's Universities" (May 3), 9–10.

Eddy, Melissa. 2018. "German Far Right and Counterprotesters Clash in Chemnitz," *New York Times* (August 28), at https://www.nytimes.com/2018/08/28/world/europe/chemnitz-protest-germany.html

Eddy, Melissa. 2017. "For Sebastian Kurz, Austria's 31-Year-Old New Leader, a Swift Rise" (October 18), at https://www.nytimes.com/2017/10/16/world/europe/sebastian-kurz-austria.html

Eisenmann, Martin, Yascha Mounck, and Limore Guitchen. 2017. European Populism:Trends, Threats, and Future Prospects. Tony Blair Institute for Global Change, at https://institute.global/policy/european-populism-trends-threats-and-future-prospects

Enders, Adam, and Jamil S. Scott. In press. "The Increasing Racialization of American Electoral Politics, 1988-2016 (ERPC 2016)," American Politics Research

Erhardt, Julian, Steffen Wamsler, and Markus Freitag. 2020. " National Identity Between Democracy and Autocracy: A Comparative Analysis of 24 Countries," *European Political Science Review*, 13:59–76, DOI: https://doi.org/10.1017/S1755773920000351

Erlanger, Steven. 2018. "As Sweden Votes, the Far Right Gains Even in an Immigrant Bastion," *New York Times* (September 17), at https://www.nytimes.com/2018/09/07/world/europe/sweden-election-far-right.html

Erlanger, Steven. 2017. "In Eastern Europe, Populism Lives, Widening a Split in the E.U.," *New York Times*, (November 28), at https://www.nytimes.com/2017/11/28/world/europe/populism-eastern-europe.html?ref=todayspaper&_r=0

Erlanger, Steven. 2015. "Poland Escalates Fight with Europe Over the Rule of Law," *New York Times* (July 10), A10.

Erlanger, Steven and Marc Santora. 2018. "Poland's Nationalism Threatens Europe's Values, and Cohesion," New York Times (February 20), at https://www.nytimes.com/2018/02/20/world/europe/poland-european-union.html

Evans, J., Gould, M., Norman, P. 2019. Drivers of Populist Radical Right Support in Britain, 2017–2018. [data collection]. UK Data Service. SN: 8474, http://doi.org/10.5255/UKDA-SN-8474-1, from https://beta.ukdataservice.ac.uk/datacatalogue/studies/study?id=8474

Feder, Shira. 2018. "Poland's Proposed New Law Limiting Kosher Slaughter Is Anti-Semitic. Here's Why," *The Forward* (February 20), at https://forward.com/food/394791/polands-proposed-new-law-limiting-kosher-slaughter-is-anti-semitic-heres-wh/

Fenwick, Clare, 2019. "The Political Economy of Immigration and Welfare State Effort: Evidence from Europe," *European Political Science Review* 11: 357–375

Ferwerda, Jeffrey. In print. "Immigration, Voting Rights, and Redistribution: Evidence from Local Governments in Europe," *Journal of Politics*, DOI: https://doi.org/10.1086/709301

Finkel, Eli, Christopher A. Bail, Mina Cikara, Peter H. Ditto, Shanto Iyengar, Samara Klar, Lilliana Mason, Mary C. McGrath, Brendan Nyhan, David G. Rand, Linda J. Skitka, Joshua A. Tucker, Jay J. VanBavel, Cynthia S. Wang, and James N. Druckman. 2020. "Political Sectarianism in America," *Science*, 370: 533–535.

Finney, Nissa, and Ludi Simpson. 2009. Sleepwalking to Segregation? Bristol, UK: The Policy Press.

Fiorina, Morris P., Samuel J. Adams, and Jeremy C. Pope. 2011. Culture War? The Myth of a Polarized America, Boston: Pearson.

Foa, Roberto. 2010. " Global Satisfaction with Democracy 2020," Bennett Institute for Democracy Centre for the Study of Democracy, at https://www.bennettinstitute.cam. ac.uk/media/uploads/files/DemocracyReport2020.pdf

Ford, Robert, and Matthew J. Goodwin. 2010. "Angry White Men: Individual and Contextual Predictors of Support for the British National Party," *Political Studies*, 58:1–25.

Ford, Robert, and Kitty Lymperopoulo. 2017. "Immigration." In Elizabeth Clery, John Curtice, and Roger Harding, eds., *British Social Attitudes* 34, London: NatCen Social Research, at www.bsa.natcen.ac.uk

Frankema, Ewout. 2011. " Colonial Taxation and Government Spending in British Africa, 1880–1940: Maximizing Revenue or Minimizing Effort?" Explorations in Economic History, 48:136–149.

Freeman, Gary P. 2009. "Politics and Mass Immigration." In Robert F. Goodin and Charles Tilly, eds., Oxford Handbook of Contextual Political Analysis, pp. 633–649. Oxford: Oxford University Press, at https://www.oxfordhandbooks.com/view/10.1093/oxfordhb/9780199604456.001.0001/oxfordhb-9780199604456-appendix-5

Freytas-Tamura, Kimiko. 2018. "British Citizen One Day, Illegal Immigrant the Next," *New York Times* (April 24), at https://www.nytimes.com/2018/04/24/world/europe/britain-windrush-immigrants.html?rref=collection%2Fbyline%2Fkimiko-de-freytas-tamura&action=click&contentCollection=undefined&region=stream&module=stream_unit&version=latest&contentPlacement=1&pgtype=collection.

Fritze, John. 2017. "Elijah Cummings Tells President Trump His Language Has Been Hurtful to African Americans," *Baltimore Sun* (March 8), at http://www.baltimoresun.com/news/maryland/politics/bs-md-cummings-trump-meeting-20170308-story.html#

Fukuyama, Francis. 2018. *Identity*. New York: Farrar, Straus, and Giroux.

Gabriel, Trip, and Dana Goldstein. 2021. "Disputing Racism's Reach, Republicans Rattle American Schools," *New York Times*, June 1, A1, A13, at https://www.nytimes.com/2021/06/01/us/politics/critical-race-theory.html

Galston, William A. 2018. "Trump's Dubious Hungarian Friend," Wall Street Journal (May 14), at https://www.wsj.com/articles/trumps-dubious-hungarian-friend-11557875311

Galson, William A. 2019b. "Anti-Semitism Soars in Eastern Europe," at (November 26), https://www.wsj.com/articles/anti-semitism-soars-in-eastern-europe-11574812176?mod=searchresults&page=1&pos=1

Garand, James, Ping Xu, and Belinda C. Davis. 2017. "Immigration Attitudes and Support for the Welfare State in the American Mass Public." *American Journal of Political Science*, 61: 146–162.

Gervais, Bryan T., and Irwin L. Morris. 2018. Reactionary Republicanism. New York: Oxford University Press.

Gidron, Noam, and Peter A. Hall. 2017. "The Politics of Social Status: Economic and Cultural Roots of the Populist Right," *British Journal of Sociology*, 68:S57–S84.

Gilens, Martin. 1999. Why Americans Hate Welfare. Princeton: Princeton University Press.

Goodman, Peter S. 2019. "Inequality Fuels Rage of 'Yellow Vests' in Equality-Obsessed France," *New York Times* (April 15), at https://www.nytimes.com/2019/04/15/business/yellow-vests-movement-inequality.html

Goodwin, Matthew, and James Dennison. 2018. "The Radical Right in the United Kingdom." In Jens Rydgren, ed., *Oxford Handbook of the Radical Right*, DOI: 10.1093/oxfordhb/9780190274559.013.26

Goossen, Mikael Ingemar Johansson Seva, and Ragnar Lundstrom. 2020. "Suspicion of Welfare Overuse in Sweden: The Role of Left -Right Ideology, Anti-Immigrant Attitudes and Gender," *Scandinavian Political Studies*, 44:115–139.

Gordon, Linda. 2017. *The Second Coming of the KKK*. New York: W.W. Norton.

Green, Joshua. 2017. Devil's Bargain: Steve Bannon, Donald Trump, and the Storming of the Presidency. New York: Penguin.

Greenfield, Jeff. 2016. "Trump Is Pat Buchanan with Better Timing," *Politico Magazine* (September/October), at https://www.politico.com/magazine/story/2016/09/donald-trump-pat-buchanan-republican-america-first-nativist-214221

Gregorian, Dareh. 2021. "Texas Lt. Gov. Dan Patrick Blames Covid Surge on 'African Americans Who Have Not Been Vaccinated," at https://www.nbcnews.com/politics/politics-news/texas-lt-gov-dan-patrick-blames-covid-surge-african-americans-n1277254

Greven, Thomas. 2016. "The Rise of Right-wing Populism in Europe and the United States: A Comparative Perspective," Perspective, Friedrich Ebert Stiftung, at http://www.fesdc.org/fileadmin/user_upload/publications/RightwingPopulism.pdf

Hacker, Andrew. 1955. *The Liberal Tradition in America*. New York: Harcour, Brace, Jovanovich.

Hainsworth, Paul, and Paul Mitchell. 2000. "France: The Front National from Crossroads to Crossroads?," *Parliamentary Affairs*, 53:443–456.

Hansen, John Mark. 1985. "The Political Economy of Group Membership," *American Political Science Review*, 79:79–96.

Hall, Peter A., and Michelle Lamont. 2013. "Why Social Relations Matter for Politics and Successful Societies," *Annual Review of Political Science*, 16:49–71.

Hanmer, Michael, and Kalkan, Ozan Kerem. 2013. "Behind the Curve: Clarifying the Best Approach to Calculating Predicted Probabilities and Marginal Effects from Limited Dependent Variable Models," *American Journal of Poltical Science*, 57: 263–277.

Hanson, Luke. 2014. The Role of Ultra-Orthodox Political Parties in Israeli Democracy, Thesis submitted in accordance with the requirements of the University of Liverpool for the degree of Doctor in Philosophy, at https://livrepository.liverpool.ac.uk/2006321/1/HowsonLuk_July2014_2002641.pdf

Harkov, Lahav. 2021. "Netanyahu Warns of African Migrants Converting after Historic Court Ruling," *Jerusalem Post* (March 10), https://www.jpost.com/israel-elections/benjamin-netanyahu-in-dialogue-with-lahav-harkov-live-in-english-661223

Hartz, Louis. 1955. *The Liberal Tradition in America*. New York: Harcourt Brace Jovanovich.

Heinisch, Reinhard, Stevem Saxonberg, Annika Werner, and Fabian Haberstock. 2021. "The Effect of Radical Fringe Parties on Main Parties in Central and Eastern Europe," *Party Politics*, 27: 9–21.

Heinisch, Reinhard, Annika Werner, and Fabian Habersack. 2020. "Reclaiming National Sovereignty: the Case of the Conservatives and the Far Right in Austria," *European Politics and Society*, 21:2, 163–181, DOI: 10.1080/23745118.2019.1632577

Heino, Andreas Johansson. 2016. "Timbro Authoritarian Populism Index 2016," at https://timbro.se/allmant/timbro-authoritarian-populism-index-2016/

Hendrix, Steve, Shira Rubin, Judith Sudilovsky. 2021. "Stampede at Religious Festival in Israel Leaves at Least 45 Dead, Dozens Injured," *Washington Post* (April 30), A1, A12, A13 at https://www.washingtonpost.com/nation/2021/04/29/israel-stampede-mount-meron/

Henley, Jon, Helena Bengtsson, and Caelainn Barr. 2016. "Across Europe, Distrust of Mainstream Political Parties Is on the Rise," *The Guardian* (May 25), at https://www.theguardian.com/world/2016/may/25/across-europe-distrust-of-mainstream-political-parties-is-on-the-rise

Hetherington, Marc, and Jonathan Weiler. 2018. *Prius or Pickup?* Boston: Houghton Mifflin.

Higham, John. 1956. "American Immigration Policy in Historical Perspective," *Law and Contemporary Problems*, 21:213–235, available at https://scholarship.law.duke.edu/lcp/vol21/iss2/2

Hjerm, Mikael, and Annette Schnabel. 2012. "How Much Heterogeneity Can the Welfare State Endure? The Influence of Heterogeneity on Attitudes to the Welfare State," *Nations and Nationalism*, 18:346–369 at https://doi.org/10.1111/j.1469-8129.2011.00523.x

Hjorth, Frederick. 2016. "Who Benefits? Welfare Chauvinism and National Stereotypes," European Union Politics, 17:: 3–24

Holtug, Nils. 2021. "Why Rawls Was Right Liberal Values and Social Cohesion." In Nils Holtug and Eric M. Uslaner, eds., pp. 133–150, National Identity and Social Cohesion. Colhester, UK: ECPR Press.

Homola, Jonathan, Miguel M. Pereiera, and Margit Tavits. 2020. "Legacies of the Third Reich: Concentration Camps and Out-group Intolerance," *American Political Science Review* 114: 573–590.

Hooghe, March, and Dieter Siters. 2020. "Regional Identities, Preferences and Voting Behavior in the Flemish Region of Belgium (2009–2019)," Presented at the Annual Meeting of the American Political Science Association, September 9–12.

Hopkins, Daniel J. 2018. *The Inreasingly United States*. Chiago: University of Chicago Press.

Hopkins, Daniel J. 2010. "Politicized Places: Explaining Where and When Immigrants Provoke Local Opposition," *American Political Science Review*, 104:40–60.

Hopkins, Valerie, 2021. "In Hungary, an Embattled L.G.B.T.Q. Community Takes to the Streets,: *New York Times* (June 24), A9.

Hulse, Carl. 2021. "G.O.P. Focuses on Polarizing Cultural Issues in Drive to Regain Power," *New York Times* (May 8), A15 at https://www.nytimes.com/2021/05/07/us/politics/republicans-culture-war.html

Huntington, Samuel P. 2004. *Who Are We?* New York: Simon and Schuster.

Huntington, Samuel P. 1981. American Politics: The Promise of Disharmony. Cambridge: Belknap Press.

Ignatiev, Noel. 2008 [1995]. *How the Irish Became White*. London: Routledge.

Illing, Sean. 2018. "How 'America First' Ruined the "American Dream," at https://www.vox.com/2018/10/22/17940964/america-first-trump-sarah-churchwell-american-dream

Inal, Nuray Nazli, and Duden Yegenoglu. 2005. "German and French Leaders' Views on Turkey's EU Membership," The Washington Institute Policywatch 1007, at http://www.washingtoninstitute.org/policy-analysis/view/german-and-french-leaders-views-on-turkeys-eu-membership

Inglehart, Ronald J., and Pippa Norris. 2018. *Culture Clash.* New York: Cambridge University Press.

Ivarsflaten, Elizabeth. 2008. "What Unites Right-Wing Populists in Western Europe?" *Comparative Political Studies*, 41:3–23.

Iyengar, Shanto, Gaurav Sood, and Yphtach Yelkes. 2012. "Affect, Not Ideology, a Social Identity Perspective on Polarization," *Public Opinion Quarterly*, 76: 405–431.

Jackson, Kenneth T. 1967. The Ku Klux Klan in the City, 1915–1930. New York: Oxford University Press.

Jardina, Ashley Elizabeth. 2019. *White Identity Politics.* New York: Cambridge University Press.

Jeremy Bob, Yonah. 2020. "High Court hints it wants to interpret Jewish Nation-State Law, not nix it," *Jerusalem Post* (December 22), at https://www.jpost.com/israel-news/high-court-holds-first-hearing-on-jewish-nation-state-law-652873

Jones, Frank L., and Philip Smith. 2001. "Diversity and Commonality in National Identities: An Exploratory Analysis of Cross-national Patterns," *Journal of Sociology*, 37:35–63.

Jones, Robert P. 2017. "Trump Can't Reverse the Decline of White Christian America," *Atlantic* (July 4), https://www.theatlantic.com/politics/archive/2017/07/robert-jones-white-christian-america/532587/

Jones, Robert P. 2016. *The End of White Christian America.* New York: Simon and Schuster.

Jones, Robert P., Daniel Cox, William A. Galstono, and E.J. Dionne, Jr. 2011. "What It Means to Be American: Attitudes in an Increasingly Diverse America Ten Years After 9/11," at https://www.brookings.edu/research/what-it-means-to-be-an-american-attitudes-in-an-increasingly-diverse-america-ten-years-after-911/

Jungar, Ann-Catherine. 2015. "Business as Usual: Ideology and Nationalist Appeals of the Sweden Democrats." In Hanspieter Kreisi and Takis S. Pappas, eds., *European Populism in the Shadow of the Great Recession.* Colchester, UK: ECPR Press.

Kagan, Robert. 2019. "The Strongmen Strike Back," *Washington Post* (March 17), at https://www.washingtonpost.com/news/opinions/wp/2019/03/14/feature/the-strongmen-strike-back/?utm_term=.3b064d55bc5f

Kalkan, Kerem Ozan. 2019. "The 9/11 Mosque and Partisan Polarization." In Brian R. Calfano and Nazita Lajevardi, eds., *Understanding Muslim Political Life in America Contested Citizenship in the Twenty-First Century.* Philadelphia: Temple University Press.

Kalkan, Kerem Ozan, Geoffrey Layman, and Eric M. Uslaner. 2009, "A "Band of Others"? Attitudes toward Muslims in Contemporary American Society," *Journal of Politics*, 71: 847–862.

Kallis, Aristotle. 2018. "The Radical Right and Islamophobia." In Jens Rydgren, ed., *The Oxford Handbook of the Radical Right.* Oxford: Oxford University Press. DOI: 10.1093/oxfordhb/9780190274559.013.3

Katznelson, Ira. 2013. Fear Itself, New York: Liveright.

Kaufmann, Eric. 2017. "Levels or Changes?: Ethnic Context, Immigration and the UK Independence Party Vote," Electoral Studies, 48:57–69.

Kautto, Mikko. 2010. "The Nordic Countries" In Linda J. Cook, *The Oxford Handbook of the Welfare State*. Oxford University Press available at https://www.oxfordhandbooks.com/view/10.1093/oxfordhb/9780199579396.001.0001/oxfordhb-9780199579396-e-40?print=pdf

Kenny, Michael. 2016. "The Genesis of English Nationalism," *Political Insight* (September), 7: 8–11, at https://journals.sagepub.com/doi/abs/10.1177/2041905816666124?journalCode=pliaKKenny,

Kenny, Michael. 2015. "The Rise of a Political Englishness?" *Political Insight* (September) 28–31. at https://www.psa.ac.uk/insight-plus/rise-political-englishness

Kinder, Donald R., and Cindy D. Kam. 2010. Us Against Them: Ethnocentric Foundations of American Opinion. Chicago: University of Chicago Press.

Kingsley, Patrick. 2019. "A Friend to Israel, and to Bigots," New York Times, at https://www.nytimes.com/2019/05/14/world/europe/orban-hungary-antisemitism.html

Kingsley, Patrick. 2018. "Hungary Criminalizes Aiding Illegal Immigrants," *New York Times* (June 20), at https://www.nytimes.com/2018/06/20/world/europe/hungary-stop-soros-law.html

Kingsley, Patrick, and Benjamin. 2019. "In Hungary, Viktor Orban Showers Money on Stadiums, Less So on Hospitals," *New York Times* (October 26), at https://www.nytimes.com/2019/10/26/world/europe/viktor-orban-soccer-health-care.html

Kirby, Jen. 2018. "Trump Wants Fewer Immigrants from 'Shithole Countries' and More from Places like Norway" (January 11), at www.vox.com/2018/1/11/16880750/trump-immigrants-shithole-countries-norway

Kornacki, Steve. 2018. *The Red and the Blue: The 1990s and the Birth of Political Tribalism*. New York: Ecco Press.

Krimel, Katherine, and Kelly Rader. 2020. "Racial Unfairness and Fiscal Politics," American Politics Research,: 1–14 at https://journals-sagepub-com.proxy-um.researchport.umd.edu/doi/pdf/10.1177/1532673X20972102

Kumar, Krishnan. 2003. *The Making of English National Identity*. Cambridge: Cambridge University Press.

Kumlin, Staffan, Dag Wollebæk, Audun Fladmoe, and Kari Steen-Johnsen. 2017. "Leap of Faith or Judgment of Deservingness? Generalized Trust, Trust in Immigrants and Support for the Welfare State." In Wim van Oorschot, Femke Roosma, Bart Meuleman, and Tim Reeskens, eds., *The Social Legitimacy of Targeted Welfare: New Perspectives on Deservingness Opinions*. Cheltenham, UK: Edward Elgar.

Kupper Beate, and Amdreas Zick. 2010. Religion and Prejudice in Europe. London: NEF Initiative on Religion and Democracy in Europe

Kymlicka, Will. 2007. Multicultural Odysseys. Oxford: Oxford University Press.

Lahav, Gallya. 2004. Immigration and Politics in the New Europe. New York: Cambridge University Press.

Lancee, Bram, and Merlin Schaeffer. 2015. "Moving to Diversity. Residential Mobility, Changes in Ethnic Diversity, and Concerns about Immigration. In R. Koopmans, B. Lancee, and M. Schaeffer. eds., *Social Cohesion and Immigration in Europe and North America: Mechanisms, Conditions, and Causality*, 38–55. London: Routledge

Larsen, Christian Albrekt. 2011. "Ethnic Heterogeneity and Public Support for Welfare: Is the American Experience Replicated in Britain, Sweden and Denmark?" *Scandinavian Political Studies*, 34:332–353.

Layman, Geoffrey, Thomas Carsey, and Julia M. Horowitz. 2006, "Party Polarization in American Politics: Characteristics, Causes, and Consequences," *Annual Review of Political Science*, 9:83–110.

Lee, Frances E. 2019.. "Populism and the American Party System: Opportunities and Constraints," *Perspectives on Politics*, 18: 370–388.

Lefkofridi, Zoe, and Elie Michel. 2017. "The Electoral Politics of Solidarity." In Keith Banting and Will Kymlicvka, eds., pp. 233–257. *The Politics of Commitment.* Oxford: Oxford Unversity Press.

Levendusky, Matthew S. 2017. "Americans, Not Partisans: Can Priming American National Identity Reduce Affective Polarization?" *Journal of Politics*, vol. 80:

Levitsky, Steven, and Daniel Ziblatt. 2018. How Democracies Die. New York: Viking.

Levy, Morris E. In print. "Once Racialized, Now "Immigrationized?" Explaining the Immigration-Welfare Link in American Public Opinion," *Journal of Politics*, DOI:https://doi.org/10.1086/711404

Lewin, Eyal. 2016. "'It's the National Ethos, Stupid'! Understanding the Political Psychology of the Israeli 2015 Elections Using Data from the National Resilience Survey," *Red Fame: International Journal of Social Science Studies*, 4:63–74, at http://dx.doi.org/10.11114/ijsss.v4i7.1651

Lieber, Dov, and Rory Jones. 2021. "Israel's Bennett Seeks New Political Order. Netanyahu Stands in the Way," *Wall Street Journal* (January 26), at https://www.wsj.com/articles/israel-bennett-netanyahu-biden-coalition-jerusalem-palestinians-11629903262

Lipset, Seymour Martin, and Gary Marks. 2000. *It Didn't Happen Here: Why Socialism Failed in the United States.* New York: Norton.

Lopez, German. 2019. "Donald Trump's long history of racism, from the 1970s to 2019" (July 19), at https://www.vox.com/2016/7/25/12270880/donald-trump-racist-racism-history

Lubbers, Marcel and Eva Jaspers. 2010. "A Longitudinal Study of Euroscepticism in the Netherlands: 2008 Versus 1990," *European Union Politics*, 12:21–40, at https://www.researchgate.net/publication/227574003_A_Longitudinal_Study_of_Euroscepticism_in_the_Netherlands_2008_Versus_1990

Lucassen, Geertje, and Marcel Lubbers. 2012. "Who Fears What?" *Comparative Political Studies*, 45: 547–574.

Mader, Matthias, and Harald Schoen. 2019. "The European Refugee Crisis, Party Competition, and Voters' Responses in Germany," *West European Politics*, 42(1): 67–90.

Marcus, Jonathan. 1995. *The National Front and French Politics.* London: Macmillan.

Martin, Christian W. 2018. "Electoral Participation and Right Wing Authoritarian Success – Evidence From the 2017 Federal Elections in Germany," at https://ssrn.com/abstract=3159320

Masci, David. 2021. "Most Poles Accept Jews as Fellow Citizens and Neighbors, But a Minority Do Not," *Pew Research Center*, at https://www.pewresearch.org/fact-tank/2018/03/28/most-poles-accept-jews-as-fellow-citizens-and-neighbors-but-a-minority-do-not/

Mason, Lilliana. 2018. *Uncivil Agreement*, Chicago: University of Chicago Press.

Mason, Lilliana, Julie Wronski, and John H. Kane. In press. "Activating Animus: The Uniquely Social Roots of Trump Support," *American Political Science Review*, at https://www.cambridge.org/core/services/aop-cambridge-core/content/view/D96C71C353D065F62A3F19B504FA7577/S0003055421000563a.pdf/activating-animus-the-uniquely-social-roots-of-trump-support.pdf

Mayer, Nonna. n.d. "Immigrants and Politics in France," at http://nationsworld.kr/cncho/paper/68-Mayer.pdf

Mayer, Nonna. 2018a. "The Radical Right in France." In Jens Rydgren, ed., *The Oxford Handbook of the Radical Right*. Oxford: Oxford University Press. DOI: 10.1093/oxfordhb/9780190274559.013.22

Mayer, Nonna. 2018b. "The Political Impact of Social Insecurity in France," *Partecipazione e Conflitto*, at http://siba-ese.unisalento.it/index.php/paco, DOI: 10.1285/i20356609v11i3p646

Mayer, Nonna. 2012. "Islamophobia" in France: Old Prejudice in New Clothes?" In Samuel Salzborn, Eldad Davidov, and Jost Reinecke (eds.), *Methods, Theories, and Empirical Applications in the Social Sciences*, VS Verlag für Sozialwissenschaften | Springer Fachmedien Wiesbaden. Germany, at 137-143 DOI 10.1007/978-3-531-18898-0_17

Mayer, Nonna. 2005. "Radical Right Populism in France: How Much of the 2002 Le Pen Votes Does Populism Explain?" Presented at the Symposium "Globalization and the Radical Right Populism," Centre for the Study of European Politics and Society, Ben Gurion University of the Negev, 11-12 April, at https://www.researchgate.net/publication/228957645_Radical_Right_Populism_in_France_How_much_of_the_2002_Le_Pen_votes_does_populism_explain

Mayer, Nonna. 1998. "The Front National Vote in the Plural," *Patterns of Prejudice*, 32:3=24 at DOI 0031-322X/3-24/003708

McAuley, James. 2020. "France Mandates Masks to Control the Coronavirus. Burqas Remain Banned," *Washington Post* (May 11), at https://www.washingtonpost.com/world/europe/france-face-masks-coronavirus/2020/05/09/6fbd50fc-8ae6-11ea-80df-d24b35a568ae_story.html

McAuley, James. 2019. "For European Jews, a horrifying sight on the other side of the Atlantic," *Washington Post*, at https://www.washingtonpost.com/world/the_americas/for-european-jews-a-horrifying-sight-on-the-other-side-of-the-atlantic/2018/10/28/0556d282-dad0-11e8-8bac-bfe01fcdc3a6_story.html

McAuley, James. 2018a "French Mayor Bans Pork Substitutes in School Meals, Saying He's Defending Secularism," *Washington Post* (January 15), at https://www.washingtonpost.com/world/europe/french-mayor-bans-pork-substitutes-in-school-meals-saying-hes-defending-secularism/2018/01/14/3442fc98-f64b-11e7-9af7-a50bc3300042_story.html?utm_term=.7ced0585a104

McAuley, James. 2018b "Struggling to Prevent Terrorist Attacks, France Wants to 'Reform" Islam," *Washington Post* (April 17), at https://www.washingtonpost.com/world/europe/struggling-to-prevent-terrorist-attacks-france-wants-to-reform-islam/2018/04/16/b81a20c6-1d67-11e8-98f5-ceecfa8741b6_story.html?utm_term=.5270cbe2b084&wpisrc=nl_todayworld&wpmm=1

McAuley, James. 2018c. "For Some French Officials, the Headscarf Is Such a Threat They Are Attacking a Teenager," *Washington Post* (May 30), at https://www.washingtonpost.com/world/europe/frances-headscarf-debate-focuses-on-a-muslim-student-leader/2018/05/30/9f190ed6-6347-11e8-81ca-bb14593acaa6_

McAuley, James. 2018d. "Why Halal Meat Generates So Much Controversy in Europe," *Washington Post* (October 9), at https://www.washingtonpost.com/world/europe/why-halal-meat-generates-so-much-controversy-in-europe/2018/10/08/e58fd16a-9439-11e8-818b-e9b7348cd87d_story.html?utm_ term=.e2d2c03b9488

McAuley, James. . 2018e. "'Yellow Vest' Protests Damage Paris Monuments, Shops and Macron's Presidency," *Washington Post* (December 3), at https://www.washingtonpost.

com/world/europe/yellow-vest-protests-damage-paris-monuments-shops-and-macrons-presidency/2018/12/03/83dec944-f708-11e8-8642-c9718a256cbd_story. html?utm_term=.1c00b45ad5d5

McCrummen, Stephanie. 2021. "The 31-Day Campaign Against QAnon," *Washington Post* (October17),athttps://www.washingtonpost.com/nation/2020/10/17/kevin-van-ausdal-qanon-marjorie-greene-georgia/

McLaren, Lauren. 2015. Immigration and *Perceptions*. Cambridge: Cambridge University Press.

Meckler, Laura, and Josh Dawsey. 2021. " Republicans, Spurred by an Unlikely Figure, See Political Promise in Targeting Critical Race Theory," *Washington Post* (June 21), A16, at https://www.washingtonpost.com/education/2021/06/19/critical-race-theory-rufo-republicans/

Miller, David. 1995. *On Nationality*. Oxford: Oxford University Press.

Milne, Richard. 2018a. "How the Remorseless Rise of the Swedish Far Right Could Leave the Country Ungovernable," New Statesman (July 4), at https://www. newstatesman.com/culture/observations/2018/07/how-remorseless-rise-swedish-far-right-could-leave-country-ungovernabl

Milne, Richard. 2018b. "Muslim Coordinate Flames Provides Opening for Sweden's Right Wing" (June 8), at http://www.savemysweden.com/muslim-coordinate-flames-provi des-opening-for-sweden s-right-wing/More in Common. 2018. Hidden Tribes: A Study of America's Polarized Landscape, at https://hiddentribes.us/pdf/hidden_tribes _report.pdf.

Minkenberg. Michael. 2018. "Religion and the Radical Right." In Jens Rydgren, ed., *The Oxford Handbook of the Radical Right*, at DOI: 10.1093/oxfordhb/ 9780190274559.013.19

Montgomery, David. 2021. "After Walkout, Texas Voting Showdown Part II Looms," *New York Times*, A20, at https://www.nytimes.com/2021/07/10/us/TEXAS-VOTING-REPUBLICANS-LEGISLATURE.html

More in Common. 2017. *National Identity, Immigration, and Refugees in German*. Washington, DC: More in Common.

Morris, Loveday. 2020 "Hungary's 'Coronovirus Bill' Hands Orba-brand Powers," *Washington Post* (March 31), at https://www.washingtonpost.com/world/hungarian-parliament-hands-orban-power-to-rule-unchecked/2020/03/30/cc5135f6-7293-11ea-ad9b-254ec99993bc_story.html

Morrow, Duncan. 2000. "Jorg Haider and the New FPO." In Paul Hainsworth, ed., *The Politics of the Extreme Right*, 33–63. London: Pinter

Mudde, Cas. 2010. "The Intolerance of the Tolerant," *Open Democracy*, October 20, at http://www.opendemocracy.net/cas-mudde/intolerance-of-tolerant

Mudde, Cas, and Cristóbal Rovira Kaltwasser. 2013. "Populism.," In Michael Freeden and Marc Stears, *The Oxford Handbook of Political Ideologies*, DOI: 10.1093/oxfordhb/ 9780199585977.013.0026

Noack, Rick. 2021. "Macron's Government Unveils Plans for New Anti-terrorism Legislation, in Part to Ward off Criticism from the Right," *Washington Post* (April 29), at https://www.washingtonpost.com/world/france-anti-terrorism-law/2021/04/28/ 27b0419a-a6c7-11eb-a8a7-5f45ddcdf364_story.html

Noack, Rick. 2019. "Polish Towns Advocate 'LGBT-free' Zones While the Ruling Party Cheers Them On," *Washington Post* (July 21), at Https://www.washingtonpost.com/

world/europe/polands-right-wing-ruling-party-has-found-a-new-targetlgbt-ide-ology/2019/07/19/775f25c6-a4ad-11e9-a767-d7ab84aef3e9_story.html

Norman, Laurence. 2021. "EU's New Weapon in Rule-of-Law Battle With Poland, Hungary: Money," *Wall Street Journal* (August 4), A4, at https://www.wsj.com/articles/eus-new-weapon-in-rule-of-law-battle-with-poland-hungary-money-11627996211?mod=world_major_1_pos5

Norman, Laurence, and Stephen Fidler. 2019. "European Elections Deepen Divisions in National Capitals," *Wall Street Journal*, at https://www.wsj.com/articles/european-elections-deepen-divisions-in-national-capitals-11559053075

Nossiter, Adam. 2018. "How France's 'Yellow Vests' Differ From Populist Movements Elsewhere," *New York Times* (December 5), at https://www.nytimes.com/2018/12/05/world/europe/yellow-vests-france.html

Nossiter, Adam, and Katrin Bennhold. 2020. "The Politics of Terrorism in a Combustible Europe," *New York Times* (November 9), at //www..nytimes.com/2020/11/09/world/europe/france-austria-terrorist-attack-macron-kurtz.html

Noury, Abdul, and Gerard Roland. 2020. "Identity Politics and Populism in Europe," *Annual Review of Political Science*," 23:421–439.423

Novack, Benjamin., 2021. "Hungary Adopts Child Sex Abuse Law That Also Targets L.G.B.T. Community," *New York Times* (June 15), at https://www.nytimes.com/2021/06/15/world/europe/hungary-child-sex-lgbtq.html.

Onishi, Norimitsu. 2021a. "Will American Ideas Tear France Apart? Some of Its Leaders Think So," New York *Times* (February 10), at https://www.nytimes.com/2021/02/09/world/europe/france-threat-american-universities.html

Onishi, Norimitsu. 2021b. "The Mayor, the Teacher and a Fight Over a 'Lost Territory' of France," *New York Times* (June 9), A8, at https://www.nytimes.com/2021/06/08/world/europe/france-mayor-teacher-islam-secularism-laicite.html

Onishi, Norimitsu. 2019. "The Man Behind a Toxic Slogan Promoting White Supremacy," *New York Times* (September 21), at https://www.nytimes.com/2019/09/20/world/europe/renaud-camus-great-replacement.html

Onishi, Norimitsu, and Aurelien Breeden. 2020a. "On the Scrappy Fringes of French Politics, Marine Le Pen Tries to Rebrand," *New York Times* (May 16), A9

Onishi, Norimitsu, and Aurelien Breeden. 2020b. "Macron Vows Crackdown on 'Islamist Separatism' in France," *New York Times* (October 2), A17.

Onishi, Norimitsu, and Constant Méheut. 2021a ."Can France's Far Right Rise to Power? One Mayor Shows How." *New York Times* (March 14), A1, A10, at https://www.nytimes.com/2021/03/13/world/europe/france-far-right-national-rally-le-pen-macron.html

Onishi, Norimitsu and Constant Méheut. 2021b. "In France's Military, Muslims Find a Tolerance That Is Elusive Elsewhere," *New York Times* (June 21), A4, at https://www.nytimes.com/2021/06/26/world/europe/in-frances-military-muslims-find-a-tolerance-that-is-elusive-elsewhere.html

Onishi, Norimatsu, and Constant Méheut. 2021c. "France's Ideals Are a Harder Sell among Diverse Youth," *New York Times* (July 22), A4, at https://www.nytimes.com/2021/07/21/world/europe/france-youth-discrimination-diversity.html

Onishi, Norimatsu, and Constant Méheut. 2020a. "France's Hardening Defense of Cartoons of Muhammad Could Lead to 'a Trap,'" *New York Times* (October 31), A11, at https://www.nytimes.com/2020/10/30/world/europe/France-Muhammad-cartoons.html

Onishi, Norimatsu, and Constant Méheut. 2020b. "A Coded Word from the Far Right Roils France's Political Mainstream," *New York Times* at https://www. nytimes.com/2020/09/04/world/europe/france-ensauvagement-far-right-racism. html?searchResultPosition=1

_Onishi, Norimatsu, and Constant Méheut. 2020c. "France's Dragnet for Extremists Sweeps up Some Schoolchildren, Too," *New York Times* (November 23), A11, at nytimes.com/2020/11/23/world/europe/france-extremism-children.html

Onishi, Norimatsu, and Constant Méheut. 2020d. "Once a Slogan of Unity, 'Je Suis Charlie' Now Divides France," *New York Times,* (December 19), A12, at https://www. nytimes.com/2020/12/19/world/europe/france-charlie-hebdo-slogan.html#:~:text= PARIS%20%E2%80%94%20In%20the%20hours%20after,%E2%80%9CJe%20suis%20 Charlie.%E2%80%9D

Oscarrson, Henrik, and Soren Holmberg. 2016. "Issue Voting Structured by Left-Right Ideology." In Jon Pierre, ed., *The Oxford Handbook of Swedish Politics*, DOI: 10.1093/ oxfordhb/9780199665679.013.14

Pancevski, Bojan. 2019. "The Iron Curtain Is Gone but Europe's East and West Are Divided Again," *Washington Post* (November 10), at https://www.wsj.com/articles/ the-iron-curtain-is-gone-but-europes-east-and-west-are-again-divided-11573405238

Parker, Christopher. 2018. "The Radical Right in the United States of America," In Jens Rydgren, ed.,*Oxford Handbook of the Radical Right*, DOI: /oxfordhb

Parker, Kim, Juliana Horowitz, Anna Brown, Richard Fry, D'Vera Cohn, and Ruth Igielnik. 2018. What Unites and Divides Urban,Suburban and Rural Communities, Pew Research Center, at http://assets.pewresearch.org/wp-content/uploads/sites/3/ 2018/05/22100715/Pew-Research-Center-Community-Type-Full-Report-FINAL.pdf

Parker, Kim, Juliana Horowitz, Anna Brown, Richard Fry, D'Vera Cohn, and Ruth Igielnik. 2017a. "What It Takes to be Truly One of Us," at http://www.pewglobal.org/ 2017/02/01/what-it-takes-to-truly-be-one-of-us/

Parker, Kim, Juliana Horowitz, Anna Brown, Richard Fry, D'Vera Cohn, and Ruth Igielnik. 2017b. "Europe's Growing Muslim Population" (November 29), at http://www. pewforum.org/2017/11/29/europes-growing-muslim-population/

Pedazhur, Ami. 2012. *The Triumph of Israel's Radical Right*. New York: Oxford University Press.

Perliger, Arie and Ami Pedazhur. 2018. "The Radical Right in Israel." In Jens Rydgren, ed., *The Oxford Handbook of the Radical Right*. Oxford: Oxford University Press , at DOI: 10.1093/oxfordhb/9780190274559.013.33

Petersen, Slothuus, Stubager, and Togeby (2010) in Sweden

Pew Research Center. 2019. "In a Politically Polarized Era, Sharp Divides in Both Partisan Coalitions," at https://www.people-press.org/2019/12/17/in-a-politically-polarized-era-sharp-divides-in-both-partisan-coalitions/.

Pew Research Center. 2018. "Being Christian in Western Europe," at http://www. pewforum.org/2018/05/29/being-christian-in-western-europe/

Pew Research Center. 2018. "The Age Gap in Religion Around the World," Pew Research Center (June 13), at https://www.pewforum.org/2018/06/13/ the-age-gap-in-religion-around-the-world/

Pew Research Center. 2021a. "Topline questionnaire: Fall 2020 Survey," at https://www. pewresearch.org/global/wp-content/uploads/sites/2/2021/05/PG_2021.05.05_ Cultural-Grievances_TOPLINE.pdf

Pew Research Center. 2021b. "Americans' Views of the Problems Facing the Nation," at https://www.pewresearch.org/politics/2021/04/15/americans-views-of-the-problems-facing-the-nation/

Pew Research Center on Religion and Public Life. 2017. "Global Restrictions on Religion Rise Modestly in 2015, Reversing Downward Trend" (April 15), at http://www.pewforum.org/2017/04/11/global-restrictions-on-religion-rise-modestly-in-2015-reversing-downward-trend/

Porter, Eduardo. 2017. "How the G.O.P. Became the Party of the Left Behind," *New York Times* (January 27), at https://www.nytimes.com/interactive/2020/01/27/business/economy/republican-party-voters-income.html

Pratto, Felicia, Jim Sidanius, Lisa M. Stallworth, and Bertram F. Malle. 1994. "Social Dominance Orientation: A Personality Variable Predicting Social and Political Attitudes," Journal of Personality and Social Psychology, 67:741–763

Pronciuk, Monica. 2021. "In Poland, an L.G.B.T.Q. Migration as Homophobia Deepens," *New York Times* (April 24), A14.

Pronciuk, Monica. 2020. "Polish Towns That Declared Themselves 'L.G.B.T. Free' Are Denied E.U. Funds," *New York Times*, July 30, at https://www.nytimes.com/2020/07/30/world/europe/LGBT-free-poland-EU-funds.html

Public Religion Research Institute. 2021. "Understanding QAnon's Connection to American Politics, Religion, and Media Consumption," (May 27), at https://www.prri.org/research/qanon-conspiracy-american-politics-report/

Public Religion Research Institute. 2020. "Dueling Realities: Findings from the 2020 American Values Survey," at https://www.prri.org/research/amid-multiple-crises-trump-and-biden-supporters-see-different-realities-and-futures-for-the-nation/

Radziemski, Lily. 2021. "Want to **Stay Long Term** in France? First **Come** the Classes on How to **Be** French," *Washington Post* (October 13), at https://www.washingtonpost.com/world/europe/france-integration-separatism/2021/08/12/4a19b3f6-f609-11eb-9738-8395ec2a44e7_story.html

Rapp, Carolin. 2017. "Shaping Tolerant Attitudes Towards Immigrants: The Role of Welfare State Expenditures," *Journal of European Social Policy*, 27:40–56.

Rasgon, Adam. 2018. "Druze Revolt: Why a Tiny, Loyal Community Is So Infuriated by Nation-State Law," *The Times of Israel* (August 8), at https://www.timesofisrael.com/druze-revolt-why-a-tiny-loyal-community-is-so-infuriated-by-nation-state-law/

Rathbun, Iakhnis, and Powers, 2012 in theory or deservingness

Roberts, Kenneth M. 2016. " Populism and Political Representation," In Carol Lancaster and Nicolas van de Walle, eds., *Populism and Political Representation*, Oxford: Oxford University Press, at DOI: 10.1093/oxfordhb/9780199845156.013.30

Rogers, Thomas. 2021 "Welcome to Germany." *The New York Review* (April 29), at https://www.nybooks.com/articles/2021/04/29/welcome-to-germany/

Rothstein, Bo. 2005. *Social Traps and the Problem of Trust*. Cambridge: Cambridge University Press.

Rothstein, Bo, and Eric M. Uslaner. 2005. "The Historical Roots of Corruption," *World Politics* (look up pags)

Rubin. Shira, and Steve Hendrix. 2021. "Netanyahu Turns to Extremist Party That Calls for Expelling Arabs from Israel," *Washington Post* (March 21), A21, at https://www.washingtonpost.com/world/middle_east/israel-election-netanyahu-ben-gvir/2021/03/19/c3992b7c-85c4-11eb-be4a-24b89f616f2c_story.html

Rydgren, Jens. 2004. *The Populist Challenge: Political Protest and Ethno-Nationalist Mobilization in France*. New York: Berghan.

Rydgren, Jens, and Patrick Ruth. 2013. "Contextual Explanations of Radical Rightwing Support in Sweden: Socioeconomic Marginalization, Group Threat, and the Halo Effect," *Ethnic and Racial Studies*, 36:4, 711–728, DOI: 10.1080/01419870.2011.623786

Rydgren, Jens, and Patrick Ruth. 2011. "Voting for the Radical Right in Swedish Municipalities: Social Marginality and Ethnic Competition?" *Scandinavian Political Studies*, 34:202–225.

Santora, Marc. 2020. "Poland's Virus-Delayed Presidential Election Suddenly Looks Tight," *New York Times* (June 28), at https://www.nytimes.com/2020/06/27/world/europe/poland-election-.htm

Santora, Marc. 2019a. "In Poland, Nationalism with a Progressive Touch Wins Voters," *New York Times* (October 10) at https://www.nytimes.com/2019/10/10/world/europe/poland-election-law-and-justice-part y.html

Santora, Marc. 2019b. "Poland's Populists Pick a New Top Enemy: Gay People," New York Times (April 7), A1, AA14 at https://www.nytimes.com/2019/04/07/world/europe/poland-gay-rights.html

Sauerbrey, Anna. 2018. "German Conservatism Is Making a Comeback," *New York Times* (April 14), at https://www.nytimes.com/2018/04/13/opinion/german-conservatism-comeback.html?smid=nytcore-ipad-share&smprod=nytcore-ipad

Schäfer, Armin. 2017. "Return with a Vengeance: Working Class Anger and the Rise of Populism," at http://items.ssrc.org/return-with-a-vengeance-working-class-anger-and-the-rise-of-populism/

Schaffner, Brian, Stephen Ansolabehere, and Sam Luks. 2021. *Cooperative Election Study Common Content*, at https://doi.org/10.7910/DVN/E9N6PH, Harvard Dataverse, V1

Schain, Martin A. 1987. "The National Front in France and the Construction of Political Legitimacy," *Western European Politics*, 10:229–252.

Schellenbergm Britta. 2013. "Development within the Radical Right in Germany." In Ruth Wodak, Majid Khosravinik, and Brigitte Mral, eds., *Right-Wing Populism in Europe*, pp. 1349–1162. London: Bloomsbury.

Schildkraut, Deborah. 2011. *Americanism in the Twenty-First Century: Public Opinion in the Age of Immigration*. New York: Cambridge University Press.

Senik, Claudia, Holger Stichnoth, and Karine Van der Straeten. 2009. "Immigration and Natives' Attitudes towards the Welfare State: Evidence from the European Social Survey," Social Indicators Research, 91:345–370.

Serwer, Adam. 2019. "White Nationalism's Deep American Roots," *Atlantic* (April), at https://www.theatlantic.com/magazine/archive/2019/04/adam-serwer-madison-grant-white-nationalism/583258/https://www.theatlantic.com/magazine/archive/2019/04/adam-serwer-madison-grant-white-nationalism/583258/

Schierup, Carl-Ullrich, Peo Hansen, and Stephen Castles. 2006. *Migration, Citizenship, and the European State*. New York: Cambridge University Press.

Schmidt-Catran, Alexander W., and Dennis C. Spies. 2016. "Immigration and Welfare Support in Germany," *American Sociological Review*, 81:242–261.

Semyonov, Moshe, Rebeca Raijman, Anat Yom Tov and Peter Schmidt. 2004. "Population Size, Perceived Threat, and Exclusion: A Multiple-indicators Analysis of Attitudes Toward Foreigners in Germany," *Social Science Research* 33, 681–701.

Shafir, Gershon, and Yoav Peled. 2002. *Being Israeli*. Cambridge, England: Cambridge University Press.

Sharon, Jeremy. 2021. "The Haredi Parties' Impact on Israel's Religious Life Under Netanyahu," (June 10), at https://www.jpost.com/israel-news/politics-and-diplomacy/the-haredi-parties-impact-on-israels-religious-life-under-netanyahu-670690

Shears, Michael, and Zolan Kanno-Youngs. 2021. "Surge in Migrants Defies Easy or Quick Solutions for Biden," New York Times (May 31), A1, A15, at https://www.nytimes.com/2021/03/16/us/politics/biden-immigration.html

Sides, John. 2017. "What Makes Someone a "Real" American? 93% of Americans Actually Agree on This" (July 14), at https://www.washingtonpost.com/news/monkey-cage/wp/2017/07/14/whats-very-important-to-being-american-93-of-americans-actually-agree-on-this/?utm_term=.60ee13506001

Sides, John, Michael Tesler, and Lynn Vavreck. 2018. Identity Crisis. Princeton: Princeton University Press.

Simmons, Harvey G. 1996. The French National Front. Boulder, CO: Westview Press.

Simonsen, Kristina Bakkaer, and Bart Bonikowski. 2020. "Is Civic Nationalism Necessarily Inclusive? Conceptions of Nationhood and anti-Muslim Attitudes in Europe," European Journal of Political Research, 59:114–136.

Slayton, Robert. 2017. "When Did Jews Become White?" Jewish Currents (September 12), at https://jewishcurrents.org/when-did-jews-become-white

Smith, Matthew, Jamie Ballard, and Lindsey Sanders. 2021. " YouGov America. 2021. "Most Voters Say the Events at the US Capitol Are a Threat to Democracy," (June 1), at https://today.yougov.com/topics/politics/articles-reports/2021/01/06/US-capitol-trump-poll

Smooha, Sammy. 2019. "The Jewish Ethnic Divide and Ethnic Politics in Israel." In Oxford Handbook of Israeli Politics and Society, ed. Reuven Y. Hazan, Alan Dowty, Menachem Hofnung, and Gideon Rahat, pp. 1–31. Oxford Handbooks Online. 201., at https://drive.google.com/file/d/1QrLQXEIa1PtJMpUtYPrmmLhOESSx4s4Q/view

Sniderman, Paul M., Louk Hasgendoorn, and Markus Prior. 2004. "Predisposing Factors and Situational Triggers: Exclusionary Reactions to Immigrant Minorities," American Political Science Review, 98: 35–49.

Sobolewska, Maria, and Robert Ford. 2020. Brexitland. Cambridge: Cambridge University Press.

Sobolewska, Maria, and Robert Ford. 2019. "British Culture Wars? Brexit and the Future Politics of Immigration and Ethnic Diversity," The Political Quarterly, 142–154.

Sombart, Werner. 1976. Why Is There No Socialism in the United States? New York: International Arts & Sciences Press, Inc.

Somnez, Felicia. 2019;. "Trump Says that Jewish People Who Vote for Democrats Are 'Very Disloyal to Israel,' Denies His Remarks Are Anti-Semitic," Washington Post (August 21), at https://www.washingtonpost.com/politics/trump-says-that-jewish-people-who-vote-for-democrats-are-very-disloyal-to-israel-denies-his-remarks-are-anti-semitic/2019/08/21/055e5 3bc-c42d-11e9-b5e4-54aa56d5b7ce_story.html

Spencer, Howes, and Michael Levinson. 2021. "Charlottesville Removes Robert E. Lee Statue at Center of White Nationalist Rally," New York Times (July 11), A21, at https://www.nytimes.com/2021/07/09/us/charlottesville-confederate-monuments-lee.html

Spyer, Jonathan. 2019. "Netanyahu Scores Another Victory for Likud's Populism," Wall Street Journal (April 17), at https://www.wsj.com/articles/netanyahu-scores-another-victory-for-likuds-populism-11555541611

Stanley, Jason. 2018. "Germany's Nazi Past Is Still Present," New York Times (September 10), at https://www.nytimes.com/2018/09/10/opinion/germanys-nazi-past-is-still-present.html

Staples, Brent. 2019. "Vicious Bigotry: How Italians Became White," *New York Times* (October 12), at https://www.nytimes.com/interactive/2019/10/12/opinion/columbus-day-italian-american-racism.html

Stevis-Gridneff, Melina, and Benjamin Novak. 2020 "Hungary and Poland Threaten E.U. Stimulus Over Rule of Law Links," *New York Times* (November 17), A1, A10, at https://www.nytimes.com/2020/11/16/world/europe/eu-stimulus-poland-hungary.html

Stevis-Gridneff, Melina, and Benjamin Novak. 2011. "Hungary's Ruling Party Breaks with Conservative E.U. Allies," *New York Times*, A13.

Stichmoth, Holger. 2012. "Does Immigration Weaken Natives' Support for the Unemployed?" *Public Choice*, 151:651–624.

Stockemer, Daniel. 2015. "The Voters of the FN under Jean Marie Le Pen and Marine Le Pen: Continuity or Change?" *French Politics* 13: 370–390.

Stockemer, Daniel, and Abdelkarim Amengay. 2015. "The Voters of the FN under Jean-Marie Le Pen and Marine Le Pen: Continuity or Change?" *French Politics*, 13:370–390.

Stokes, Bruce. 2017. "What It Takes to Truly Be 'One of Us,'" at http://www.pewglobal.org/2017/02/01/what-it-takes-to-truly-be-one-of-us/

Sullivan, Eileen. 2019. "Trump Again Accuses American Jews of Disloyalty," *New York Times* (August 21), at https://www.nytimes.com/2019/08/21/us/politics/trump-jews-disloyalty.html

Taras, Raymond. 2018. *Nationhood, Migration and Global Politics*. Edinburgh: Edinburgh University Press

Tesler, Michael. 2016a. "Trump Voters Think African Americans Are Much Less Deserving than 'Average' Americans" (December 19), at http://www.huffingtonpost.com/Michael-tesler/trump-voters-think-africa_b_13732500.html

Tesler, Michael. .2016b. *Post-Racial or Most-Racial? Race and Politics in the Obama Era*. Chicago: University of Chicago Press.

Tesler, Michael, and David O. Sears. 2010. *Obama's Race*. Chicago: University of Chicago Press.

Tesler, Michael, and John Sides. 2017. "How Political Science Helps Explain the Rise of Trump: the Role of White Identity and Grievances," at https://www.washingtonpost.com/news/monkey-cage/wp/2016/03/03/how-political-science-helps-explain-the-rise-of-trump-the-role-of-white-identity-and-grievances/

Tharoor, Ishaan. 2019. "A Cautionary Tale about Dealing with the Far Right," *Washington Post* (May 21), at https://s2.washingtonpost.com/camp-rw/?e=ZXVzbGFuZXJAdW1kLmVkdQ%3D%3D&s=5ce385e8fe1ff666ca124e2a

Theiss-Morse, Elizabeth. 2009. *Who Counts as an American?* New York: Cambridge University Press.

Therborn, Goran, Anders Kjellberg, and Staffan Marklund. 1978. "Sweden before and after Social Democracy: A First Overview," Acta Sociologica, 21:37–58.

Thiebault, Reis. 2021. "Joint Chiefs Chairman Feared Potential 'Reichstag Moment' Aimed at Keeping Trump in Power," *Washington Post* (July21), at https://www.washingtonpost.com/politics/joint-chiefs-chairman-feared-potential-reichstag-moment-aimed-at-keeping-trump-in-power/2021/07/14/a326f5fe-e4ec-11eb-

Trofimov, Yaroslav. 2019. "The New Anti-Semitism," *Wall Street Journal* (July 12), at https://www.wsj.com/articles/the-new-anti-semitism-11562944476

Troianovski, Anton. 2016. "Europe's Nationalist Politicians Tap into Deep-Seated Frustration," *Wall Street Journal* (May 21), at https://www.wsj.com/articles/europes-nationalist-politicians-win-voters-hearts-1463689360

Troianovski, Anton, and Zeke Turner. 2017. "In the Heartlands of Support for German Right-Wing Party, Voters Express Angst over Immigration and Democracy," *Wall Street Journal* (September 28), at https://www.wsj.com/articles/in-the-heartlands-of-support-for-german-right-wing-party-voters-express-angst-over-immigration-and-democracy-1506510647

Uslaner, Eric M. 2021. "National Identity and Political Polarization." In Nils Holtug and Eric M. Uslaner, 241–251. *National Identity and Social Cohesion*. Colchester, UK: ECPR Press.

Uslaner, Eric M. 2018. *The Historical Roots of Corruption*. New York: Cambridge University Press.

Uslaner, Eric M. 2012. *Segregation and Mistrust*. New York: Cambridge University Press.

van Oorschot, Wim. 2006. "Making the Difference in Social Europe: Deservingness Perceptions among Citizens of European Welfare States," *Journal of European Social Policy*, 16: 23–42.

van Oorschot, Wim. 2010. "Who Should Get What, and Why? On Deservingness Criteria and the Conditionality of Solidarity Among the Public," Politics and Policy, 28:33048.

Van Spanje. 2010. " Contagious Parties: Anti-Immigration Parties and Their Impact on Other Parties' Immigration Stances in Contemporary Western Europe," Party Politics, 2010, 16:563–586.

Vavreck, Lynn. 2017. "The Great Political Divide Over American Identity," at https://www.nytimes.com/2017/08/02/upshot/the-great-political-divide-over-american-identity.html?mcubz=0&_r=0

Vasilopoulou, Sofia. 2018. "The Radical Right and Euroskepticism." In Jens Rydgren, ed., *Oxford Handbook of the Radical Right*, DOI: 10.1093/oxfordhb/9780190274559.013.7Veuglers, John W.P., and Roberto Chiari, 2002. " The Far Right in France and Italy." In Martin Schain, Aritstede Zolberg, and Patrick, Hossey, eds., Shadows Over Europe: The Development and Impact of the Extreme Right in Western Europe, pp. 83–103. New York: Palgrave Macmillan.

Wang, T. Y. 2017. "Changing Boundaries," In Christopher H. Achen and T.Y, Wang, eds., *The Taiwan Voter*. Ann Arbor: University of Michigan Press.

Waxman, Dov, and Ilan Peleg. 2019. "The Nation-state Law and the Rightwing Populist Challenge to Israeli Democracy," Presented at the Annual Meeting of the American Political Science Association, Washington DC, August 30, at https://convention2.allacademic.com/one/apsa/apsa19/index.php?cmd=Online+Program+View+Paper&selected_paper_id=1512163&PHPSESSID=uk0n35kkg3uds3cn8vkafre3b4

Weisskircher, Manès. 2019, " Germany's Far-right AfD Party Might Be the Big Winner in Tomorrow's Regional Elections. Here's What That Means," *Washington Post* (August 31), at https://www.washingtonpost.com/politics/2019/08/31/germanys-far-right-afd-party-might-be-big-winner-tomorrows-regional-elections-heres-what-that-means/

Whitehead, Andrew L., Samuel L. Perry, and Joseph O. Baker. 2018. "Make America Christian Again: Christian Nationalism and Voting for Donald Trump in the 2016 Presidential Election," *Sociology of Religion*, doi: 10.1093

Widfeldt, Anders 2018. "The Radical Right in the Nordic Countries," In Jens Rydgren, ed., Oxford Handbook of the Radical Right, DOI: 10.1093/oxfordhb/9780190274559.013.27

Widfeldt, Anders. 2002. "Scandinavia: Mixed Success for the Populist Right," Parliamentary Affairs, 53:486–500.

Williams, Joan C. 2017. *White Working Class: Overcoming Class Cluelessness in America*. Boston: Harvard Business Review Press.

Williams, Michelle Hale. 2018. "The Political Impact of the Radical Right." In Jens Rydgren, ed., *Oxford Handbook of the Radical Right*, DOI:0.1093/oxfordhb/9780190274559.013.16

Wilson, Graham K. 2017. "Brexit, Trump and the Special Relationship," *British Journal of Politics and International Relations*, 19:543–557.

Witte, Griff. 2019. "Hungary's Viktor Orban Has Bashed Europe for Years. Will Europe's Most Important Political Party Kick Him Out?," Washington Post, at https://www.washingtonpost.com/world/europe/hungarys-viktor-orban-has-bashed-europe-for-years-will-europes-most-important-political-party-finally-kick-him-out/2019/03/17/66fb7430-402d-11e9-85ad-779ef05fd9d8_story.html

Witte, Griff. 2018. "Once-fringe Soros Conspiracy Theory Takes Center Stage in Hungarian Election," Washington Post (March 17), at https://www.washingtonpost.com/world/europe/once-fringe-soros-conspiracy-theory-takes-center-stage-in-hungarian-election/2018/03/17/f0a1d5ae-2601-11e8-a227-fd2b009466b   c_story.html?utm_term=.e939beb4a73b

Witte, Griff and Luisa Beck. 2018. "Merkel's Bavarian Allies Tried to Pander to the Far Right.Now They're Paying the Price," *Washington Post* (October 12), at https://www.washingtonpost.com/world/europe/merkels-bavarian-allies-tried-to-pander-to-the-far-right-now-theyre-paying-the-price/2018/10/12/cc1df1aa-c71d-11e8-9c0f-2ffaf6d422aa_story.html?utm_term=.d1d247972cc5

YouGov America. 2021. CBS NewsYouGov Poll July 17–21, at https://drive.google.com/file/d/1l6lRDU1_cRTHirbRo7GFxcyMP2lK7QCu/view

Zerofsky, Elizabeth. 2019. "Letter from Hungary: Viktor Orbán's Far-Right Vision for Europe," *New Yorker* (January 14), at https: newyorker.com/magazine/letter-from-hungary.

Zick, Andreas, Beate Küpper, Andreas Hövermann. 2011. Intolerance, Prejudice, and Discrimination: A European Report. Berlin: Friedrich Ebert Stiftung Forum, at http://library.fes.de/pdf-files/do/07908-20110311.pdf (September 5), at https://www.washingtonpost.com/outlook/boris-johnson-will-do-anything-for-brexit-even-destroy-his-own-party/2019/09/05/6a64d96e-cff1-11e9-87fa-8501a456c003_story.html

Zick, Andreas, Thomas F. Pettigrew, and Ulrich Wagner. 2008. *Prejudice and Discrimination in Europe*. Oxford: Blackwell Press.

Index